Lifespan Journey

ourselves and others

Pamela Linsey

LifespAn JOURNEY
ourselves and others

Pamela Linsey B.A. Hons., D.S.A., D.A.S.S., C.Q.S.W., F.E.T.C.

Hodder & Stoughton
A MEMBER OF THE HODDER HEADLINE GROUP

DEDICATION

*In loving memory of Jack,
my dearest husband and best friend,
who shared his love with me and showed me how to be.*

British Library Cataloguing in Publication Data

Linsey, Pamela
Lifespan Journey: Ourselves and Others
  1. Developmental psychology
  I. Title
  155

ISBN 0 340 670215

First published 1996
Impression number   10 9 8 7 6 5 4 3 2 1
Year   1999 1998 1997 1996

Typeset by Fakenham Photosetting Limited, Fakenham, Norfolk
Printed in Great Britain for Hodder & Stoughton Educational, a division of Hodder Headline Plc,
338 Euston Road, London NW1 3BH by The Bath Press, Bath

CONTENTS

INTRODUCTION

The purpose of this book is primarily practical, showing how psychological theories can be integrated and usefully applied in everyday living and in remedial situations. It aims to provide a summary of different approaches, and to simplify some of the complicated areas in current debate and theory.

The material has been tested in practice and found useful for students training for the caring professions in teaching, nursing, ministry and especially counselling.

The book is also intended for general readers who are interested in psychology, and for those who wish to gain a better understanding of themselves and others. It is suitable for use in self-help groups, voluntary or pastoral training groups; because several of the theories discussed are familiar to professional workers, people working in a voluntary capacity will find some common ground in their discussions with them.

Erikson's lifespan framework, and the additional complements drawn from other theories, are those found on many professional training courses, where this book may be found useful. Application of theory, with practical examples, follows each theoretical focus. Remedial processes are discussed, ranging from those requiring professionally skilled help to the personal development of insights that promote confidence and well-being.

Empathy is invited by the frequent use of 'we' and 'our', bringing the reader alongside whoever is under discussion. Social dimensions and personal relationships are included in this integrated approach, which includes a basic introduction to psychoanalytic, behaviourist, humanistic, transpersonal, cognitive, developmental and social psychological approaches.

Exercises and discussion suggestions at the end of the book are intended to help tutors, students, self-help groups or individual readers make the most of the text ... examples drawn from the reader's own observations are the best way to consolidate understanding. No previous knowledge is assumed, and conventional psychological terminology is explained as it occurs.

Research and book references are given. Note that research and first publication dates do not always coincide with later publication dates given. Earlier dates therefore appear in brackets in the Reference section. Guidance to further study is provided throughout the chapters by the device (see *Texts) which refers to titles marked with an asterisk in the Recommended reading and *Texts for further study section, so that the book may be used as a springboard.

ACKNOWLEDGEMENTS

Many people have been responsible, in their different ways, for the production of this book. The list below leaves out many I would like to include, since I am aware how much the contents have depended upon my own training, working and family relationships and friends. The following people all deserve mention for reasons given; those who are not mentioned will know who they are.

First, mature students at the Bournemouth and Poole College of Further Education, whose requests were responsible for shaping the book, and colleagues Arnold Mason, Jim Watson, Tony Udall and Laurie and Deirdre Baynes for their professional comments and their friendly encouragement.

Valuable comments and encouragement were also given by fellow tutors and students on the Wessex branch of the British Association for Counselling (WESBAC) Training Course for Counselling, in particular by course leaders Sheila Murray and Roger Fulcher. My own understanding, and the contents of these chapters, owe much to many others: Bryan Pechey, who introduced me to Jung and the transpersonal approach; all those who taught and trained me and those who have been my clients.

I am grateful to Kay Bader who first read and checked my script, and to Pam Judd, for reading and commenting on the text, and for her friendship and pearls of wisdom that have enriched some of the examples given here. Thanks are also due to Julie Hill, Project Editor at Hodder & Stoughton, for her editorial support and helpful suggestions for the book's presentation, Eiméar Crawford, Senior Designer at H & S, for her wonderful cover design, and Matthew Cooper for his cover artwork.

Especially and most relevantly for a book of this kind – I want to thank my family for the rich living, learning experience and for the perspectives they have given me: my husband, Jack, for his kindness, wisdom and lifelong support and encouragement; his parents, Theodore and Tryphena, and my aunt Kitty, who all showed me how to grow old gracefully and not to fear death; my parents, Basil and Kay, my sister, Betty, and our adopted sisters, Mollie and Betty Mary, who have all taught me so much about human nature; our cousins, Lucianne, Vera and Peter, for sharing some of their different experiences in their caring professions; my elder son, Peter, for his willingness to discuss and comment on ideas; my younger son and daughter-in-law, David and Cindy, for their interest and support, and for encouraging me to master a word processor; their children, Benjamin and Emily, for giving me some time off from playing with them to get the book written.

Lastly, I would like to thank the reader, for whom I have written this book in the hope that it may be useful.

PROLOGUE

The following chapters contain ideas and theories drawn mainly from the developmental approach of the discipline of psychology, especially Erikson's lifespan stage theory, which is used as a framework. Our ideas about ourselves and others have a long history, and there are many separate disciplines and contrasting approaches in psychology that focus on import- ant aspects of our human living and help our understanding. Some of these are outlined, as a background to more intensive study, in **Appendix I, Historical Background and Modern Psychology**. Read it first, if you wish; by tracing how our ideas have evolved, you can gain a 'You are here' per- spective. Chapter 1 focuses on the influences of heredity and environment, and different perspectives on aggression; you may prefer to carry straight on to this when you come to the end of the prologue.

Modern psychology spans many areas of interest and kinds of study from which we may choose to inform our understanding. The framework offered here is intended to leave room for individual experience and choice. Perhaps the ultimate test that we apply to information we may wish to retain is how well it works out in our daily living. Our selection also depends on whether our outlook is sufficiently mature to perceive the choices that a deeper understanding may give us.

A parable attributed to Buddha, of which there are many modern versions in circulation, illustrates the variety of our approaches and perceptions. It shows the very different conclusions we may draw from them, and our fre- quent reluctance to examine other points of view or to consider more pen- etrating questions:

'Six blind men were sitting by the roadside when an elephant was led past. With great curiosity, they approached to find out more about the animal. The first to reach him touched the great tusks. "What a fine structure this creature has ... his bones even come out through his skin!" he exclaimed, and went and sat down again to contemplate his discovery.

The second man, close behind, encountered the elephant's trunk, and felt its strength and flexibility. "Hmm! ... Some kind of large snake with big nostrils in the front," he muttered to himself as he, too, went and sat down again to consider his findings.

The third man came in contact with a flapping ear. As he backed away, he wondered how well this animal could fly, since it obviously had wings.

The fourth rested his hands on the huge body and felt a bit of mud that was caked onto the elephant's skin. "This is a creature of the water … very large, no fur … probably an amphibian," he decided.

The fifth man, who moved more slowly than the others, arrived in time to touch the elephant's tail, which soon moved away from him. "Must be some kind of tall cow," he concluded, and went back to join the others.

But the sixth man was more interested in the sounds made as the elephant walked along … gentle plodding and the shuffle of his keeper's feet, accompanied by the chink of the chains that dangled from his load. "Why does he allow himself to be led along like this?" he wondered. "Where did he spend his early days?" he asked. "Was he always in captivity?" No one knew. "How does he behave with others of his kind?" But the elephant had gone before anyone could give him an answer.

He wandered thoughtfully back to the others. They were arguing quite fiercely, flatly disagreeing with one another. But peace was restored among them as they united in condemning the stupidity of their questioning companion.'

(Based on many sources, adapted and 'embroidered' for the purpose of this book.)

NATURE–NURTURE AND OUR CAPACITY FOR LEARNING

1

Whether our purpose is to make sense of human behaviour, to encourage creative growth, or to find ways of resolving personal and social problems – or all of these – it may help us to know which aspects of ourselves are laid down genetically (heredity) and which are acquired through life experience (environmental effects). The Nativist–Empiricist debate, more commonly known as the Nature–Nurture controversy, arises because we suspect that there are many human characteristics (traits) that depend, at least partially, upon genetic programming, and we are unsure about how far environmental experience influences our development.

Research reflects these two questions. On the one hand, geneticists and psychologists try to discover evidence of genetic transmission, through the painstaking examination of genes and by studying twins, adopted children and their adoptive and biological parents, and by recording the patterns and frequency of certain traits in family trees. On the other hand, the effects of different environmental factors are explored, using as research subjects, both genetically related and genetically mixed groups of people.

Research findings show that many human traits, either aptitudes, or vulnerability to some diseases, appear to be genetically determined tendencies. These seem to be set in motion, or inhibited, by environmental events, which supports the commonly held view that our traits are the result of a complex interaction of both inherited and environmentally produced factors. Like other 'some of each' views, this position is known as Interactionist. However, it can still help us to know more specifically which of our own, our children's or other people's traits and tendencies are part of a genetically inherited physical make-up. We can then make the most of them, encouraging, avoiding or mitigating them, by changing the environment or our attitudes towards it.

Let us look first at the genetically inherited traits for which we have good evidence – our physical formation.

HEREDITY

Details of our biological 'programme' are carried in genes arranged in strings of DNA (deoxyribonucleic acid) called chromosomes. There are approximately a thousand on each chromosome. Human cells carry forty-six chromosomes, twenty-three from each parent. It is during the process of cell division of the reproductive cells, called meiosis, that genetic material is exchanged between the two sets of chromosomes, as they gather together in a crossing-over stage, shortly before the single cell divides into two. In this way, new genetic combinations are formed, resulting in the many individual variations in each family, and in the gene pool of a population.

The ovum, usually released at a rate of one each month, carries more cell material and is much larger than the sperm, of which millions may be produced each day. Several sperm are needed to dissolve the covering of the ovum to allow fertilization by one successful sperm to take place. The fertilized egg (zygote) now contains its full forty-six chromosomes, half from each parent, and is known as the genotype.

At this point, further genetic determination takes place, as only one gene in each pair present, the more dominant one, will be expressed. Thus genes may be dominant or recessive, those which are recessive only becoming active when paired with another recessive gene. Several genes combined are responsible for some traits, and there are many traits and tendencies for which we have not yet established the genes involved (see **Biology *Texts**). We know that blue eyes and baldness are each carried by a recessive gene, while brown eyes and curly hair each come from a dominant gene. Recessive gene disorders include phenylketonuria (PKU) and cystic fibrosis among others, with a one-in-four chance of the disease being suffered by the children of carriers, a one-in-four chance of being clear altogether, and a two-in-four chance of being a carrier. Down's syndrome is a chromosome disorder, where, instead of just one twenty-first chromosome from each parent, there is a third, extra, twenty-first from one of the parents, due to imperfect cell division during meiosis.

Sex determination

The twenty-third chromosome determines the sex of the embryo, and may carry sex-related disorders such as haemophilia or colour blindness. It is shaped either like an X (the female ovum always carries an X) or like a Y (the male sperm carries X or Y in equal numbers). When paired at fertilization, XX produces a female genotype and XY produces a male. However, variations occur, and include XO (only one chromosome present) which is known as Turner's syndrome, where a female child, who may be affected mentally, fails to mature at puberty. XXY (Klinefelter's syndrome) produces a female child, also failing to mature at puberty. XXX is female and shown by research to have a high incidence in hospitalized cases of schizophrenia. But unless we have extensive evidence of the incidence in the general population, it would be unsafe to draw any firm conclusions concerning a chromosomal link. Likewise, we need to be cautious when considering the higher incidence of XYY (male development) in aggressive prison inmates. There could be XYY men, perhaps with a high creative drive, in the general population whose genotype we do not know, but only extensive studies could allow us to do more than speculate.

Fertility clinics have provided us with much of the information we have about chromosomal variations, but these are not the only factors that can affect the sex development of the embryo. Hormones are also involved. These are chemical 'messengers' carried by the bloodstream, and are the products of the endocrine system. Approximately seven weeks after fertiliz-ation, XY embryos produce testosterone from their rudimentary testes. If this fails to occur, the embryo continues to develop as a female, or, if testos-terone is partial or late in production, part-male, part-female development may result, causing problems of gender identification and allocation at birth. An XX (female) foetus may undergo partial or full male development if there is a shortage of cortisol production, or if there are excessive androgens or some drugs in the mother's bloodstream, and here also, gender may be dif-ficult to identify at birth.

Genotype into phenotype

Thus we can see that our original genetic material is the foundation of our development. The first task of this genotype is to undergo the sorting out of the dominant and recessive genes, determining which of each pair will be ex-pressed in what then becomes known as the phenotype. The phenotype is immediately subject to conditions in the fallopian tube and the womb, as it takes in nutrients and progresses to the establishment of its placenta. The genetically programmed process of maturation has already begun with the first division of the zygote, unfolding throughout life until our last breath and the final breakdown of our body cells. The uterine environment, the first we experience, is itself programmed to enhance early development, but harmful events may interfere. (See **Environment** below.)

The occurrence of twins challenges any assumption that our individual identity is always established at fertilization. Twins resulting from two sep-arate zygotes (fertilized ova) are known as fraternal, or dizygotic, twins, and present no identity dilemma. However, twins resulting from one zygote are a different matter. These monozygotic twins may be formed very soon after fertilization, producing identical twins, or after several cell divisions have taken place, when mirror identical twins can be recognized. Siamese twins result from a much later division into two individuals, and there are vari-ations in the amount of body that is shared and in the prospects for survival and surgical separation. All these different kinds of monozygotic twins share a placenta, which is differentiated during the first few cell divisions, so that these twins have at least the very earliest part of their biological existence as a single organism, and mirror and Siamese twins apparently longer. At what point can we say that human individuality has begun, or must we logically accept that the moment in time can vary?

Notwithstanding this mystery, we can assert that heredity provides our basic biological potentials, including sensory organs, brain, nervous system and reflex responses, together with a range of spontaneous random move-ments. These gradually come under voluntary control as we interact with our environment, and our maturation programme unfolds in the context of our own immediate surroundings.

ENVIRONMENT

Our environment affects us even before conception. Geographical factors, climate and land features, all shape the economic basis of our society and our cultural values. In different cultures, and in different groups within our culture, we are affected by the level and kind of economic conditions into which we are born. Our occupations, available diet, living accommodation, amenities and education all form the framework within which families bear and rear the next generation. These conditions, along with the related value-hierarchy of our family, strongly influence whether our conception is lovingly planned and provided for, accepted as natural, inevitable and usually welcome, or occurs with no thought or provision for our welfare, often unwelcome and accompanied by varying degrees of disaster suffered by struggling parents or parent.

Gestation

We know well the harmful effects of certain drugs taken by the gestating mother, or of a poor diet, and that some diseases, such as rubella, contracted during pregnancy affect foetal development. Other agents of serious injury, such as the AIDS virus or syphilis, are passed on directly through the placenta into the foetal bloodstream.

It is more difficult to establish the effects of stress, physically and psychologically, as close observation without intervention to mitigate causes would be unethical, but the hormones of pregnancy might appear to offer at least some protection in many instances, many mothers of apparently physically healthy babies having experienced stress while pregnant. Psychoanalytic theory suggests that we are probably psychologically vulnerable during gestation, and this hazard certainly cannot be ruled out.

At more moderate levels of stress, ethical respect for privacy impedes the gathering of potentially useful information (data), but evidence of foetal response to parental voices, music and other sounds and pressures is now accumulating. We can state with confidence that we can interact with our environment, even during gestation, and are probably influenced by it to an extent as yet unknown.

Culture and family

Cultural and family patterns surround our gestation period with more or less consideration and assistance, and birth is a very variable experience. Apart from physical and procedural factors, opportunity for parental bonding is now known to be very important as a foundation for our emotional development. Attention is given to ensuring that babies needing incubators or special care after birth are handled by their parents as early and as much as possible so that bonding may 'catch up' from an initial setback. (See chapter 4.)

From birth onwards, maturation continues to unfold, influencing the way we adapt to our environment physically, emotionally, socially and cognitively, through our interaction with it. For example, our development of language depends both upon brain maturation and upon exposure to language during our language-sensitive early years. The physical appearance bestowed on us by our genes, whether we are large or small, plain or beautiful by cultural standards, clumsy or graceful, will influence the response of others towards us, which in turn will help form the expectations and attitudes with which we approach our world.

Cultural norms expressed in family child-rearing practices shape our values, attitudes and behaviour patterns. Opportunities and encouragement to explore new ideas and ways forward are environmental openings for the development of our aptitudes. Some potentials may be ignored or discouraged, or considered unsuitable for development in particular sections of a population. Evolutionary theorists show the advantage to our species of high levels of adaptability, while ecologists remind us of our environmental restraints. Politicians and sociologists argue about how best our social framework may perform the balancing act between our genetically inherited human motivations and the ecology of our planet.

Figure 1.1 *Nature–nurture. This child may have an inborn musical talent, but to fulfil its potential, the talent will need nurturing by teacher, parents and social milieu*

Ethics

From this very complex task, and influencing those in power to a greater or lesser extent, there has arisen in the ethos of each culture a system of moral rules and principles. Here psychologists can add their understanding of individual moral development and human capacity to the philosophers' more general discussion of ethics and the very variable, often ethically questionable, pronouncements of religious leaders and institutions. These, in turn, have always reflected their cultural and historical shaping and accumulated traditions, or have embodied rebellion against the constraints of an established religious order, or the prevailing beliefs about the nature of Divinity or about the concepts of what constitutes good or ill.

Ideological leaders have historically attempted to impose their own widely ranging, similarly often questionable, ethical beliefs, sometimes inspiring unthinking acceptance or unquestioning fervour in a substantial part or all of a population. Both religious and ideological institutions have had huge influence, beneficial and harmful, on the environmental conditions that we experience in our different cultures. They help shape our development as individuals, as we interact with and adapt to their material and moral effects. As we become critically aware of the strengths and fallibilities of our institutions, we are constantly trying to find ways of improving our conditions, our ethics and the nature of our interactions within them, and this often necessitates institutional change. Sociologists have closely studied these aspects of our environment.

Can we learn from the mass of experience we can find in recorded history and in the studies of our different disciplines? Many psychologists believe that we can. They define learning as 'a relatively permanent change in behaviour brought about by experience', and offer different approaches, each emphasizing social, emotional, cognitive or biological aspects of the process. Later chapters in this book will explain some of them, but the theory of learning that focuses most closely on the effects of external, environmental factors is the stimulus-response (SR) theory of the Behaviourists, based on the learning of associations, and this is outlined next.

THE DEVELOPMENT OF BEHAVIOURISM AND SOCIAL LEARNING THEORY (SLT)

John Watson's establishment of the Behaviourist approach (1914) incorporated the findings of Edward Thorndike (1898) and those of Ivan Pavlov, working during the 1900s (1927). Thorndike was an educationalist who made observations of the training of circus animals before designing his own experiments. He studied the escape behaviour of cats placed in a basket, finding that they quickly formed an association between moving a piece of string with a paw, at first by accident, and the opening of the basket lid that allowed their escape. He formulated the Law of Effect, which states that a behaviour will tend to be repeated if it has a satisfying effect. The learning thus acquired he called 'instrumental' learning.

Classical conditioning

Ivan Pavlov, a physiologist, was investigating the salivation of dogs, when he noticed that the dogs would begin to salivate before their food appeared, at the sight of a trainer. When the alternative stimulus of a bell, or of a light, was presented just before the food, on a few occasions, the dogs began to respond with salivation even when only the bell or the light was presented on its own. The dogs' normal salivation response to food was called an 'unconditioned response' (UCR) to an 'unconditioned stimulus' (UCS), while the salivation response to the bell or the light was called the 'conditioned response' (CR) to a 'conditioned stimulus' (CS). The process is known as 'classical conditioning' and is effective, in animals and in humans, for a range of responses operated by the autonomic nervous system, not normally under voluntary control. These include our emotional responses, both pleasant and unpleasant.

John Watson not only demonstrated classical conditioning, producing a conditioned fear response in a child subject, but also desensitization (or 'extinction' of the conditioned response), by gradually introducing the conditioned stimulus (object producing conditioned fear response) while a conditioned child subject was in a state of enjoyment, eating. Watson thus arranged new pairing of stimuli, producing new associative learning (see *Texts). He convinced many psychologists that only observable behaviour could be studied scientifically, not thought processes, and this approach became known as behaviourism.

Operant conditioning

During the 1930s, Burrhus F. Skinner carried Behaviourist theory another stage further with his work on the response behaviour of pigeons and rats. By rewarding the birds with seed as they moved towards the 'target behaviour', Skinner was able to shape their pecking behaviour, for example, into playing ping-pong. Similarly, as rats explored their cage, food rewards were delivered, at first as they approached, later as they pressed a lever. This process is called 'operant conditioning', and is a more refined and versatile example of Thorndike's instrumental learning. Skinner showed that, once a behaviour was learned, intermittent 'reinforcement' (reward) was the most effective way of maintaining it (Skinner, 1938).

This potent intermittency is exactly what our environment provides – we are seldom rewarded for every effort we make, but learn that persistent effort usually brings satisfying results. Operant conditioning is effective for responses that are normally under voluntary control, a good example being learning to drive. We find the brake pedal and carry out other actions as voluntary responses to our instructor's directions. As we repeat all the movements in practice, we are rewarded by our instructor's approval and by an improvement in our driving skills and self-esteem. Once we have passed our driving test, we seldom think about our movements as we make them – they have become operantly conditioned responses to the stimuli of our vehicle and road conditions. Operant conditioning theory can help to explain why it is difficult to change our habits.

Effects of punishment

Unpleasant events also exercise conditioning power over responses that become associated with them. Skinner showed that rats would learn to climb into another part of their cage to avoid an electric shock, but it has been found, especially with human beings, that reinforcement of desired behaviour is longer lasting than aversive associations with undesired behaviour. Even to have this lesser effect, the aversive experience has to be at a crucial, individually variable level of unpleasantness, and has to be applied *at the time of the undesired behaviour*. Punishment applied other than instantly forms an association with the punisher or with being found out, bypassing the tendency to behave undesirably.

Deferred punishment can only deter people with a capacity for deferring *reward*, that is, those with a sufficiently developed *association* system brought about by enough experience of reward. Most social signals that have a deterrent effect are the spontaneous reactions of others with an immediate change in their current behaviour, which 'nips in the bud' the undesired behaviour. However, much will depend on the stronger individual patterns laid down by the previous experience of positive reinforcement, or lack of it. Also potent are *both* the strength of motivation for the socially undesired behaviour and the perceived alternative.

Learned helplessness

Learned helplessness processes have also been uncovered by Behaviourist research. M. Seligman (1972), working with dogs, was investigating how quickly they could escape if given prior experience of unpleasant stimuli. They were therefore harnessed into a shuttle box (a box with two compartments) and given electric shocks from which they could not escape. Seligman discovered, contrary to his expectations, that when shocks were given after the harness had been removed to allow them to escape into the other compartment, they failed to do so. They had learned that they were helpless.

Our environment, consisting of our circumstances and our parenting, sometimes conditions this learned helplessness into individuals or whole communities, who cannot then perceive the possibility of action on their own behalf. Seligman found that a lot of effort was needed by the trainers repeatedly dragging dogs into the safe compartment before they could establish new, useful learning.

Classical and operant conditioning theory can explain avoidance behaviour, helpless inertia, or periodic bouts of helplessness accompanied by anxiety or panic. It suggests that aversive stimuli or pain, in the absence of crucial, counteracting early assistance and reassurance, have formed associations with certain environmental stimuli or situations. To overcome this conditioning, we need new learning experience of associations with non-disaster and with coping adequately. Behaviourist therapy is therefore based on providing this new experience.

Observational learning

Albert Bandura (1960s, 1977, 1985) has made a major contribution to Social Learning Theory, explaining how we also learn by observing others. Where we see someone else, especially someone we regard positively, being rewarded for their behaviour in some way, such as enjoyment, gain or approval, we are very likely to imitate them, learning vicariously from their experience. If they meet discomfort or disapproval, in the absence of apparent gains or increased esteem, we are similarly likely to avoid doing whatever they were doing.

Banduras and his colleagues' research (see example later in this chapter) has generated several studies of the effects of watching television, especially violent films. Results show that other environmental factors (called 'variables'), such as the presence of critical others, affect the outcome, and personality studies suggest that the state of maturity and personal integration of the viewer are also crucial determinants of outcome. Bandura later broke with strict Behaviourist tradition by including in his analysis of our social learning the cognitive interpretations we make of a situation, which govern the selection of conditioned responses we produce. Thus we distinguish between a celebration and a dangerous situation, or between a formal or informal occasion, and respond differently (Bandura, 1985).

Although Behaviourists can make useful suggestions about how we may achieve desirable individual and social change, and have pioneered successful programmed learning techniques in education, there are further questions of ethics, self-determination and the role of reasoning that Behaviourism does not address. It is therefore a good idea to complement its findings with the contributions made by other approaches, and an example of this 'eclectic' approach is shown in the next section on aggression.

AGGRESSION

Any debate must begin with a definition of its subject, and a nature–nurture discussion is no exception. Aggression has been described by psychologists as behaviour that makes uncomfortable or harms another person, or his or her property, and has further been identified as either hostile or instrumental. Hostile aggression is directed primarily at a person or persons, while instrumental aggression is incidental to the pursuit of some other goal. There may or may not be present in aggressive behaviour: anger, animosity, intention or even awareness of the aggression perceived by others.

There is moral disagreement about when aggression may be acceptable or desirable, for example in sport or salesmanship, and there is uncertainty about where the borderline lies between aggression and competition, or between aggression and assertiveness. Here it can be useful to view aggression as one end of a continuum that spans assertiveness, firmness, gentle effectiveness through neutral flexibility, compromise and giving way to open acceptance. This scale can also be used to select an appropriate, conscious level of response.

Finally, we can recognize a form of aggression, often overlooked as such, where passivity adversely affects others by placing oppressive demands on them. This is known as 'passive aggression'. There is, as we can see, a very wide range of behaviour that may be experienced as aggression by those on the receiving end. Explanations of how aggression arises are therefore likely to be diverse, some emphasizing genetically programmed tendencies, while others point to environmental shaping.

Social learning

Beginning with the Behaviourists' Social Learning position, let us return to the contribution of Albert Bandura referred to above. He and his colleagues carried out 'naturalistic observations' of nursery school children through a one-way mirror. Some of the children had been playing individually beforehand in a room where there was an adult 'model' who, with half of the children had behaved nurturantly towards a large doll. The other half of the children, referred to as the second experimental group, saw the adult model behaving aggressively towards the doll, as they played individually alongside. When both experimental groups joined the 'control' group of children, who had not played beside the adult model, to play in the large observation room, they all saw most of the toys being removed from the room as they entered, thus producing a level of frustration likely to evoke reactions.

The most aggression was observed in the children who had seen the aggressive adult model. The group exposed to the nurturant model showed the least aggression, while the control group were in between. Social Learning theorists believe that observational learning accounts for a great deal of human aggression, but that children are also conditioned directly when young. The positive reinforcements of advantages gained over other children, the satisfaction of 'getting away with' disallowed behaviour, and, where it occurs, encouragement to 'toughness', all shape aggressive patterns of behaviour. For the Behaviourists, then, aggression is overwhelmingly an environmental product, and their hard, scientific evidence cannot be ignored in any practical discussion.

Psychoanalytic view

In strong contrast with this view, the psychoanalytic approach, beginning with Freud, emphasizes a biologically based drive, present at birth. Initially, Freud thought that aggression was closely linked with libido, these two drives forming the basic, raw energy of the 'id' (1923). (See chapter 3.) His later theory of 'Eros' (Life) and 'Thanatos' (Death) instincts (1920) views aggression as not only linked with the desiring, creative, self-preservative drives of Eros, but as a secondary part of the drive towards a Nirvana-like peace that was the essence of Thanatos.

Freud had three sons fighting in World War I, and he had come to understand that human beings 'fight for peace' and try aggressively to remove obstacles to that goal. As Eros and Thanatos counterbalance one another's energies, aggression could be inhibited, allowed appropriate expression, or 'sublimated', a term used by Freud to describe the redirection of basic drives into socially acceptable channels. Ego development enabled this balancing process between id drives, external reality and superego evaluation (see chapter 3).

Psychoanalyst Anthony Storr has written extensively about human aggression (1968), which he views as a biologically based necessity for survival that is also essential to enable us to free ourselves of dependencies and achieve self-direction. He argues that we need the capacity to oppose influences that would maintain our dependent subservience, and that we cannot and should not try to get rid of all aggression. He advocates social outlets for this valuable aspect of our nature in sport and democratic politics, and, in his later writing, he incorporates many references to the necessity of early loving relationships, in which we may feel and learn to handle aggression, to develop our capacity for self-control and to usefully direct of our aggressive energies.

Animal studies

Comparative psychologists are people who study animals in order to compare their responses and behaviour with those of human beings. This approach is itself controversial, but even in subhuman species, evidence has been produced in support of both the nature and the nurture side of the debate concerning aggression (see *Texts).

Ethologists also study aggression in animals, and Konrad Lorenz (1963) has observed that intra-specific aggression (between animals of the same species) serves several purposes. Individual survival needs intensify when food supplies are short, and aggression, or the threat of aggression, surrounding mating behaviour ensures for the species that the fittest animals are those who pass on their genes to future generations.

Social animals, living in groups, maintain their social structure and compete for their place in the 'pecking order' by aggressive threat or action. They enhance cohesion by co-operative and mutually bonding behaviour, and Lorenz suggests that this necessity for co-operation in mating and rearing the young, and in achieving the greater security of an integrated group, is the evolutionary origin of devotion and love. Intra-specific aggression, biologically programmed to ensure individual survival and mating advantage, is therefore an essential precursor to the bonding necessary to bridge its antagonisms. This theory can readily be extrapolated (extended) to human love that 'overcomes the differences'.

Social environment

Social psychologists look for explanations of behaviour in the social environment, and their research has produced evidence of aggression based on a number of factors. Respect for authority and the carrying out of orders has been demonstrated in war studies following World War II and the Vietnam conflict, and by the series of 'electric shock' experiments by Milgram in the 1960s and 1970s. In these, he showed that a substantial majority of ordinary people were ready to administer severe shocks to 'learners' when asked to do so by a research psychologist they respected. His results were replicated in other cultures, suggesting that respect for authority is a common human characteristic that can bring about extraordinary aggression in otherwise apparently ordinary individuals. A prison role-playing study similarly showed how normally well balanced people are influenced by stereotyped social perceptions or 'blindnesses' (Zimbardo, 1972).

Deindividuation (the loss or submergence of a sense of identity) has been shown to increase aggression in crowds, and to reduce responsible behaviour generally (Festinger et al., 1952). It has thus become a common practice for employees, including professional people, to always give their names, often wearing labels in their work. Studies of social prejudice have associated prejudice with aggression, and social psychologists have suggested social changes indicated by their research that can reduce both (Cook, 1979). Policy-makers, at local, national and international levels, need to be fully aware of the range of research findings that together give insight into human responses, especially, perhaps, intraspecific human aggression.

Interactionist view

This has been only an outline of some of the arguments concerning aggression, and of the kinds of evidence on which they are based, but hopefully it has been enough to show how complex the nature–nurture issue is. More advanced argument must take into account larger bodies of research that can be found in other texts (see *Texts), but the interactionist position is overwhelmingly dominant today. However, because there are so many possible factors involved, it can be that just one single factor – biological, psychological or environmental – can be crucial to the development of one particular individual at a particular time.

Another example of the importance of carefully considering both biological and environmental factors and their interaction is in the research into Asperger syndrome, a mild form of autism. Research investigates biological disorder, perceptual dysfunction, possible environmental factors that exacerbate the condition and especially the environmental remedial potential of training and public awareness (Frith, 1991). We need, therefore, in seeking an effective understanding of any particular issue, to consider carefully the potential of each of the approaches in psychology and of other disciplines, while not losing sight of the complex, interactionist whole.

The next chapter focuses on the biological base of temperament and on the association between our nervous system and different kinds of activity; later chapters will include references to the kinds of experience that have been observed to affect our development over our lifespan.

INDIVIDUAL TEMPERAMENT AND THE NERVOUS SYSTEM 2

Temperament theorists believe that temperament is inherited and have shown that it is consistent over time. Research into the reactions of new-born babies (neonates) has demonstrated considerable individual differences, as well as general sex differences, in the sensitivity and intensity of their reactions to stimuli such as noise, light, movement, touch and handling. Some appear to be highly sensitive to stimulation and more likely to display irritability when older. Those with 'high threshold' responses react much less to environmental stimuli.

Twin studies have supported the existence of genetic elements in temperament, especially for activity rate and persistence, but not all identical twins are alike in temperament, suggesting that other factors must also be involved (Goldsmith and Gottesman, 1981).

Traits and tendencies

Evidence that early individual differences persist is provided by *longitudinal* studies (observations of the same individuals at intervals over a period of time. *Cross-sectional* studies consist of observations of different age groups at the same time). Jerome Kagan et al. (1964) showed that children have a characteristic tendency to be either impulsive or reflective in their 'conceptual tempo'. This means that either they tend to react quickly or impulsively, or they tend to think about or reflect upon an object or event before responding. Each approach has its advantages, but the longer concentration span of the reflective child favours learning, especially learning to read.

Like most categories devised by psychologists, there is no sharp dividing line between them, but being aware of the different reactions they describe can help parents, carers and teachers. They can more easily recognize and make the most of a child's natural, impulsive or reflective tendency, while carefully encouraging him or her to develop at least a little of the opposite cognitive approach for use in situations that require it.

Buss and Plomin (1975) identified four bi-polar dimensions of temperament (opposite qualities of temperament that can be scaled along a continuum (line running between them). Thus they were able to rate children as more or less active along an active–lethargic continuum, and similarly as more or less emotional–impassive, gregarious–detached or impulsive–deliberate. This last dimension was similar to Kagan's distinction of impulsive or reflective categories. Buss and Plomin also demonstrated that these qualities persisted over time.

Thomas and Chess (1977) rated their child subjects on a list of nine aspects of temperament, including activity level, rhythmicity (predictability of daily pattern), approach or withdrawal, adaptability, response threshold, reaction intensity, mood quality, distractibility and, finally, persistence and attention span. They found that these qualities clustered together to suggest three basic types of child: the 'easy', the 'difficult' and the 'slow-to-warm-up' children we can recognize among those we have known, or can remember that we were ourselves.

In our labelling of children, or adults, with psychologists' categories or with commonly used stereotypes, we need to monitor whether we might be making impulsive, invalid or unreliable assumptions about individuals. However, used with care, such labels can often be a useful aid in discussion, or a short-cut when individual differences are irrelevant to the context of our comment.

Effects of experience

Qualities of basic individual temperament are thought to arise initially from the inherited sensitivity of our nervous system, though we have evidence that experience is also important in the shaping of our characteristic responses. Experience provides the kinds and levels of stimulation as we interact with our immediate environment, so that we can develop defensive withdrawal tendencies if we encounter traumatic or prolonged excessive stimulation, or we can suffer delay or impairment in wide areas of our development if we are inadequately provided with appropriate stimulation at critical periods early in life. Emotional support is also vital, freeing us to explore our environment by providing us with a 'safe base', which we gradually internalize into the quality of confidence as we mature.

Experience, therefore, not only shapes patterns of response, as is set out in classical and operant conditioning theory, but, as described by cognitive developmental theorists, experience also programmes our memories. In our thinking, we use information stored in memory as we interact with our environment and try to make sense of incoming information, distinguishing between familiar and new elements.

Input from memory, and from current thought processes, together with input from all other parts of the body, is relayed into the hypothalamus. This is a small organ of the brain which controls homeostasis (the balancing of our internal body conditions), our endocrine system (glands secreting hormones circulated in the bloodstream) and our nervous system activity. It is thus quite difficult to separate out basic temperament from developing patterns of personality, and most psychology textbooks include temperament under the broader heading of 'personality'. Although nervous system activity is closely associated with temperament and characteristic kinds of response, details about its form and function are usually to be found under 'biopsychology', or a separate section of its own, in psychology textbooks.

In this chapter, we are especially concerned with the autonomic branch of the nervous system, but we need to be aware of its close links with the brain, other parts of the nervous system and other body systems, as well as with our thinking processes. The integration of all these is mediated by the hypothalamus, enabling us to exercise at least some 'mind over matter'.

THE NERVOUS SYSTEM

Our nervous system has evolved from a simple, elongated string of nerve cells that began specialization by the development of olfactory properties able to register the chemical odours of threatening predators or desirable sources of nutrition – our sense of smell. Using our control of movement and our senses of hearing, seeing and touch, interaction with our environment down the ages has favoured the evolution of increasing complexity, producing our present brain and spinal cord, which we call the central nervous system (CNS). Our spinal cord still contains clusters of cells (nuclei) capable of initiating reflex movements without brain processing, and dancing is believed to contain an element of control from spinal nuclei.

The most basic of our processes, such as respiration and arousal, are under the control of nuclei in the brain stem, the most anciently evolved part of the brain. More flexible behaviour required further specialization, and the various organs of the limbic system came into being, making possible the experimental and 'practice' behaviour observed in play.

The most recently evolved part of our brain is the cerebrum (or two cerebral hemispheres), also called the cortex or neo-cortex. This enables more detailed processing of information, and a wider and more flexible range of responses. Verbal language capacity is the most striking recently evolved feature in the cortical evolution of our brain, usually found in the left cerebral hemisphere (although in some, but not all, left-handed people, it may be found in the right hemisphere).

Research has shown that our two cerebral hemispheres have evolved to develop 'lateralization': that is, not only does each side control the opposite side of the body (decussation), but each side specializes in the kind of thinking it does. Studies of subjects who have undergone the surgical separation of the two hemispheres in the treatment of epilepsy (Sperry, 1974) and various studies using an electroencephalogram (EEG) have shown that the left hemisphere is active during tasks involving speech, reading, writing, calculation, logical and analytical skills, and in focusing on detail.

The right hemisphere registers greater activity during thought processes involving musical and artistic abilities, imagery and dreaming, in spatial and pattern perception and in holistic overviewing. Emotional, and sometimes impulsive, responses have also been associated with right-hemisphere activity, as has intuitive feeling. In addition to these differences in hemispheric activity, EEG studies have shown a high degree of co-ordination between them, even in their specialized tasks.

Thus the central nervous system regulates and controls our internal processes and our behaviour, sending out impulses to different parts of the body and receiving input, through the peripheral nervous system (PNS), which consists of two parts. One part, the somatic system ('soma' means body), conducts information to the brain from the sensory receptors of sight, hearing, taste, smell and touch, and also from the sense that registers internally the position of our bodies (proprioception). The somatic system also conducts nerve impulses from the CNS that control all our body movements. The other part of the peripheral nerve network, the autonomic nervous system (ANS), serves the internal (visceral) organs, and the processes involved in metabolism (that is, in energy production and conservation, and in cell maintenance).

The autonomic nervous system

The autonomic nervous system is further divided into two: the sympathetic and the parasympathetic networks, which function both antagonistically (in opposition) to one another and in co-ordination. The sympathetic branch is often called the 'fight/flight' part of the system, since it prepares our bodies for emergency activity when we become alarmed, but it is also responsible for the mobilization of energy at more moderate levels and for maintaining alert concentration. It dilates the pupils of our eyes, inhibits saliva flow and digestive processes, accelerates heartbeat and increases oxygen intake by dilating the bronchi of our lungs. It increases the secretion of adrenalin and noradrenalin (called epinephrine and norepinephrine in some texts) and inhibits bladder contraction, arousing us and generally preparing us for activity.

The parasympathetic branch, in contrast, promotes the cellular processes that restore our energy reserves and nervous tissue. It contracts the pupils of our eyes, stimulates the flow of saliva and other digestive juices, aids digestion and intestinal activity, and enables the bladder to contract and pass urine. Introspective processes, such as meditation, require parasympathetic activity, which is also responsible for reducing levels of arousal and for our sense of release sometimes accompanied by a flow of tears.

The ANS, sympathetic and parasympathetic, is under the control of the hypothalamus, which lies below the thalamus, from which is relayed sensory information to various parts of the brain. The ANS is thus closely associated with the endocrine system, whose specialized glands secrete the chemical hormones circulated in the bloodstream. An example is the hormone adrenalin, which is produced by the adrenal medulla (the inside part of the adrenal gland) when activated by sympathetic nerve impulses.

A healthy ANS is resilient and able to flow smoothly from the dominance of one branch to the dominance of the other, which co-operate, for example, in enabling us to use only routine and relevant mental processes when physical energy output is high, or in keeping us mentally alert yet physically inactive. Thus it can produce the high energy and intense concentration needed in competitive sport, or, at the other extreme, it can provide for heightened states of awareness combined with complete physical stillness. Excessive sympathetic activity, unrelieved over a period, biochemically builds up tensions requiring discharge, while excessive parasympathetic dominance can result in lethargy and loss of fitness.

Maintaining ANS health

There is much we can do to ensure a healthy nervous system. Diet is important generally in supplying elements essential to all cellular function, and in particular, sodium and potassium are vital to the production of electrochemical nerve impulses and to the restoration of the capacity to pass further impulses (see **Texts** under neuron function). Citrus fruits, bananas and some vegetables supply potassium, while enough sodium chloride (salt) is necessary to replace loss through sweat-glands, especially in excessive heat or in gastro-intestinal infections. A basic understanding of body systems, processes and nutritional, exercise and rest needs, so closely affecting and affected by our nervous system function, is invaluable in helping us to regulate a sound biological base to our lives.

Just as our bodies are individually different with varying nutritional, exercise and sleep requirements, so will the appropriate balance of nervous system activity vary with individual temperament. Resilience is ensured by a suitable balance of activity and relaxation, both physical and mental, so that we remain able to respond to the normal stresses and sometimes sudden demands in our individual patterns of living. Essential occupations need the balance of contrasting recreation, as well as sufficient rest, and to review periodically the demands we make on ourselves, or allow others to make, will help us considerably. We can then arrange or negotiate desirable adjustments in our accumulated commitments, and match our pattern of replenishment accordingly. The greater the stresses we experience, the more important it becomes to plan our coping strategy.

Electronic bio-feedback is just one of the ways that have been developed to help us gain awareness of, and capacity to influence, our ANS functioning. There are also a number of approaches to relaxation and altered states of awareness, such as meditation, that use carefully designed and taught exercises. Different methods will suit different individuals, and a careful choice can be made to fit in with personal needs, aims and temperament patterns.

Figure 2.1 *Maintaining health. Both exercise and relaxed enjoyment are essential for autonomic nervous system resilience, mental efficiency and physical fitness*

Relaxation

In a simple example of learning how to relax, starting with a comfortable sitting or lying position, each group of muscles is focused on in turn, beginning with the feet and ankles. First, the muscles are strongly contracted into a state of tension (sympathetic activity), for a count of about five, and then they are suddenly released, counting for the same period (parasympathetic activity). Meanwhile, the learner concentrates on how it feels to 'tighten up' and to 'let go', thus learning to recognize the tensions that can build up, and the restorative possibilities of release that can become part of a daily routine.

The release of these tensions is why short breaks in our work improve performance and output, and why, as our ANS 'feels like a change', we are naturally inclined to 'get tired' of what we are doing and move, by choice, from one occupation to another during our day. When high motivation to persevere and complete a task or target overrides inclination, there is a corresponding glow of satisfaction as our ANS is released from its imposed pattern, to find a new balance in our next phase, adding to a cognitive recognition of the value of our output for ourselves and others. Motivation to 'work' is thus strengthened.

Physical relaxation exercises can be used alone, or as a preparation for mental relaxation, which can also be approached directly. Here again, several different methods have been developed. These all involve a 'letting go' of sensory input and thought processes, resulting in the release of restorative processes in our brains. Sometimes this is sought by a focus on stillness or silence beyond environmental sounds, or there may be a focus on an image, a word, sound (mantra) or a sequence of words, which all have the effect of 'resting' those parts of our brain normally in use, without producing the patterns of mental activity and loss of consciousness characteristic of sleep.

Increased awareness Some of these methods can induce a deep sense of spiritual awareness. As we 'allow' the restoration of body and brain cells under heightened parasympathetic influence, we can become aware of our self as part of an infinitely creative peacefulness. Such practices need to be completed by focusing on a return to our surroundings, to restore our ANS balance to the range of responses needed to interact with mundane realities. The neurotransmitters (chemical substances) of our brains need a little time for the essential process of readjustment, aided by outward focus and sometimes a counting back to it (5, 4, 3, 2, 1...).

Similarly, to be of any overall benefit, a reliable and ethical framework of down-to-earth meaning is needed to safeguard the connectedness and mental balance of any individual undertaking these exercises, and an appropriate method, or teacher, needs to be carefully chosen, bearing this in mind.

Awareness of a need for balance is also expressed in eastern spirituality, for example, in the concept of Tao, consisting of a sensitively flexible interaction between Yin (female, passive dynamics) and Yang (male, active energies). East or west, the most heavenly spirituality requires a well functioning ANS for its inner experience and for its full expression in practical living.

Further discussion of our ANS and the effects of stress will be found later in the book (see chapter 9). At this stage, it is sufficient to perceive the important role of the nervous system as the basis of our individual temperament and in the development of individual personality and patterns of living. Another such crucial concept in this study of lifespan psychology is described in the next chapter. We identify a psychological, rather than a biological function, but the 'ego', as Freud calls it, is also essentially concerned with reality and with balance.

THE MATURING EGO: FREUD, ERIKSON AND BERNE

3

Erik Erikson's lifespan theory is used on training courses in many professions because it has been found to provide a useful framework for understanding human development and the characteristics of the different stages of our lives. It has therefore been chosen to provide the main structure for the material presented in this book. Having indicated some of the different perspectives in psychology, and having examined the importance of both environmental and biological factors in shaping our individual differences, we are ready to consider, chapter by chapter, the way in which our personality and our experience interact, during our lifetime of continuing development.

Erikson's central focus is the emergence of ego strengths, or qualities, as we mature through eight stages of development from birth until we die, thus completing our own unique life cycle within the historical and cultural setting into which we are born. It will help us to understand his ideas if we look first at how they were based on Freud's psychoanalytic theory (although Erikson's viewpoint extends usefully, and with a greater sense of hope, well beyond Freud's pioneering work).

SIGMUND FREUD (1856–1939)

After an earlier period of collaboration with Josef Breuer, in which they used hypnosis, Freud began investigating the contents of the unconscious mind by interpreting his own and his patients' dreams (Freud, 1900) and by the process of free association. Although his initial theory later underwent a little modification by himself, and more by others, he laid down a description of personality development that has proved itself to be a useful tool for therapeutic purposes and a fruitful aid to discussion.

Personality structure

He perceived three main elements of personality: the 'id', present at birth, consists of basic raw instincts, the source of all our energy; the 'ego', emerging at about eighteen months of age, as we interact with our surroundings, consists of a developing capacity to balance id drives, and a little later superego morality, with reality; the 'superego', forming around four or five years of age, consists of moral values incorporated during the resolution of the Oedipus (boy) or Elektra (girl) conflict.

The id is concerned with gratification of desire (libido), and this is at first oral. Aggression accompanies libido, ever ready to further gratification, and these two id drives were seen as our raw motivation and energy source which underlay our behaviour throughout life. By stating that libido, biologically energized, was basically sexual in nature, even in infancy, Freud ignited an intense controversy, which only modern hindsight is capable of resolving, but he had the courage of a pioneer, and set forth the truth as he saw it. It is inevitable that every major theory in psychology (and, indeed, other disciplines) is shaped by the cultural background, training and experience, and by the personal life of the theorist. Let us therefore take a brief look at the factors influencing Freud's perception.

Biographical factors

Culturally, Freud was affected by living in Vienna from 1860, when he was four years old, where 'Victorian' attitudes to sex were, if anything, even more forbidding than those of the British Victorians. The population of Europe was expanding rapidly, and contraception was unreliable and met with wide disapproval. Ethological studies of reproduction in animals suggest that, in conditions of crowding and over-population, some deep-level, biologically based reaction occurs that has the effect of regulating reproductive activity. In humans, this may have found its expression in negative attitudes towards sex. Because it was a taboo subject, there actually were, in Europe and especially in Vienna, a large number of people who had problems arising from repressed sexuality that they could not talk to anyone about, and many of Freud's patients were among them.

Freud's personal life was also going through crisis. His intense grief after the death of his father in 1896 had precipitated his need for self-analysis, and he recovered a great deal of material from his childhood (see **Biographies**). He had also reached the point of having as many children as he felt able to provide for, three sons and three daughters (the youngest, Anna, being born in 1896). In the absence of reliable contraception, he had apparently adjusted his relationship with his wife, and found himself under uncomfortable sexual pressure. Taking all these facts into consideration, it is not surprising that his theory contains what many people consider a disproportionate emphasis on sex.

Psychoanalytic theory

The id was thus seen as sexually libidinous and aggressive, and it could only become civilized by the balancing activity of the ego, especially in the process of 'sublimation', whereby id energies were directed by the ego into socially acceptable behaviour. Freud's later, modified theory of Eros and Thanatos (see chapter 1) retained the concept of sublimation, which is considered superfluous by many who regard libido (a flow of desiring energy) as broadly creative.

Freud distinguished five 'psychosexual' stages to describe the changes he observed in the libido's erogenous aims. As a brilliant neurologist, he understood how our nerve fibres become more effective as they develop a fatty substance around them called myelin. At birth, the nerve fibres that serve the mouth are already well myelinated, making this our most sensitive area, and therefore the one associated with early libido (gratification and aggression)

Figure 3.1 *The oral stage. Because his mouth is well supplied with myelinated nerve fibres, this baby can enjoy exploring anything he can grasp and put into his mouth*

– sucking and exploring with the mouth and biting. He therefore called the first psychosexual stage the 'oral' stage.

The second major area to become myelinated, and therefore under voluntary control and more sensitive, is the area around the anus. Thus, during the 'anal' stage, lasting from around eighteen months until about three and a half years of age, gratification shifts its emphasis to sensation and control in the anal area. By about three years, further myelination in the genital area begins a change into the 'phallic' stage, after which libido becomes quiescent during the 'latency' period. Latency lasts from around five or six years of age until puberty, when a renewed upsurge of libido begins the last stage described by Freud, the 'genital' stage, which brings the maturing capacity for adult relationships by about eighteen years of age.

Id drives, though remaining primitive, immediate and producing primary thinking (e.g. 'I want what I want ... now!'), change their emphasis as we grow towards adulthood. Freud believed that experience and development during the first three stages – oral, anal and phallic – laid down each individual's personality by the age of six years, and Erikson's descriptions of this psychosexual shaping of personality among American Indians (Erikson, 1963) illustrate well the Freudian foundation of his training.

Freud's second major component of personality, the ego, is formed from id energies, beginning when interaction with the source of oral gratification, the mother, makes it evident to us that her response is not always instantly forthcoming, and we find that aggression, especially biting our mother, is not always the most productive answer to frustration. Some of our basic energies thus become concerned with a balancing of drives with reality, with perceived possibilities, producing reasoning that Freud called secondary thinking (e.g. 'I want what I want, but I will have to wait a bit.'). Whereas the id operates on the pleasure principle, the ego operates on the reality principle.

*Defence
mechanisms*

Because pain and anxiety interfere with its balancing act, the ego develops unconscious 'defence mechanisms' that keep painful and threatening information from entering consciousness, acting as a kind of gate. Thus pain and fear beyond a tolerable level are 'repressed', and often, with the feelings, the memory of associated events. We can observe the healthy function of this defence in injury or emergency, when survival may depend upon action, or at least the conservation of energy by not responding emotionally until later. Freud found that repression may produce physical symptoms and 'nervous disorders', and he specialized in treating them.

'Fixation' (failure to develop emotionally beyond the point where trauma occurred) may accompany repression, which may affect substantial areas of a personality, or only become evident in certain situations. Fixation may also occur when over-indulgence has failed to equip our ego with the capacity to consider the needs of others as well as our own. 'Regression' (reverting to behaviour typical of earlier developmental stages) is another commonly observed defence emerging under stress. Like repression, regression can be temporarily advantageous, giving us a 'short-break' period, and perhaps eliciting a little cossetting that can restore our ability to enjoy life, or at least to carry on coping with it. Freud maintained that all material held back in the unconscious remains dynamic and can only come under ego-control by being made conscious. This is the central principle of his method of treatment, 'psychoanalysis'.

The third component of personality, the superego, is the product of another major ego-defence, 'identification'. This occurs, Freud believed, when we greatly fear someone, or when we perceive them to be getting what we want, or being what we want to be. These conditions are present in what he described as the Oedipus and Elektra conflicts, affecting boys and girls respectively. Once again, we need modern hindsight and capacity for interpretation to make any sense of his findings.

His formulation of this unconscious process states that, during the oral and anal stages, both boys and girls direct their libido towards their mother. With the onset of the phallic stage, the boy begins to see his father as a rival, who may be angry with him for his desires towards his mother and punish him by castration. To this fear is added the boy's admiration, and his wish to acquire for himself his father's success with his mother. The double dilemma is resolved by identification with his father, during which he 'introjects' (incorporates as his own) his father's values, thus beginning to feel all his 'oughts' and 'ought nots'. These strictures are derived from personal and family values, which are usually infused by social and cultural standards.

As the superego develops to take over these values and norms, fear of punishment becomes a capacity for self-condemnation that we usually call 'guilt'. A punitive superego can make life a misery and a great deal of extra work for the ego, which now has to take superego moralizing into its balancing process according to the reality principle (e.g. id: 'I want this now.'; superego: 'It is wrong and no proper person would behave so.'; ego: 'But I can't see any harm to anyone. Is it really wrong?'). At the other end of superego variation, weak moral values allow irresponsible behaviour, and the absence of a capacity to feel guilt results in an amoral personality.

More has been written about the unhealthy effects of too much guilt, common in a punitive culture, and about the antisocial effects of too little, common in a materialistic society, than about the productive guidelines and loving attitudes incorporated by the healthy superego. However, Freud believed that as a boy's identification with his father is accomplished, and his superego established, he gives up his libidinal urges towards his mother, and so enters the latency stage.

For the little girl, the Elektra conflict is necessarily different. Freud explained that, for her, the onset of the phallic stage is marked by 'penis envy', and that the girl concludes that she has been castrated, blaming her mother. Feeling let down, she transfers her libidinal direction to her father; her mother then becomes both a hated and admired rival. This conflict is resolved in the same way as the boy's, by identification, during which the mother's values are introjected, and the superego comes into being. The latency stage is entered as desire for the father is abandoned.

Greek mythology was taught as part of a good education in Europe, so Freud was choosing commonly recognized names for these phallic conflicts and fantasies he believed that he observed. Oedipus was the son who murdered his father and married his mother; Elektra killed her mother and married her father. Our understanding of both the myths, and Freud's theory, benefits from a consideration beyond their literal content.

Modern hindsight

A great deal more sense emerges from his faithfully reported observations of adult dreams and memories, if we accept the more recent view of many that libido is broadly creative, not basically only sexual. Freud himself had moved a little in this direction in his later formulation of our Eros and Thanatos instinctual drives, and both Alfred Adler (in 1911) and Carl Jung (in 1913) had broken off their collaboration with Freud over a disagreement about the nature of libido. Adler believed that it was primarily a 'will to power', and it is interesting to note that he was a man of small stature. Jung perceived that libido encompassed many facets of creativity besides sexuality, out of which insight he developed a major theory of his own (see chapter 9). Moreover, he explained that sexual symbols in dreams, and in art and myths, represent a person's general creative potential.

From this viewpoint, castration fears in the Oedipus conflict can be interpreted as a fear that other forms of creativity may be 'cut off', and authoritarian Viennese society provided ample reason for them. The little boy would be expected to relinquish any softer 'feminine' tendencies, along with his close attachment to his mother, and to follow whatever 'masculine' training and education his father decided upon. The little girl might well have envied her brother's comparative freedom to look forward to a life outside the home, already lost to her, as her mother had obviously given in to the system. Usually all she could hope for was domesticity and child-bearing. Only father had any real freedom of creative choice, and the only solution appeared to be becoming like her mother, and growing up to marry a man with whom she could at least come first.

In discussing the nature of libido, it would be possible to argue further, and thus account for the compulsive nature of immature and of distorted sexual behaviour. Libidinal energies may be, to some extent, relatively fluid. Frustrated energies from other facets of creative drive may therefore be readily converted into sexual urge, along with distortions caused by experience or trauma. Thus, a biological goal, or distorted activity, achieves a discharge of tensions and forms a habitual pattern through id gratification and repetition. Superego – and especially ego inadequacies – result in the lack of control evident in compulsiveness, and the sexual urge, a natural drive in its own right, only comes under ego-control with full, adult ego-maturity. Perhaps Freud's concept of sublimation is in reality a more flexible, two-way process allowing the maximum likelihood of libidinal expression. Supporting this view is the recent verification of the proximity of the brain areas involved, facilitating their suggested interconnection.

Although his theory is most widely known for its emphasis on psychosexual development and personality formation, it would be a mistake to overlook his later interest in social psychology. He believed that we seek to belong to a group with whom we can identify our ego, that is, on whom we can rely to balance up aims and possibilities in the same way that we do. Our superego, he concluded from his observations, is invested in any authority we accept as legitimate, and therefore obedience to that authority carries a moral obligation to us.

Above all, Freud's pioneering focus on the importance of the biologically determined basis of the dynamics of our minds and of the effects of early experience on that basic programming has opened up a whole range of psychodynamic theories, arising from discussion and criticism of his own and others. Whatever the shortcomings of Freud's ideas, he has certainly pioneered great changes in our understanding of psychodynamics, and has introduced concepts that have aided further discussion. Erik Erikson is a major contributor to these further developments, and we return to an outline of some of the principles of his theory, leaving more detailed description of his stages to appropriate later chapters.

ERIK ERIKSON (1902–1979)

As with all theorists, Erik Erikson's background, training and later experience shaped his theory, so it will be useful to consider briefly how he acquired his insights and biases. He was born in Germany in 1902; his father was Danish, but his parents had separated, and he was brought up by his Jewish mother and stepfather. Teased as a child by his Jewish schoolmates for his Danish appearance, Erikson was sensitized early on to cultural differences. Gaining much from his German paediatrician stepfather, and after an uncertain and exploratory period during which he studied art and moved around Europe, Erikson trained as a Montessori teacher. In 1927, he was invited to teach at a school in Vienna, founded by Anna Freud (Sigmund's youngest child) and Dorothy Burlingham. Here he studied child analysis, trained and analysed by Anna Freud. He married a Canadian art critic, Joan Serson, when he was twenty-seven.

By 1933, psychoanalysis and Jewishness had come under increasing threat from the Nazis, and the family, with two small sons, was obliged to leave the country. They fled to Boston in the USA, where Erikson practised as a child analyst. Encountering the relaxed informality and extroverted, adolescent 'bobbysoxers' of American society, in contrast with the more restrained and formal society and the growing harshness of the Nazism he had left behind, again highlighted for Erikson the cultural differences that so significantly shape a child's upbringing and personality.

In his study of cultural influences, he found common ground with anthropologists, including Margaret Mead, and gained much from his discussions with them and from the observations he made when accompanying their field trips to study American Indians (the Sioux Indians studied by Scudder Mekeel, and the Yurok observed by Alfred Kroeber). He compared his findings with data collected not only from his child patients, but from children drawn from the general population who were not under psychoanalytic treatment. He also exchanged ideas with social psychologists, such as Robert Havighurst, who was especially interested in the way that different personality patterns affected adjustments necessary in later life and old age.

Erikson's key principles

As the many strands of his experience came together, Erikson formulated a lifespan theory of human development that encompassed historical, cultural and social dimensions as well as the biological and psychological progressions of existing Freudian theory (Erikson, 1950, 1963). He called this need to take into account social, biological and psychological aspects of development, 'triple bookkeeping', stating that they are interdependent and should always be considered in relation to one another. Thus he approached his major focus on ego-development, which Freud had said took place at the interface of biological and social experience, and which Erikson now described in much greater detail.

Another important concept in his theory is that of 'epigenesis', which is associated with concepts of embryonic development. Although each stage develops out of the growth of previous stages, there is a difference in the form of what is developed, distinguishing it from other stages. Moreover, during early stages, the rudimentary foundations of later stages are already forming, while in later stages, some of the growth associated with earlier stages may still be taking place. Joan Erikson, herself a published writer, has likened her husband's stage theory to a tapestry, where the different colours are woven into the whole fabric, but appear on the face of the fabric predominantly at one particular stage. This epigenetic viewpoint substantiates Erikson's belief that unsuccessfully attempted ego-development from earlier stages can re-emerge to be worked on at later stages, within the context of the whole lifespan.

At each stage, ego-strengths emerge, as a 'favourable ratio' is achieved between bi-polar (opposite) qualities. For example, we acquire the capacity to hope during the first stage as we become able to trust appropriately, and learn what needs the opposite response of mistrust. Like Jung, Erikson recognized that opposites are necessary for full function, for without them, we would have no range of flexibility.

Because of the fairly holistic dimensions it offers and the fact that it was the first psychological theory to cover the lifespan, Erikson's framework has had wide appeal, and its more modern, 'user-friendly' expositions are to be found in many settings. Another theory, developed by Eric Berne, a student and analysand (person undergoing analysis) of Erikson's, offers a different approach to understanding the ego, and is also widely used in therapeutic and some training settings.

ERIC BERNE (1910–1970)

Eric Berne was already qualified in medicine and psychiatry when he entered training in psychoanalysis with Erikson. However, he disliked the in-depth exploration based on Freudian id-ego-superego terminology, and breaking off his analysis with Erikson, he began to formulate his own theory, using instead the concept of three ego-states, based on his clinical experience with his own patients.

Parent, Adult, Child (PAC) and Transactional Analysis (TA)

He noticed that statements they made seemed to come from distinctly different states of mind. The first to be identified was the 'Child' ego-state, as more and more of his patients spoke of having 'felt just like a child'. These were perfectly capable, competent people who usually felt and behaved according to an apparently 'Adult' ego-state. In therapy, they also made statements followed by comments such as, 'That's just what my father would have said,' and Berne identified a 'Parent' set of ideas and feelings. He found that it helped his patients to recognize these ego-states and to analyse the 'transactions' they had with him and with others in the therapy groups he frequently used.

In this way, he developed a method he called 'Structural Analysis', based on discovering how each of the Parent, Adult and Child ego-states had been 'scripted' (programmed) during earlier life experience, thus shaping the different kinds of reasoning we use. This is followed by 'Transactional Analysis', in which interchanges between two or more individuals are analysed to determine which of the ego-states are in operation, and whether they are operating appropriately. This method provides a way of monitoring ego-function in some detail, and of making any desirable changes by 're-writing the scripts' (Berne, 1961, 1964).

In rejecting a biologically based focus on unconscious, instinctual drives from Freud's theory, and the more global, triple book-keeping extension of Erikson, Berne showed how the nitty-gritty of everyday transactions can be used to reveal and enhance ego-function. He found a stage theory superfluous, believing that all three ego-states are active from birth, the Parent and Child acquiring their scripts, and the Adult learning from the beginning how to calculate pragmatically and objectively. Mature ego-states, in Berne's view, co-ordinate with each other appropriately, without 'playing games'. His method, when simplified, lends itself to use by individuals or self-help groups as a tool for personal growth (Harris, 1967; Harris & Harris, 1985). It can also be used alongside more holistic approaches.

These three theories – Freud's, Erikson's and Berne's – all have in common the central concept of an ego that balances up feelings and information, and exercises some measure of control over our responses and our initiatives. Each theory can complement the others to enrich our understanding of that abstract, invisible, difficult-to-define, individual capacity for rational, integrated self-direction that we recognize as the maturing ego.

Other theories will be introduced appropriately in subsequent chapters, and we next consider Erikson's first stage and an outline of the contribution made by John Bowlby and Michael Rutter to our understanding of necessary parenting.

INFANCY: ERIKSON, BOWLBY AND RUTTER

4

The first half of the twentieth century brought major changes in our understanding of human development and, in particular, of the critical importance of infancy and childhood. Erikson evolved his lifespan theory during the 1940s and published his first exposition of the *Eight Ages of Man* in 1950 (revised edition 1963). Meanwhile, in Europe, Freud had reluctantly fled from the Nazis in 1938, joining his daughter, Anna, in London, and continuing his work until he died in 1939, just before the outbreak of World War II. During the 1940s, psychoanalysis was becoming more widely accepted, and the Tavistock Clinic was developed, where several psychoanalytically trained practitioners and researchers continued to expand our knowledge about the effects of early experience on later life.

Prominent among them was John Bowlby (born 1907), who saw the need to establish empirical evidence (based on repeatable observations and testing) in support of psychoanalytic insights, which were hermeneutic (based on interpretation). Bowlby and his colleagues carried out a considerable amount of research, especially into the effects of maternal separation and, in 1951, he published a paperback bestseller, *Child Care and the Growth of Love*, based on his consultant's report to the World Health Organization, *Maternal Care and Mental Health*. Bowlby's theory of Attachment has revolutionized our understanding of child-rearing principles, and Michael Rutter's later research, also in the UK, has further refined and added to Bowlby's contribution. Rutter published *Maternal Deprivation Reassessed* in 1972 (second edition 1981), in which he has clarified essential elements of parenting, and has offered insights into the possibilities of remedial processes and preventative action.

Another major developmental psychologist, whose theory we shall examine over the next few chapters, is Jean Piaget (1896–1980). His cognitive developmental research began while he was still a student, and expanded in his native Switzerland during the 1920s and 1930s, continuing throughout his life. Delayed by World War II, translations of his French texts spread widely during the 1950s, adding to the explosion of our understanding.

We have only to compare modern baby manuals with their earlier counterparts to find evidence of this explosion, and many more research psychologists have contributed to it. European research findings have often corresponded closely with those of Erikson and others in America, and there have been many cross-cultural studies carried out that have increased our awareness of human universalities and of cultural differences. We are in a better position to make wise choices than ever before, as we gaze in awe at a new-born infant, and ponder how best to guide his or her upbringing.

ERIKSON: TRUST V. MISTRUST

Zones and modes

Infancy, the first of Erikson's stages, is when our ego emerges as we develop a very basic intuitive discernment about who and what is to be trusted or mistrusted, in relation to the needs and motivations we experience from birth onwards. Erikson has expanded on Freud's description of this oral stage beyond the biologically sensitive oral 'zone' to include other physical and social senses in what he calls the 'incorporative mode'. Hence his stages are called 'psychosocial', in contrast with Freud's 'psychosexual' labelling.

Erikson explains that the sensitivity of our oral zone registers a sense of 'taking in' that extends to our other senses as well. Thus we take in visual and auditory information with our gaze and listening, recognize the smell of mother's milk as we draw in air, and take in the pleasure of movement, as our proprioceptive sense feeds back to us the freedom of kicking out, or the different satisfaction of being held upright, with a sense pattern of being on our feet.

Parenting

At first, this incorporative mode is experienced as 'being given', and depends on provision and on our involuntary reflexes, such as sucking and grasping, and on our random movements, such as kicking and arm waving. As 'being given' becomes a known experience, we become more active in seeking it, practising and gaining voluntary control of our movements, so that we also experience 'getting'. We learn to reach out and move towards as well as grasp a wanted person or object, and to bite off small pieces of food to ingest. The important factor to notice here is that these familiarized experiences, prelinguistically acquired, are vital components of our intuitive 'felt knowledge' accompanying our 'gut reaction' in later years.

It can be argued that satisfying experience of being given, and of getting, is a necessary foundation for feeling motivation and satisfaction in giving empathically to others, or helping them to get for themselves. We can then act from a deep understanding and wish to promote another's well-being, as opposed to giving and helping because we feel we 'ought' to do so, or because of unmet needs of our own that can blind our sensitive empathy with a drive for vicarious satisfaction.

Trust in being given begins before we are born, rooted in the symbiotic relationship with our mother where, provided that her health and intake are adequate, our needs are constantly met. Oxygen and nutrients are 'on tap' through the umbilical cord and the placenta, while the uterus and amniotic fluid provide an ever-present support for our earliest development.

It is now known that we begin to respond to external sounds and pressures well before birth, and it is possible that, if any stimuli are experienced as unpleasant, mistrustful reactions may begin to form, though we also know that hormonal changes in the mother's bloodstream induce in her a state of relative serenity, and may give some similar protection to her unborn foetus. Ethically, this is a prohibited area for research, and we must rely on naturalistic observation and inference to support or discount our ideas about it. Certainly, we need to regard the gestation period with the greatest consideration and respect.

Erikson notes that the change that takes place at birth is from a symbiotic relationship to a mutual one. Symbiotic constancy needs to be replaced with consistency in provision of nutrition, physical contact, care, protection and holding, if the potential for trust with which we are born is to be realized. Mutuality begins between baby and care givers, especially the mother, whose heartbeat and pattern of movements are already familiar. Mutuality means, on the part of the care givers, getting to understand the needs and preferences of this particular baby, and from the baby, a free expression of infant needs and satisfactions, together with adjustment of expectations in accordance with the realities of provision.

If, in the early, new-born days of mutuality, we are given a foundation of 'felt knowledge' that our needs will be satisfied when we express them, for example, even our early signals that we are getting hungry meeting with a caring response, the trust so engendered enables us to begin to overcome the discomfort of waiting. We begin to wait without needing to protest, especially if there is another form of 'taking in' available. Erikson says that our first 'social achievement', based on a growing sense of trust, is 'willingness to let the mother out of sight without undue anxiety or rage, because she has become an inner certainty as well as an outer predictability'. He emphasizes the value of predictable patterns of provision, so that familiarity may provide a secure framework for 'adventures of the senses' during our increasing waking hours. Thus begins, he says, 'a rudimentary sense of ego identity', in other words, the beginnings of our self-awareness, including our place in our environment (Erikson, 1963).

Fear and mistrust are felt when a situation seems threatening in relation to our needs and urges, for example, realizing we are alone in an unusual place, or held by a person who doesn't feel as if he or she will respond reliably to us. Gradually, we learn to approach strangeness with caution rather than immediate withdrawal, exercising an appropriate amount of mistrust.

In addition to trust and mistrust felt in relation to other people and our environment, we also become familiar with our own increasing abilities, and with our limitations. We discover we can reach the toys in our cot for ourselves and can make things move as we gradually develop voluntary control of our movements. When we overreach ourselves and topple, we learn a valuable lesson in caution, to counterbalance growing hopes of achievement. Too much trust leads to disappointment or downfall, followed by withdrawal, just as too much mistrust brings withdrawal of responses, pathological in their inhibiting effect on exploration and progress in learning.

Hope and withdrawal

Erikson identifies withdrawal as the pathology of this stage, in contrast with the ego strength of hope, the fruits of which are the capacity to wait in anticipation, to tolerate some frustration, to explore with curiosity and appropriate caution and to respond with realism and growing resilience to anxieties and uncertainties.

Realism and resilience may sound a tall order so early in life, but a baby who feels basically secure can accept a finger or his own thumb to suck, draw comfort from a 'transitional object' (usually a teddy bear or doll, whose familiarity can enable relinquishment of a parent's presence, for example, at bedtime), or, as he progresses during his second year, seek an extra cuddle from another familiar care giver when missing his parents and wanting reassurance. Psychoanalysts believe that a lack of this capacity to cope with anxieties and uncertainties is responsible for relapse into the withdrawal of depression later in life, and Erikson says that 'the re-establishment of a state of trust has been found to be the basic requirement for therapy in these cases' (Erikson, 1963).

This ego quality of hope arises from the favourable ratio of basic trust and basic mistrust, and Erikson argues that this balance needs to be realistic in relation to our family and culture, and to our developing abilities or limitations. Where conditions are adequately benevolent, a favourable ratio would be weighted towards trust, but in a harsh environment, for example with inconsistent, immature or uncontrolled parents, or in the Mundugamor tribe described by Margaret Mead (1949), survival might depend upon a high level of mistrust.

In conditions where, prior to the middle of this century, infants were kept in cots and prams for much longer, and crawled and walked later, Freud viewed ego development as emerging only with the second, anal stage, resulting from the interaction of the biologically driven id with the environment, as mobility brought increased contact. Erikson, however, viewed the ego as already active, albeit in a rudimentary way, in our early days of interaction with the realities of our new environment and mutual relationships. He also gave more attention than Freud to describing the qualities of parenting that would enhance ego development, and stated that for parents to succeed in nurturing hope in their children at this stage, it was essential for them to have a faith of some kind in which their own trust was evident, so that it would be communicated at a 'feeling' level to their child.

Erikson distinguished between 'individual spirituality', which he described as 'pure self ... the pre-parental core of creation', and 'communal and social religion' (1958), which he saw as society's unconscious attempt to provide, in its institution, for the nurturance of trust in spiritual being and in created cosmological order. At the social and cultural level, Erikson helps us to look with new eyes at the significance of our social institutions, linking these with the different stages of our lifespan needs.

Social institution: religion

Thus religious institutions are associated with the primary needs of infancy, and express a replication of a culture or sub-culture's core values. Reliable, consistent and explanatory nurturance, characteristic of good parenting, is embodied in a secure framework of predictable pattern, ritual, symbolism, narrative and exhortation, that have arisen to minister to our residual dependencies and expectations of guidance. For many, this ideal is substantially realized, and a vital faith provides meaning in daily living, and trust in an overall framework beyond themselves that can be felt and incorporated by their children.

Others, in different sects or denominations in all religions, find that their religious framework provides little room for a maturing process and spiritual growth. For them, it obscures, rather than reveals, a living faith, acquiring a rigidity, narrowness and exclusiveness that, like bad parenting, has tragic consequences. Thus it can foster dependency, obedience and conformity, while stifling the development of understanding, responsible evaluation and the capacity for love. When this tragedy occurs, Erikson suggests that core values are often recognized to be more truly honoured and expressed in social action, or in pursuit of truths about the world we live in, than in religious institutions of an imperative, monopolistic or exclusive nature. He observes that '... many are proud to be without religion whose children cannot afford their being without it but many seem to derive a vital faith from social action or scientific pursuit, and many profess faith, yet in practice breathe mistrust both of life and man.' (1963).

In his retrospective study, *Young Man Luther* (1958), Erikson mentions historical and cross-cultural examples of the failure of religious institutions to overcome their own corruptions and anachronistic practices. However, his stronger focus is on how they have also attempted to provide a 'vertical' for our spirituality and for the maturing of our ego, so that we can release our fullest potential in the 'horizontal' of everyday living. He continued to emphasize the value of faith and a sense of cultural integration, not only in infancy (and parenting), but in the later stages described in his lifespan theory.

Social meaning

Erikson believed that we need a sense of social meaning behind restraints on our satisfaction, and that, provided that care is sufficient, familiar and consistent, we can accept these restraints. If our basic sense of 'being given' is established, we can tolerate having to wait, share or take our turn, or being denied something for which we have reached. For example, as a baby's grasp gets strong enough to hurt a parent's face or hair, learning can begin to 'touch gently', parental guidance and gentle tone of voice conveying clear, social meaning about what is acceptable and liked by others and what is not.

Social meaning is necessary, not only to guide restraints, but also to add purpose to our enjoyment and involvement with others. This sensitivity enables positive feedback from them to engender the feeling of social satisfaction that helps develop our sense of purpose and social contributiveness. In all these ways, the social aspect of Erikson's 'triple bookkeeping' becomes functional.

APPLICATIONS OF THEORY: RESIDUES, REALITY AND REMEDIES

One of the encouraging features of Erikson's theory is his attitude to 'residues' (left-over emotional tasks of development). He believed that these may be reworked at later stages, so that it is never too late to achieve at least some growth in deficient areas, and some remedial re-learning in areas where we may have been over-stressed, over-indulged or traumatized (emotionally injured).

Some residues remain, even where we have been brought up in a mostly favourable environment, and it can be a rewarding endeavour to identify and redevelop gaps and distortions, thus releasing more of our individual potential. An understanding of the first-time-round stages of childhood provides a valuable guide for this process, within a framework of our own, consciously applied parenting principles. Some of the residues from the first stage, for which we may find we can 're-parent' ourselves, include mistrust of opportunities, inability to face the uncertainties and demands of creative effort, or an idealistic expectation of others, along with accusing disappointment when they fail to satisfy us and we feel 'let down'.

Friendships and partnerships benefit from our growth as we leave behind dependent demands and compulsive supplying, and develop mutual awareness and respect for each other's actual needs, preferences and limitations. Often there is a need to rebuild the foundations of our sense of basic personal worth and self-trust, or of the fundamental separateness and worth of other individuals.

Figure 4.1 *These parents gaze in awe at their newborn baby. What choices can they make about its upbringing?*

If we can also recover our sense of pure fun and enjoyment, which good parenting is able to discover and foster in infancy, we shall indeed have revitalized one of life's greatest treasures. All too often, capacity for relaxed enjoyment can be stifled by anxieties beyond toleration level, or labelled as 'childish' and left behind with childhood. It can also be corrupted by parental or cultural examples, based on substitutes or shoddy social values, making the remedial task more difficult, but one that it is not impossible to address.

Remedial processes   Faced with this incapacity in adulthood, we need to begin again, examining people, objects, our surroundings and experiences with the left-behind eyes and wonderings of infancy. 'Adventures of the senses', free movement of our bodies and a readiness to laugh with others at the incongruities we encounter can help considerably in shaping new approaches to remedy and recreation. Many of these 'adventures' can be undertaken by individuals on their own, but similarly appreciative others, in an accepted cultural context, are a vital part of relearning to participate gainfully and harmlessly in social recreation. Given thought and adequate provision of a framework, this treasure from infancy can be restored!

Erikson recognized the curative value of play in childhood, using it as a two-way means of communication with his child patients, and as a framework within which a child could explore different outcomes to concurrent situations and events. In much the same way, an adult may construct such a framework of discussion, perhaps using art forms to aid insight and relaxed exploration.

Depression

Depression, consisting of withdrawal of responses, may be a residual pathology linked with this stage, not only by Erikson, but notably by Melanie Klein (who was John Bowlby's training analyst, and, like him, was less hopeful about remedial possibilities). In its milder forms, it may fade spontaneously, or yield to individual effort along the relearning lines suggested above, though a mature and understanding person with whom to discuss feelings and progress can be invaluable.

Skilled help is indicated where depression is more severe, or where there are other problems accompanying it, but alongside chemotherapy and some other forms of professional treatment, Erikson's approach of reworking childhood residues in the self-parenting framework of adult reality can usually help towards recovery. Past realities may have shaped our current emotional patterns, but our ego can work with present realities, at least to improve the skills and strengths we may have missed out on, and to find ways of healing, or handling more bearably, our past traumas.

Three basic principles serve these remedial processes. Firstly, we need to acquire and incorporate a set of wise and loving parent references. We may gather them from others we have seen being good parents, from our reading, and by the active construction of our own thinking as we build on good examples, criticize bad instances and work out constructive alternatives. We become the kind, wise, nurturant parent of our own development, remembering to balance our own recognized needs with consideration for the needs of others, so that mutuality and good relationships are also fostered.

Secondly, we need to become the eager explorer and learner we see in a young child, discovering the miracle of our own creativity and wondering about the amazing world around us and the joys it offers as well as its hazards. This is where our motivation and energy for change and productiveness are rooted, along with the basic feeling values accompanying our needs. It is this *felt sense of value* that we seek to recover as we experience and learn to handle both need and creative urges.

Self-help of this kind has often been viewed as selfish interest or self-indulgence, as it can frequently evoke egocentric feelings and attitudes or strong feelings of guilt. As all good parents discover, a child has to experience both regard for his or her own needs, worth and capacity, and a felt regard for the needs, worth and capacity of others. Only in this way, can both a happy confidence and a capacity for relationships unfold together, as our ego works with increasing comprehension of inner realities and realities about other people. During this remedial process, like children, we grapple with learning how to balance our own feelings with feelings for others, their needs and their creative aims, and it is this gradually learned counterbalance, denying neither element, that prevents self-concern from becoming selfish lack of concern towards others, and avoids the opposite pitfall of crippling self-denial.

As awareness and feelings of motivation increase, like young children, we find that constant repetition establishes new abilities. This is especially true in remedial work, as the newly established neural pathways need to become very well used if they are to supersede the earlier habits and attitudes laid down in the neuronal networks of our brain. Repeated opportunities to practise new learning, to feel and explore freely like a child again, will open the way to redevelopment, so we need to incorporate these spaces into our adult living.

Thirdly, we need to progress at our own pace, though sometimes events will precipitate growth in certain areas to meet current contingencies. As with children, patience is needed, but the developmental and remedial process can continue to unfold and enrich us throughout life. Infancy has its own special gifts to bestow. The qualities and gifts of later stages, together with appropriate parenting and re-parenting, will be discussed in each relevant chapter. Meanwhile, we shall turn to further major contributions to our understanding of childhood and parenting, in the work of John Bowlby and Michael Rutter.

BOWLBY: FOUR PHASES OF ATTACHMENT AND THE GROWTH OF LOVE

Bowlby gathered evidence from scientifically valid and reliable experiments and observations from several sources, evidence which led him to conclude a biological basis for the bonding of mothers and infants from birth. It is only more recently that fathers have been considered to have any role at this time, but Bowlby did recognize that, at first, an infant displays bonding behaviour to any carer who responds appropriately, including the father.

During what he calls this first, 'pre-formative' phase, babies spontaneously behave and respond in biologically programmed ways. Besides crying and reflexes such as turning towards a touch on the cheek, sucking, and closing the fingers round anything touching the palm of the hand, babies soon begin to focus and follow with their eyes and to snuggle when held. Smiling follows, and captivated carers ensure survival.

Mothers are hormonally sensitized to respond to all these actions, and provided that her baby's bonding behaviour is maintained by enough appropriate responses, a mother can learn the pattern of care that suits her own particular infant best, an infant already accustomed to her voice and characteristic movements before birth. In turn, the baby continues to adapt to the mother's responses and to those of other carers involved, so that by about six or eight weeks old, the second, 'formative' phase has begun. With the establishment of regular patterns of interaction, the baby begins to show preferences, favouring the carers who consistently provide the most satisfying relationship, usually the mother. By six or seven months, the third, 'established' phase is reached, recognizable by the baby's protest and distress when left or separated for a period.

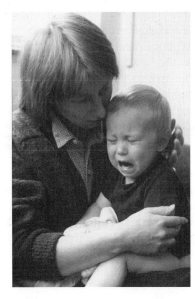

Figure 4.2 *Nurturing hope. Distress is not the end of the world when the caregiver is on hand to offer comfort*

Bowlby thought that, until this primary relationship with the mother or central caregiver was established, the infant could not form other relationships, but the research of Peggy Emerson with Rudolph Schaffer in Glasgow (1964) and of Mary Ainsworth working in Uganda (1967) showed that where caring was shared among several family members or close neighbours, babies 'bonded' in several relationships simultaneously (multiple attachment), though the mother was usually the primary figure. Though recognizing these findings, Bowlby continued to believe strongly that, during the critical period for bonding, between birth and five years, a child needed the constant presence and availability of mother.

In this way, a close, dependent bond could be formed, an essential basis for the gradual change of the fourth, 'separating-out' phase, where a cooperative working relationship can be established. During this period, the child achieves some independence, and learns to recognize the mother's separateness, as a person in her own right, with different preferences and goals. This, said Bowlby, is the necessary foundation for the satisfactory formation of any future affectional bonding.

Distress syndrome
Separation from the mother during the first five years was shown to be associated with disturbed behaviour during adolescence, including delinquency, in a study Bowlby published in 1944.

Further research by a former student and later a colleague of Bowlby's, James Robertson and his wife Joyce, identified the distress syndrome found to be responsible for much of the damage caused by separation.

They studied children in hospitals and residential nurseries, where it was customary to forbid any visiting, with the well-meaning intention of avoiding the upset of the children when their parents left. Rotational duties for staff meant no consistency of carers, who were encouraged not to form relationships with children in their care, again from the well-meaning motive of avoiding separation upset for both children and staff. Children in institutions were kept with others of their own age-group – babies, 'tweenies', toddlers – so that there were similar levels of need competing for the attention of their nurses. In these heart-rending conditions, each child's initial reaction on separation from his or her mother was protest, crying and anger. This first 'protest' stage could last for up to a week.

Then despair and hopelessness set in. Intermittent miserable crying and general apathy, lasting for variable lengths of time, marked the second, 'despair' stage. The third and last stage of this frequently confirmed syndrome was misleading, as the child now appeared to have 'settled down', recovering some cheerfulness and interest in play, toys, food and sweets. But the Robertsons pointed out that the child's attitudes to people were now impersonal, and that he or she appeared to care for nobody. When returned home, disturbed behaviour was frequent, and research had already shown that adolescent problems were likely to occur.

The Robertsons demonstrated, in a series of films, how good foster care could mitigate the despair stage of the syndrome by providing a consistent substitute source of responses to the child's emotional needs. Following these studies, institutional care of children was revolutionized, to try, as far as possible, to provide for this consistency and substitution. Gradually changes took place, and hospital visiting became a right. In institutions, 'family grouping' (children over a range of ages with relatively permanent staffing in small groups) became the norm, and each child had a 'special' carer (and off-duty substitute). Even with these improvements, separation was still a traumatic ordeal for a child. It became recognized that disturbed behaviour on returning home was a natural, healing regression, which enabled the child to regain earlier securities and trust, when responded to in a warm, understanding and encouraging way. (This is an important feature of remedial work.)

Childhood grief   Bowlby remained pessimistic about those children, especially the very young, who did not have adequate early attachment relationships, or who suffered the trauma of separation. He also drew attention to a child's need to grieve for any loss suffered, especially by death, before any new attachments could hope to form, and then only if a capacity for attachment had already been sufficiently developed. He believed that the inability to cope with loss or bereavement in adulthood had its roots in inadequate attachments or unresolved grief in childhood. Childhood dependencies that had never been adequately met and then transformed into mutuality, he said, were responsible for many of the stresses in later relationships, including poor parenting of the next generation.

Bowlby's ideas have generated a great deal of research into the nature of mother-child interaction that includes, for example, the work of Rudolph Schaffer (especially *Mothering*, 1977) and of Daniel Stern, who has described the quality of mother-baby relationship as 'the mutual creation of shared pleasure ... including interest, curiosity, boredom, delight, laughter, surprise, silences and resolving distress ... the stuff of friendship and love' (Stern, 1977). A major contribution, in recent decades, has been the work of Michael Rutter, briefly outlined next.

RUTTER: MATERNAL DEPRIVATION AND REMEDIAL FACTORS

Rutter, who qualified in medicine in 1955 and then trained at the Maudsley Hospital, realized that, although separation of children from their parents was frequently followed by problems during adolescence, this was not always the case. He carried out a study on the Isle of Wight to gather evidence in support of his hypothesis (a statement capable of being disproved), and then set out to discover the factors that seemed to give some children resistance to the ill-effects of separation. In a series of studies during the 1970s, he investigated the contributions made to a child's stability or vulnerability by parents' health, by housing, education and social group. With Nicola Madge, he published a widely read book, *The Cycles of Disadvantage* (Rutter & Madge 1976), in which there was much evidence to support the serious and cyclical effects of the different kinds of disadvantage.

But Rutter was especially interested in identifying factors that seemed to offer children some resistance to environmental effects. These included a child's temperament, which to some extent helps to shape experience, the qualities of their early parenting, and those factors associated with the post-traumatic period that point the way to the provision of remedy.

In a longitudinal study (the same individual subjects studied over a period) with David Quinton (1984), he was able to show the beneficial and cumulative effects of positive educational experience on the mothering behaviour of women who had themselves been brought up in institutional care. With a greater sense of hope in the control of their own future, several of the young women had married 'non-deviant' spouses, and these combined factors were associated with an observed quality of mothering better than in those lacking this experience, and comparable with similar women with a non-institutional childhood.

In *Maternal Deprivation Reassessed* (1972, 1981), Rutter also analysed the several aspects of a child's attachment needs, and in addition to recognizing actual separation, he addressed the problems of relationships with deprived areas, distinguishing between 'privation' (absence of) and 'deprivation' (loss of) the different aspects of essential parenting.

Essential child-rearing qualities

His evidence shows that the kind of relationship that can endure some separation has the vital qualities of stability, consistency, warmth, affection with physical contact, social stimulation and interaction, and cognitive stimulation, especially language interaction. These are in addition to the already accepted necessities of adequate physical care and feeding. He has also shown that some aspects can usefully be supplied by a trusted person other than the parent, both where there is parental disability and where remedial experience is indicated.

Rutter's interest in the different qualities of attachment and child care has done much to enhance our understanding of mothering and fathering, and also of the qualities, kind of arrangements and prerequisite introductions necessary for satisfactory child care while parents are at work. He urges that we focus on preventative education, so that basic features of parental care, already known to be essential, become more universally known and practised. Secondly, he advocates that we continue to research and promote those qualities of personality developed in childhood that increase resilience and offer some resistance to the ill-effects on health and social adjustment of unavoidable misfortunes during childhood.

Preventative action   An example of preventative action is provided by the recent follow-up studies of the American Head Start programme begun by David Weikart (1972), Irving Lazar and Richard Darlington (1982), E. Zigler and W. Berman (1983) and added to by several others. Between them they have provided crucial evidence that, for every dollar originally spent in providing assistance to under-privileged mothers, visiting the home and showing them how to play and interact with their children, six dollars now has to be spent on mental health, criminal proceedings and social security on a similarly under-privileged control group who did not receive Head Start. Not only does preventative action bring humanitarian individual and social benefits, but it is six times less expensive in the longer term.

Erikson, Bowlby and Rutter, despite, or perhaps because of, the fact that their daily work consisted of treating disturbances in children, have all tried to identify the positive processes in development, and their findings have much in common in this respect and in the qualities of parenting they advocate. Lest parents become discouraged by the formidably demanding recommendations, Donald Winnicott introduced the phrase 'good-enough mother', which has since been extended to 'good-enough parent'. We can be reassured that parental errors are unlikely to have serious consequences when counteracted by interactions enabling the development of trust, attachment, caution and some resilience to disappointment. Where these predominate during infancy, we can expect the ego-quality of hope to emerge, with all its promise of exploration, discovery and creative fulfilment.

EARLY CHILDHOOD AND THE PLAY AGE

5

EARLY CHILDHOOD: AUTONOMY V. DOUBT AND SHAME

In the second stage of his theory, Early Childhood, Erikson again expands on Freud's foundation of insights, this time concerning his 'anal' stage. Freud said that myelination in the anal zone meant that libidinal pleasure is now centred in the experience and control of the anal function and in exploring its product (faeces). Aggression can be expressed by withholding, or faecal smearing. He also made connections between a child's anal emotional experience and later sublimated enjoyment of handling garden soil, clay or dough, and identified anal personality types characterized by obsession (urgent necessity), parsimony (withholding) or a need to 'perform' for others' expectations.

Freud thought that the ego emerges as increased mobility brings a greater need to balance the realities of id drives and external opportunities for their satisfaction. Erikson built on these findings, though he believed that the ego has already begun its balancing function during infancy.

Like Freud, Erikson recognized the emergence of voluntary anal and urethral control due to nerve myelination. It is this biological fact that distinguishes toilet training in *voluntary* control from any earlier training resulting from conditioning. The latter is much less reliable or flexible, as the classical conditioning involved operates at an involuntary level.

The experience in our retentive-eliminative biological zone of 'holding on' and of 'letting go', Erikson said, extends to our social modalities ('modes'). Based on our first stage foundation of 'taking in', of 'being given' and of 'getting', we now add to our felt knowledge the generalized, behavioural experiences of 'holding' and 'releasing'.

Voluntary control and autonomy

Our feeling responses cover a wide range, at one end of which is a harsh gripping or restraining, as we clutch a toy, refusing to let it go, and at the other a destructive or anarchical letting loose, as we tip out a box of small objects or a kitchen drawer! Given enough respect for the feelings behind them, these raw responses can, thus recognized, gradually come under voluntary control. When we are feeling secure and relaxed, arising from our own 'taken in' experience of care and cuddles, we can also respond with carefulness, a tender holding – 'to have and to hold', as Erikson describes it, or a more gentle 'to let pass' or 'to let be'. Increasing dexterity, locomotor development, and rapid learning about the world around us widens these experiences in all directions.

As we discover our increasing control over our bodies and the space and objects around us, and over our interactions with our parents and others, our ego develops a sense of autonomy. We feel increasing power and make choices about using it. Choices such as moving to another spot or selecting a toy are often made spontaneously, but we also need to learn to consider before choosing. Erikson advises parents to offer plenty of simple choices within a framework of protection from our untrained discrimination and discretion. Some experience of mistakes naturally occurs, and we also encounter the choices and rights of others, so that autonomy does not become autocratic supremacy.

Mistakes and failures

Doubt occurs when we experience failure of our own abilities, make mistakes, regret choices, or meet with unreliability in people or objects around us. Our early caution matures to deal with the greater hazards of our increasing adventures. As with shame, 'a better way' becomes the resolution we learn to seek, and there is often some overlapping in doubt and shame as we 'feel exposed', as Erikson puts it, in failure or mistake. Too much doubt may leave us prey, in the future, to indecisiveness, or to anxiety-provoked compulsive responses in the presence of uncertainties, and too little doubt may lead to foolhardiness or gullibility.

We experience shaming exposure, especially when disapproval spells out the wrongness of our actions, and unless care is taken to make clear that it is the action, not the child, that is the cause of disapproval, a basic sense of unworthiness can accumulate and remain. Experience of seeking 'a better way' to replace undesirable actions, is the constructive resolution that we need to practise, so that we develop a feeling sense about what to do when mistaken or in the wrong.

Doubts about our own abilities, worth and autonomy yield to gradually increasing, guided extensions of our physical endeavours, and to interactions with 'good-enough', caring parents and others. Play with other children brings practice in finding 'best ways' of managing our actions, of handling objects, of negotiating uncertainties and disputes, and of maintaining our autonomy by exercising some choice about 'joining in'. There is much repetition of 'me' and 'mine' while these boundaries to autonomy, and its extension to possessions, are established.

As with giving, it is believed by many that it is only when we have developed a 'felt knowledge' of our own autonomy, through the respect and nurturance accorded to us, that we can feel any respect for the autonomy and rights of choice of others. Without these feelings, we learn how to get our own way regardless, or are left feeling that we, and they, must comply or compete with the choices and compulsions of others.

BOUNDARIES AND LIMITATIONS

While most of our development desirably takes place with positive encouragement and the fostering of mutual co-operation, negatives are necessary to the learning of practical and moral limitations. Within this balance of encouragement and restraint, gradually internalized, secure guidelines need to emerge, which are the origin of discretion, and furthermore begin to imprint the meaning and 'feeling sense' of the word 'right'. This may acquire connotations of 'kind', 'perceptive', 'thoughtful', 'compliant', 'conventional', 'tough', 'clever' or whatever principles shape the approval, the responses and especially the example of those caring for us. 'Wrong', at this stage, is what brings disapproval, and we become especially sensitive to variations in facial expression and tone of voice (see chapter 6).

Denial and disappointment

We have inevitably met some frustration and denial of our wishes during the first stage, and have some idea about what is fruitless and must be relinquished, about what and who may yield to persistence, and what can be held in hope. Increasing autonomy and choice now add a working understanding to what was formerly a seemingly arbitrary 'no' or denial.

Denial of what we want may also be experienced because a situation or attempted activity is too difficult for us. Parental guidance is invaluable in advising persistence. 'Try it this way' – or postponement – 'When you're bigger' – or in accepting that which cannot be changed, preferably with some explanation – 'I'm sorry, there aren't any peas today. We've run out. We must remember to buy some tomorrow. Would you like some beans instead?' Finding an alternative can be fostered by offering a suggestion or choice, and later by asking for ideas. In this way, a pattern is laid down which becomes part of us, and we learn to discriminate where persistence is desirable and where acceptance and adaptation are the 'best ways' of responding to denial of our wants.

As part of our gradual learning about denial, we also need to learn how to handle our feelings of disappointment, and that it is all right to want to receive the understanding and perhaps the comforting hugs of someone else when we are feeling hurt by denial, alongside preparing to deal with the practical situation. Only from this starting point, can we begin to offer empathetic understanding to someone else, as opposed to behaving coldly and correctly, or obliviously, towards their disappointments. These lessons are especially well learned through observation of how our parents handle their own set-backs and hurt feelings, and how they comfort and empathize with one another. Verbal expression will gradually replace tantrums and some of the tears, but only if the example of 'good-enough' parenting shows the way.

Saying 'no' and saying 'yes'

There are three basic kinds of denial and its verbal expression, 'no', that we need to acquire felt knowledge about: when 'no' is said to us, when we say 'no' to others, and when we say 'no' to ourselves. Unless we can accomplish this learning, many of the joys of saying 'yes' will remain out of reach.

During infancy, we have become familiar with the meaning of a parental 'no'. With emerging autonomy, we begin to discover some control over our response to it, and first we must find out if persistence is fruitful or otherwise! This will need testing out from time to time, so that we can be sure of the security of our framework and that our parents really will protect us from the hazards of our own spontaneity. It is at this crucial point that future attitudes to practical and social ordering and to authority are shaped; if we can feel our parents *firmly alongside us*, helping us to co-operate and to understand why, or at least that there is some reason for restraint, we shall avoid the 'too much' of over-compliance, or of compulsive rebelliousness or amoral attitudes. Thus is patterned and internalized the capacity for moral choice.

During infancy, mute or protesting refusals have already made clear our negative feelings, and we have become familiar with the responses of our carers to them. To this established pattern is now added our ability to say 'no'. A fast developing sense of autonomy means that we constantly need to test out new areas and to discover how far our choice can be extended, and how safe are the boundaries we are given. Much experimentation is needed if we are to learn to handle this social regulator wisely. Parents and other carers have the difficult task of showing respect and allowing enough practice without either over-indulgence or over-repression, so that we can develop our own sense of judgement. Saying 'no' appropriately is an important part of learning to choose.

Finally in this process, we just begin to learn the wisdom of saying 'no' to ourselves on some occasions, to stop and consider consequences if we follow some impulse. It is here that we begin to be aware of, and to learn how to handle, our natural human range of raw impulses with their accompanying feelings, essential if we are ever to experience full freedom of choice.

Emergence of will   With encouragement and clear guidance, we can just begin to combine feeling and awareness concerning our own motives and needs, and therefore to have the beginnings of felt knowledge about how others may be feeling, to help us choose an appropriate response. Understanding helps us to feel first, and then to 'stand beside' and consider, as our ego balances our increasing awarenesses of internal and external realities.

The capacity to exercise will sensitively, which includes the 'yes' of permission and encouragement as well as the 'no' of restraint, is the ego quality that Erikson says is associated with this second stage. It is the essential forerunner of a healthy sense of self-direction, developed during the next phase of our unfolding. Our capacity for a chosen 'yes' develops alongside these three kinds of 'no', and needs the same firm framework within which to explore. Based on the 'yes's and 'no's, and on the example of our carers, this internalized self-regulation will be very intermittent in early stages, and will need plenty of patience, encouragement and respect. It is on the respect which we receive, as this ego strength emerges from the 'favourable ratio' of autonomy v. doubt and shame, that our own self-respect is built.

We can thus come to feel ourselves as essentially of value and worth loving, able to love and to make wise choices, and with a reliable ability to handle our mistakes and our wrong-doing, and to enjoy the good things in life. The firm, loving structure and example of good-enough parenting becomes an internal structure within which autonomous choice, questioning doubt, and the moral indicator of shame, which is nature's prompting to the finding of a 'better way', will continue to bestow their gifts during the rest of our life cycle.

Parental needs

Parental needs at this stage are that they have themselves an autonomous sense of self-worth and regard for others, internalized guiding principles, and that they are able to impart, at a feeling level, a sense of freedom about choosing in the many areas of living where choice and preferences can be discovered and exercised. They need, also, with an ability to convey by example, a capacity for coping with feelings aroused by frustration and denial, and for handling their own mistakes and shortcomings.

To some extent, if they wish to do so, they can enhance these areas in themselves as they nurture and learn alongside their children, thus strengthening the spirit of co-operation that can so enrich family life and individual development. Toddler groups involving parents are a potent opportunity for supporting and nurturing good parenting at this vital, pattern-setting stage of unfolding.

Residues from this stage are very many, and can be seen in habitual helplessness and self-effacement, and in manipulative and autocratic behaviour. Frequently these are worked out and modified during schooldays under the influence of peers and of teachers and other adults trained in the encouragement of self-reliance and responsible choice as well as ability. Where teachers, for whatever reason (large classes, parental pressures or inadequate training), heavily emphasize obedience and conformity, this valuable opportunity can be minimized, compounding a residual, pervasive sense of 'having to', the compulsion that, Erikson says, is the pathology of this stage.

Figure 5.1 *Parental needs. These parents and their young children find mutual support, advice and opportunity to chat and play; whether groups are self- or community-organized, skilled input is invaluable, educationally, remedially and preventatively*

Compulsion

It is the absence of a sense of choice that is the key malfunction in compulsion, the inability to exercise will or willingness. For many people, this can preclude any sensitive consideration based on personal values and priorities, and any goodwill that might accompany choice, is also lost. Life can then become a series of more or less resented, burdensome chores. Another residue from this stage is the obsessional importance that may be attached to always being 'in the right'. Here, shame is felt to be too painfully exposing, so that it is, of necessity, avoided.

Remedially, we need to recover and develop our capacity to embrace our own fallibility, common to all humanity, admit our mistakes and find a 'better way'. Like a young child, we need to discover that we do not 'have to' act on our doubtful or shameful impulses, and until we have consolidated this learning about feeling and choosing, we cannot develop the sense of responsibility which the next stage brings. Autonomy is concerned with internal emotional and thought processes as well as with situational events.

Choices and decisions

Difficulty in making decisions accompanies an undeveloped capacity for making choices, and may result from either too much freedom of choice beyond a child's ability to consider wisely, or from the replacement of choice by demands for obedience and appreciative acceptance of arbitrary provision. Inability to say 'no' to others, with an excessive sensitivity to disapproval, is another common residue that accompanies the absence of a felt sense of choice. Alternatively, and arising from the same lack of guided practice in a safe framework, there may have arisen a characteristic tendency to exploit the reluctance of others to say 'no'.

Unless clear guidance and example have been provided, there may be a residual need to test out what others will tolerate in any new situation, or there may be obliviousness or indifference to the boundaries of others. Above all, both in early childhood and in remedial endeavour, it is the spirit of autonomous co-operation that needs to be fostered, if the boundaries of self and others are to be sensitively established, and the practical and moral limitations to our choices become healthily internalized.

Social institution: law and order

Just as religious institutions have arisen to serve needs related to the first stage, Erikson identifies the institution of law and order to support the needs related to the second stage. This has enormous implications in the understanding behind our social policies and political will, when we consider how to remedy and maintain our freedoms and our social framework, though we need also to take into account the residues and remedial potential of the third stage when formulating effective public policies and designing relearning experiences for offenders.

The agents of law and order step in where internalized and 'felt' co-operative attitudes towards others and respected authority have failed to develop, and a lawless lack of self-restraint has resulted. Commendably, the inadequate, stretched resources of instituted law and order try, where they are able, to provide an attempt at a relearning framework, where the emphasis is on co-operative effort, with emotional support, and the encouragement and modelling of 'yes's and 'no's, by 'good-enough', trained leaders.

Where communities assist parenting by providing such a framework, there is significantly less need for the penal and judiciary agents of instituted law and order to apply the restraint that is missing in those who, for lack of adequate earlier experience, are unable to say 'no' and fall prey to drug dependency or peer pressures, and commit anti-social offences. As we shall see in the discussion of the next stage, this learning framework for choice is a vital precursor to making responsible choices, including those involved in our social behaviour, and in becoming and behaving as 'good-enough' parents to the next generation. Not to provide these foundation aids to parenting, and appropriate remedies, has been shown in the American Head Start research and follow-up studies to compound cyclical disadvantage and to become increasingly costly, in every sense of the word.

The rules and regulations established by a variety of other institutions also contribute to this social provision with familiar patterns, and a sense of security about 'how things are done properly', providing the framework within which choices can be made. Thus Erikson's 'triple bookkeeping' principle, at this stage of early childhood, is nurtured through to adulthood in all its biological, psychological and social aspects.

Re-parenting

Remedial re-parenting in later years requires that we set up for ourselves, or with help that is then internalized, a safe framework for practice and, as a child does, proceed from simple choices, like tea or coffee, peas or beans, to more open choices of what, when and where. Against the grain of long-established assumption, we need constantly to remind ourselves that we actually have choice in so much, if we can only perceive it, and have the will to exercise it. As we become familiar with choosing, our capacity for freedom will extend into other areas of our lives, and into our offering of choices to others. Only then can we make truly responsible choices, associated with the next stage, instead of compulsive compliance with, or denial of, our own needs and urges, and those of others.

This is the point of our development at which it becomes easier to say 'no', as we stop offering them choices that encroach on our true willingness or capacity. Our relationships are then freed from the souring of resentment, however much we succeed in denying our unwillingness, as we strive to preserve a 'helpful' self-image. What marks our emancipation from the disapproval of others, and from any active or passive manipulation, is our more mature concession to their developmental rights to experience their own feelings and boundaries, and to choose what they will do about them. If we begin our refusal with acknowledgement of, and perhaps sympathy with, their disappointment, the effects of denial are softened and any manipulativeness disarmed.

Saying 'yes' then becomes a pleasurable choice, since we respond because we really want to help and not because we think we ought to want to help. Chill duty, that we may unconsciously still obey, is a poor substitute for warm willingness arising from an autonomous sense of choice. If concern for others is included in our personal values, we shall often want to respond with a 'yes', but unless we have a sufficiently developed internalized 'parent', concerned also for ourselves, we shall naturally and inevitably overreach our limitations, fall short of the demands we place on ourselves and, thus diminished, reduce the actual value of our offerings to others. It is in their interests, as well as ours, that we need to exercise wise choices about saying 'yes' as well as about saying 'no'.

Residual inability to handle negative emotions and reactions can be remedied by adopting the role of the 'good-enough' parent and recognizing that the raw reactions of our human nature need to be experienced before they can be handled uncompulsively. Thus we might say to ourselves something like, 'I am fully human, and therefore have angry, hostile and rejecting tendencies as part of my necessary survival, defence and developmental programming. Like a child, I can learn to experience them without fear, to let them pass and to choose how I will respond to a person or situation'. This pattern, however we may have worded it, needs to be internalized so that it can take over, gradually, from its destructive usurper. Until we have recognized and allowed for our innate negativity, its power in us will remain potent. Here again, we may have to work against the grain of a long-held assumption that negative feelings must be blocked out, because the shame of having them is too painful. Instead, shame needs to be perceived as a useful indicator for the beginning of a search for a better 'action readiness' (see chapter 12), such as trying to understand whoever or whatever has aroused our negative reaction.

Freeing ourselves from fixation

Fixation at an early stage of dependency, when to hate our parents for temporary frustrations would have been too destructive to risk, may mean either that we cannot allow ourselves to register, or that we feel in excess, hostility to others or society generally. At an early stage, we cannot realize that our destructive impulse is not the same thing as actual destructiveness, so that we may not have learned that it can pass harmlessly before choosing our response.

To remedy this and acquire the capacity to register feeling and then direct our responses, we need to unlock the threatening fears of 'hating our parents', experience for ourselves that waves of hatred pass and do not need to be acted upon, and set free our capacity to behave lovingly unhampered by frozen, unconscious, but still potent, chilling hostility. We can practice this on our 'pet hates', especially on powerful figures or institutions, as do many teenagers and young adults. The crucial next step, often not taken, is to pass beyond our hatred and to focus on how best to deal constructively with the person, people or situation confronting us, which means trying to gain some understanding of them. As always, patience and practice are needed for new learning.

If we have been traumatized, the blocked-off feelings and defences will be much stronger, and we may need help and support to allow their experience and wise handling, with the same compassion and space for recovery for ourselves as we would accord to others. Post-traumatic help is now more commonly offered as a result of the increasing awareness of its value, and psychotherapy can often assist the handling of past traumas.

With autonomous choice, ability to experience and learn from doubt, shame and other feelings, and the unfolding of our will, the epigenetic seeds of wisdom germinate in us, and some growth can be expected, even if injury has occurred, or early childhood experience has stunted these potentials. The principles of their development remain the same, from wherever and whenever the framework of parenting comes, and are woven into the continuous process of our life cycle.

The next stage, which Erikson calls the Play Age, has already shown recognizable, rudimentary elements during 'Infancy', is increasingly observable during 'Early Childhood', and emerges to accomplish its task of ego development around the age of three or four. With this continuity in mind, we turn now to examine the 'Play Age', with its glorious potential for creative blossoming.

THE PLAY AGE: INITIATIVE V. GUILT

Freud's third, 'phallic' psychosexual stage is again the basis of Erikson's insights. Myelination of the nerve fibres in the genital area brings new sensitivity and interest, and the term 'phallic' is applied to girls as well as boys. This is in symbolic accord with Erikson's emphasis on creative purpose and direction as the ego strength to emerge from this stage. Freud's description of the formation of the superego, through identification with the same-sex parent during the Oedipus or Elektra conflict, is echoed by Erikson, and both of them point out the pathological results of an over-zealous superego – 'an overconstriction to the point of self-obliteration'.

Erikson's own description of the emergence of the third stage from the second is poetic. 'There is,' he says, 'a new miracle of vigorous unfolding which constitutes a new hope and a new responsibility for all.' We seem to 'grow together' both in person and in body, with newly released energies ready for our next major adventure. Without waiting until people or circumstances present us with choices and ideas for interesting activity, initiative begins to form around ideas of our own, and with our new sense of control, we form some plan of action towards our purpose and put it into operation.

Erikson describes the impetus of initiative as 'making' and of being 'on the make'. His description of the kinds of initiative differently undertaken by boys and girls reflects the biases of culture and decade, but allowing for this, we can recognize that both boys and girls can exercise 'masculine' initiative in directive and active ways, and 'feminine' purpose in selective response, and in persuasive or attractive presentation.

Self-direction

Nowadays, we are increasingly less rigid in our perception and encouragement of gender characteristics and sex roles, but research has consistently shown greater average rates of muscular activity in boys and greater average verbal ability in girls. However differences persist, both boys and girls can gain through their play and family experience, a sense of so many wonderful things to enjoy making, doing, creating, so many goals worth achieving, and this 'felt knowledge' will motivate self-direction and endeavour throughout life.

Founded on choice, initiative adds the capacity to plan ahead, and it is this extra dimension that contains our vital sense of personal responsibility. New games are invented, constructions become imbued with more purpose, and adventures and projects are undertaken. Interactions with family and friends are sustained by reciprocal and common purposes. If our initiative has a successful outcome, we experience a sense of personal achievement and are encouraged to further efforts. Our autonomy now expands into bursts of

Figure 5.2 *Initiative. This small girl has planned and completed her construction successfully*

creativity, persistent application of new skills and a growing independence. Our relationships blossom.

Responsibility and handling guilt

If our endeavour meets with failure or disaster, and especially disapproval or blame, we experience guilt, for in addition to the shame of wrong choice or action, we now have a sense of responsibility. We need to learn how to identify where our planning and actions went wrong, and to focus our feelings of regret into a new direction for 'a better way'. This progression does not always come easily, but patience in fostering the ability to admit a mistake and to allow disappointment and regret is the first step. Where others are involved, this needs to be in conjunction with consideration for what they, too, may be feeling. Our capacity for reasoning is very limited at this stage, and we rely heavily on our own feeling reactions and those we learn to perceive in others. Yet it is now that the foundations of moral reasoning are laid as parents repeatedly and simply explain their own reasons alongside their prohibitions, prescriptions and encouragement. Many of these are internalized, along with observations of how our parents actually behave (see chapter 6).

Where regret is not present, and we are feeling gratified by the success of a destructive impulse, some gain, or by the discomfort of a rival or antagonist, even more patience is needed. Underlying values need to be made clear – for example, kindness, turn-taking and reciprocity, and the rights of ownership – so that these will gradually become our internalized guidelines as we mature. Choice for self and others, especially regarding participation, is important here, within clear boundaries, for without choice within boundaries, reliable, self-directed moral choices cannot begin to form.

Disapproval needs to be clearly attached to the irresponsible act and its consequences, not to our core potential and planning capacity, and needs to be discussed, together with our feelings, vulnerabilities and intentions, by our parents and carers 'with and alongside' us, not 'poured down from above'. Without this discussion, sensitive moral considerations are unlikely to form, though there may be some blind, automatic guilt reactions based on parental modelling.

Mere compliance or obedience are notoriously unreliable in adolescence and beyond, though they have some place before co-operation and responsibility become possible for us. Regret needs to be attached to the nature and consequences of our blundering or ill-intentioned initiatives, and we have no 'felt measure' of what is wrong, unless we have felt and internalized a 'good-enough' ethos of nurturance and regard with which to compare what is happening. Only then can we learn to deal effectively with our own guilt and with injury and resentment caused by the offences and failures of others.

Forgiveness

Experience of being forgiven for real, recognized transgressions, be they thoughtless, accidental, angry reactions, or maliciously intended, has long been acknowledged as an essential precursor of forgiving others and of forgiving ourselves. Without the expectation of openness and forgiveness, regret and hurt feelings are habitually repressed, whether they result from offending actions or from being offended against, deprived or separated. These feelings then form an unresolved sense of wrongness, a reservoir of guilt that affects the whole personality, especially emotional health. Alternatively, repressed regret and hurt feelings may trigger a self-preservation reaction that blunts or defends against guilt, personal or parental, and causes asocial, antisocial or perverted development.

False forgiveness, where the necessary issue of perception of the offence, and 'felt' regret for it by the offender has been bypassed, produces equally undesirable consequences. This 'writing off' often occurs during early childhood and throughout life when a penalty or punishment has confused the vital element of *regret for the transgression*, essential for the emergence of reliably 'better' behaviour, under the control of our own initiative and direction. This is why deterrents and retributive methods are notoriously unreliable.

Consideration and co-operation

Consideration, practical, moral and imaginative, is therefore the skill that we need to have fostered and expanded during this crucial period, and during any later remedial efforts. Co-operation is again the key for parents and carers, as we experience and internalize guidelines for our initiative and thus become aware of the meaning of responsibility.

So tender is this new sensitivity during the time of its emergence that we frequently feel responsible for family events that are not of our doing. It is enough that our feelings have been involved, for example, in the death of a familiar grandparent, in the break-up of a marriage, or especially in the illness or loss of a mother, father, brother, sister or close friend.

Parents need to become aware of this hidden hazard, and to give reassurance, which may require repeating, when events of a disturbing kind happen within a family, saying something along the lines of, 'Sometimes children feel it is their fault when things like this happen in a family, but it really isn't. Just being part of a family (or being a friend) is enough to make them feel that what has happened is somehow because of them, or what they might have done. It really *isn't* like that. They don't need to worry, though they will probably feel quite sad for a while.' Opportunity to grieve for any loss, to share sad feelings and to talk about both happy and sad times is essential.

It is important that we learn to distinguish this guilt of involvement, closely associated with the guilt of failure to act in a situation, from the personal guilt of action, intention or of failing to act. Our sense of failed responsibility towards others is the counterpart of the increased pleasure we feel in shared enjoyment and effort, both guilt and enjoyment being part of close involvement with others. Collective guilt is another form of guilt experience we may recognize later in life. Like a sense of collective achievement based on the past, it often reaches back to collective 'wrongness' before and beyond our own individual lives, but its resolution can be learned alongside that of involved guilt.

Paradoxically, if we would take our part in remedial action for involved or collective 'wrongness', we must first leave it behind and thus free our creative initiative, now responsible only for what is possible and realistic for us. Regret and a new forward focus are again the key to the change in self-direction. As we become able to handle guilt of all kinds, through discussion, consideration and appropriately associated feelings of disappointment and regret, our initiative is tuned into increasingly productive endeavours, our self-direction tempered by new awarenesses that release newly creative potential.

Inhibition

Erikson says that inhibition, 'too much' holding back of urges and responses, is the pathology that may develop at this stage in the absence of a favourable ratio of initiative v. guilt. Enough successful achievement is necessary, along with trial-and-error experience of a sense of 'good' and 'bad' or 'wrong'. Parental praise and blame are powerful factors, and are internalized alongside the potent, *apparent* values that we perceive expressed in our parents' full range of initiative and response. Where these are consistently 'good enough', parental verbal expression will reinforce the underlying values, but where there is discrepancy between what is done and what is said, what is done will become the internalized pattern.

Parental example

Parental example in the handling of their own shortcomings and feelings of guilt is likewise very potent. In fact, it is possible for parents with very few apparent shortcomings to leave their child without this necessary experience, so that a sense of guilt in being unable to live up to perceived, impossibly high standards becomes the pathological result. It seems that parents also need to be 'bad enough', to provide and communicate an example of grappling 'well enough' with the inadequacies and distortions that are a part of our human experience.

Parental needs, at this time, in addition to those especially associated with earlier development, are that they are able to model the qualities and skills of self-direction that their child will need as independence increases in leaps and bounds during the next stage of 'Schooldays'. They also need enough social integration to provide for their own continuing needs, and to provide for their child's increasing needs of social contact and experience. Artistic awareness, and ability to play 'Let's pretend' and other games, will enrich both their own and their child's development.

Play

Play provides an excellent milieu for the exercise of initiative, for imaginative exploration and for the testing out of the guidelines that are gradually being internalized. Playmates supply added stimulus, enjoyment in sharing and co-operation, and experience in handling discord and disputes over ownership or dominance. With our playmates, we begin to discover the value of peer relationships, and these become increasingly important to us as we grow.

Erikson expanded on Freud's insights into the value of play in the resolution of emotional conflict. Freud had observed a 'repetition-compulsion', that prompted the 'playing-out' of conflict through fantasized enactment and resolution, already evident by eighteeen months of age. He had also described how both dreams and play could replicate the joys of wish fulfilment. Often very Freudian in his language, Erikson built on these findings and showed, in his research and writings, how important is this treasure of childhood, giving it pride of place in naming his third psychosocial stage the 'Play Age'. More of his insights and methods will be discussed in the next chapter.

Social institution: drama

The social institution that Erikson has associated with continuing provision for the play needs of this stage is drama. Anthropological and historical accounts have amply documented this activity in many different ages and cultures, and drama appears to be fundamental to human society. Traditional festivals, rituals and rites of passage enable a 'playing-out', in symbol and enactment, of important dynamic events and interactions within our human nature and in society. Myth, narrative and, in our own culture, early mystery plays and celebrations of Christ's nativity are examples. In more recent times, each period has produced its own drama of subtly or radically changing cultural perceptions, social comment, insight and vision, portrayed in ritual, theatre and other art forms.

In societies such as our own, we are rediscovering the potency of role-play and socio-drama in training and in re-educational programmes, not to mention the even more potent psycho-drama used in psychotherapy. We are beginning to realize the potential, for good and ill, of the vicarious effects of watching and listening to drama, on stage, film, video and broadcasting, on people of different levels of maturity. The dynamic effects of identification, in role portrayal, are also being exploited in advertising. Unfortunately, we have not yet learned to apply the understanding about drama, albeit only a *part* of the shaping of individuals and our society, that Erikson and others have provided for us. As yet, we prefer to rely on partially informed or commonly confused 'hearsay' opinion, and on commercial demand and profit, for our guidelines.

Drama, and other art forms, can offer priceless opportunities for older children and adults to continue this formative and therapeutic process throughout life – recreation in its full sense. To maintain this treasure, the *continuity* of suitable provision is of crucial importance for our whole society during the fourth, 'Schooldays' stage. Drama, especially, and musical, visual, literary and other imaginative arts and crafts can thus bestow on us, individually and socially, their rich, natural, formative and remedial potentials. Erikson has offered strong evidence in support of this epigenetic, triple bookkeeping approach, and plenty more lies around us, as we consider the social aspects of our unfolding nature. (The benefits of rule-governed play, as opposed to imaginative, freely creative play, will be discussed in the next chapter.)

Remedial processes

Residues from this stage include a wide range of inhibited responses and asocial or antisocial attitudes and behaviour. These problems are often caused or compounded by residues from Infancy and Early Childhood stages, and remedies and re-parenting must consider how far this is the case, otherwise efforts towards change will be hampered by more basic inadequacies.

Misdirected initiative of many kinds, inertia, and the complexities of guilt and resentment associated with this stage all require considerable skills of re-parenting, and professional help may be indispensable. At least warm support and understanding encouragement are needed. Above all, our willingness to cultivate new awarenesses at a feeling level and to undertake responsibility for our own direction are prime essentials.

Once again, the establishment of a 'good-enough' re-parenting framework is the first task. It will depend on what has been internalized in the past or has developed in the absence of guidance whether external provision is required, skilled according to the nature of the residual problem, whether criminal, psychiatric or less severe in nature. Though the institutional setting and attendance may be custodial or compulsory for some, and their exposure to stimulus material, example and discussion may be unavoidable, the actual capacity for conscious self-direction and creative initiative can only occur on the stage two basis of will or willingness. Hence the value of art, music or drama therapy, within a firm framework, whether this structure be institutional or the strengths and circumstances of an individual's life.

Unethically tortuous 'brainwashing' and 're-education' techniques focus on breaking down existing patterns by aversive means, 'Mr Nasty', and gaining this necessary 'willingness' by mitigating the discomfort, or by introducing 'Mr Nice'. Though there is often considerable discomfort in the breakdown of internalized patterns, resulting from imprisonment, detainment in hospital, other life changes or losses, or from intensive psychotherapeutic processes, the ethical difference from brainwashing methods needs to be vigilantly maintained.

This difference lies in emphasis on concern for the individual as a developing person, balanced by concern for other developing persons, both in immediate surroundings and in society generally. Creeds, ideologies, training programmes or even therapeutic methods can lose sight of this basic ethic, overemphasizing either personal interests or corporate needs and dogma. To this ethic we now add some awareness of our need for a felt, integrated relationship with our material and natural environment, of the effects on each person of squalor, ugliness and pollution, and of the benefits of natural beauty, harmony and sustainable husbandry. This awareness is becoming part of our personal and social sense of responsibility.

For less severe residues, the re-parenting framework consists of consciously recognized values whose principles imbue patient nurturing. Whether this is self-parenting, or a mixture of self- and peer-parenting, will depend on individual choice and circumstances. Just as we internalize our parents' nurturing and move from a dependent relationship to maturing independence and self-direction, the nature of support we draw on, from therapist, counsellor, friends or groups, needs to change and move with us beyond initial dependence, compliance and conformity, and progress towards internalization and independent mutual regard. This progress is best achieved, as with a child, at our own, sometimes uneven, natural pace, giving time for our relationships to accommodate the changes.

Gradually, we can increase the creative output of our initiative, and discover new productive, recreational and restorative joys. We can reassess our actual responsibilities, and those of others, in the light of an increasing ego capacity to balance realities and growth needs of ourselves and of others. By posing the question 'Why?' and giving deep-level consideration to roots and consequences, we can re-examine the 'oughts' that have dominated our lives. We can sift out those which actually correspond with our prime values, and those which are rooted in compliance and conformity, or in identification with no longer relevant values.

Prime values, which include biological, emotional, intellectual and ethical needs and considerations, are our basic source of motivation and energy, and we can transform an abrasive 'ought' by releasing this motivation, so that our action becomes a response to a spontaneous urge, a 'want to'. Thus we find it easier to assess realistically and handle wisely the conflicting disinclinations attached to the cost in time, comfort or the lost alternative that accompany an 'ought'. Our hierarchy of priorities becomes clearer and our values better expressed in our lives by our initiatives and considered responses. Any 'ought' that does not stand up to this scrutiny, in the light of principles, priorities and use of resources, can be beneficially jettisoned, and it is surprising how many of these we carry unsuspectingly.

Stages two and three are inseparably intertwined, here, as reactions to disapproval and our sense of responsibility are both involved. Guidelines from Early Childhood and from the Play Age will be helpful in developing the new awarenesses we need for these reassessments. (See discussion of values in chapters 6 and 8.)

In remedial work for this stage, a momentum of creative initiative will greatly aid any reworking of guilt conflicts by providing the necessary counterbalance and sense of positive achievement. It cannot be too strongly emphasized that an undistorted, felt sense of 'good' and of 'worth' is indispensable, both as the source of transforming and redeeming energy, and as the internalized measuring 'standard' for all kinds of personal or involved guilt. In extreme cases, this building through experience may have to begin from foundation level and to straighten out distortions as it proceeds, but it has long been said that 'there is at least some good in everyone', and remedial work consists of finding this starting point, releasing its expression, and fostering existing and developing strengths. Guilt and regret have no felt meaning except in relation to injured, felt, internalized 'good'. Neither cognitive recognition alone, nor punishment or reward, can substitute for this, since they can produce only amoral and unreliable, calculated or conditioned changes.

Arts as therapy

The arts provide a medium for creative imagination to express, explore and consolidate initiatives, to gain insight and to develop this yardstick of 'good', as does play in childhood. Some form of art is therefore often invaluable in a remedial process. Occupational therapy, frequently used institutionally, has progressed a long way in its remedial insights since early basket making, and now includes a wide range of occupations. Similarly, in everyday living, cooking, carpentry, gardening, engineering, crafts and many other activities may all provide, for a particular person, the enjoyable creative outlet necessary for a sense of freedom, personal worth and achievement. Some exploration may be needed before a person who has lost the capacity to play, or to find creative enjoyment in his or her work, can release this pleasurable flow of initiative in a well-suited field of activity. Even where the means of livelihood or home circumstances do not easily allow this, it is essential to carve out some space where creative enjoyment and freedom can be found.

The remedial process needs to be tailored to the person undertaking it, and there are some severe residues that require considerable effort to overcome. Analytical psychotherapy deals with a complex mixture of gaps, distortions and effects of trauma, but the principles of identifying malfunction and stage of origin, followed by appropriate re-parenting that becomes internalized and independent, remain the same.

Analytical psychotherapy

Residual guilt of involvement is an example that will be outlined to illustrate such an analytical psychotherapeutic approach, which offers maximum understanding of self and others, in comparison with other methods of bringing about change. With that understanding, we have better hope of prevention or mitigation of damage and suffering in the future. The effects of involvement in obviously traumatic events are now more widely recognized because of this accumulated understanding, and help is increasingly being offered.

Unbearable guilt of this kind, repressed at the time of trauma, may have been too painful to express, even if there had been someone potentially available to share the feelings with, and the burden may have been carried throughout life with emotionally crippling consequences. The critical sensitivity to 'feeling responsible' can remain past its natural period, and in extreme cases, the bewildered adolescent and adult may unconsciously and repeatedly uncover this potently menacing vulnerability in a search for its natural progression to resolution. As already described, a natural progression would be: recognition of the falsity of personal responsibility, arrived at by consideration and discussion; experience of regret (probably preceded by a considerable amount of anger) about events; the finding of a 'better', more balanced perspective about responsibility and misfortune.

The repressed pain of involved guilt may cause the sufferer to perceive an internal threat or deficiency, sometimes projecting it outwards, and experiencing paranoia associated with circumstances and surroundings. It may even feel like the 'bottomless pit' of collective guilt and suffering, to which involved guilt is closely related. Often the repressed feelings emerge, so that in addition to the fear of perceived threat, the sufferer feels, in some irrational way, agonizingly responsible.

Stepping stones

The way out of this hell, having identified the crucial areas, is consciously to construct 'stepping stones' to provide new, more balanced experience and learning. Skilled help is indispensable, both to supply the missing insight and perspective and to nurture its internalization.

The stepping stones are made, firstly, out of recognitions of the falsity of involved guilt. This often means that the originating traumatizing event, or pattern of traumatic events, sometimes spanning generations in a family and the guilt of others, needs to be identified and considered. Repressed fears, grief and anger emerge during this process of psychoanalysis, sometimes mercifully contained by dreams and their interpretation, often spilling into, or 'colouring' current situations, as they have probably been doing for some time. These would normally be passing states of emotion, but when they arise from repressed, immature origins, may be intensified and recurrent until we learn to 'pass through' them, accepting their naturalness under the circumstances, expecting them to fade, and 'climbing out the other side'. As in childhood, the sufferer needs the kind of listening, affirming, sharing support that fosters the healing process of grief and readjustment, and restores self-trust, self-worth and a sense of free will, that also having been affected by the trauma of involvement.

The analogy of stepping stones emphasizes that the 'left-foot' stones of new understanding, just described, need to be followed by 'right-foot' stones of readjustment. Regret is the release factor that enables a step forward to be made, and needs to include any deficient response of our own as well as the hurtful or deficient actions of others. Initiative can then be self-directed into 'better' openings.

Persistent anger and resentment towards others may trap potential initiative, and at least some understanding of their guilt is helpful. Consideration of the oblivious, immature or distorted qualities of involved others, together with the facts or possibilities that contributed to their deficiencies, may pave the way to 'letting go' the injurious past, even to healing feelings of compassion for them and their forbears. The swirling torrents of fears, of inadequacy and pain then become less potent, their energy gradually being appropriated by new initiatives and positive achievements.

Forward scanning

Perception of 'better' openings for initiative and emotional investment will increase at a rate corresponding to changes achieved, in a 'chicken-and-egg' fashion, since progress in remedial work of this kind will be impeded by the as yet unresolved residues. There may be a delay between perception and understanding of causes, and the feelings and concepts of new possibilities, and it is important to 'keep scanning' in a forward direction during this re-alignment.

Courage, perseverance and patience are needed by the sufferer, as a nurturant, encouraging re-parenting framework is internalized, and a growing independence is achieved. An inability to function in major areas of life, or 'breakdown', may have necessitated re-learning, or the process may be undertaken side-by-side with adequate functioning in basic home and work situations. Pace needs to match individual capacity and circumstances, and time needed for this working-through will vary, both during the process and overall.

Roughly the same process may be observed in art therapy, psychodrama and other methods, where awarenesses gained about the internal dynamics will vary. Whatever the method, enjoyable creativity that feels like play will help consolidate released initiative and provide counterbalancing relief from grappling with uncomfortable emotions.

*Multidisciplinary
approaches*

It is important not to overlook possible biological impairment when considering the residual effects of any stage or stages. Valuable though psychoanalytic insights are, a grave weakness may be an exclusive focus on their explanatory and remedial framework that can discount simple factors that impede communication, such as less obvious sight or hearing defects, or Asperger syndrome.

In the example of Asperger syndrome especially, failure to diagnose this perceptual impairment, however it may have developed (see chapter 1), can lead to lack of skills-training facilities, support networks and public understanding. All of these deficiencies of recognition add cruelly to the painful experiences of the sufferer and his or her family, and until recent years, diagnosis was rare (Wing, 1981). A multidisciplinary approach can be the most useful for this and other perceptual disorders which may be hard to distinguish from residual emotional problems and can be compounded by them.

Both Freud and Erikson believed that, by around five or six years old, personality patterns are already formed. Erikson was more optimistic about the possibilities of some continued development and modifications in the patterning arising from the experiences of the first three stages, albeit requiring the concentration of even more effort and resources than during the critical, formative period. A high proportion of psychoanalytic therapy, and of more informal re-parenting endeavours, focuses on the psychodynamics of these early years. Hence the lengthy discussion in this chapter of the principles that are necessary for effective remedial procedures. Further discussion of some of the practicalities will be found in later chapters.

The work of good-enough parenting is to release a creative potential that is already there, and to awaken and nurture a capacity to draw all kinds of nourishment and inspiration from our universal and more local environment, according to the faith that sustains this capacity in all good parenting. From this comes our sense of integration with our community and our planet, and our release from many of the otherwise stressful insecurities of human experience.

Many of the experiences we need for our development are found in play. Toys, games, stories, role-play and film extend our understanding of ourselves and other people as well as of facts and processes. Play will be discussed in its emotional, social, cognitive and moral dimensions in chapter 6, and as we have already seen, its potential is immense. We shall also consider some of the theories of Jean Piaget.

PLAY: FEELING, RELATING, REASONING AND JUDGING

6

lay is a form of behaviour that occurs only in animals emerging recently enough in the phylogenetic (evolutionary) process of development to have evolved a limbic system. These organs of the forebrain permit a flexibility of behaviour that includes spontaneous, motivated actions that may not have any obvious, immediate consequence apart from intrinsic pleasure and sometimes the satisfaction of curiosity. In the young of many species, we can observe exploration and the make-believe practice of skills that will be required in adult life, for example where mother's tail substitutes as a vine to climb, or as future prey.

Primates display facial expressions akin to our smiling, apparently communicating playful intent in their mock-fighting and chasing, which nevertheless serve to establish and maintain social ordering. Human play, therefore, has deeply instinctive origins, and moreover we share with the animal kingdom a preference for 'optimum-level' arousal that motivates us to seek relaxation when arousal has been high for a period, and activity that will alleviate boredom after a period of low arousal. Novelty and stimulation have a basic biological as well as a human cognitive value, while familiarity and repetition increase feelings of security and relaxation at all levels.

PSYCHOSOCIAL DEVELOPMENT

Erik Erikson described play as 'a function of the ego, an attempt to synchronize the bodily and social processes with the self'. Not only does play provide for a wide range of exploration and enjoyment, but when stressed or traumatized, Erikson stated that 'playing it out is the most natural self-healing measure childhood affords' (1963). He developed a method of encouraging his child patients to play with a doll's house and a family of dolls, finding that they replicated in their play whatever emotional turmoil they were undergoing. The dolls were in the child's control and could safely be made to act out feelings and experiences that the child could not handle in reality. Erikson would sometimes communicate his understanding to his small patient by setting the scene himself and inviting the child to take over.

Play therapy

Play therapy consists, firstly, of communicating understanding of whatever the child is revealing about his or her feelings, and secondly, of the provision of materials and a safe space for following through the problem sequence of feelings and events. This allows for the discovery of alternative resolutions, as the child becomes more secure through the calm acceptance of the therapist and safe repetition, and begins to imagine and try out new responses arising from new feelings that are now becoming possible. An excellent, detailed example of this therapeutic process is Virginia Axline's study of 'Dibs' (1971). Another, more interactional method, using a drawing game, was developed by Donald Winnicott during the 1960s.

This basic principle of having control over a medium of expression, with space to exercise it, can be extended to sand or water play, modelling, drawing and painting, and games of 'Let's pretend'. All these are used as therapeutic tools, for adults as well as children, and they also provide a natural means of 'playing it out' for children dealing with the conflicts of ordinary developmental tasks, when they have enough uninterrupted access to them. Adults can similarly use such opportunities to 'unwind' as well as to release creative expression.

In addition to specific parent and child representations, other imagined figures of monsters, ghosts and fairies, story heroes and villains, and a variety of animals or robots, play out stresses and explorations in a variety of houses, caves, castles, forests, seas and skies, using earth or space vehicles, or glorious imaginary flight. Magical fantasy permits what is not possible in concrete reality, and the child is aware of the difference, though limited knowledge of the physical world may lead to false assumptions about it.

Imaginary companions

A common and interesting phenomena is the imaginary companion, who may 'appear' in particular situations or may become an extra 'member of the family' over a period of time. Feelings that the child cannot yet cope with, or regressions that are sometimes a precursor to progress, may be projected into this figure, or occasionally figures, so that the child can 'play out' the feelings of inadequacy, need or conflict. Parents and carers can learn much from this revealing process, and, aware that the 'companion' represents a very tender, as yet unintegrated part of the child, can make appropriate and reassuring responses to 'it', through the child. Though acceptance supports the 'playing out' process, care is needed not to prolong the projection beyond its usefulness by ascribing to its existence an extended adult 'reality' that the child could have difficulty in dismantling.

In children's play generally, the adult role can vary from a safe presence, or an occasionally commenting observer and provider of materials, to full participation. Children who rarely play on their own at home may benefit from the opportunity of play space in the care of another adult, and Erikson suggests that aunts or grandmothers have often provided this therapeutic experience of undivided attention and free, unshared access to play materials. No parent can possess completely the awarenesses, knowledge, qualities and skills that each particular child may need, and the compatible input of other adults and older children, especially in play situations, is of great potential benefit as a supplement to home play with peers and siblings.

Psychosocial theories, based on a mass of gathered evidence, show us that, along with good-enough parenting, and especially during these formative years, good play experience can develop our capacities and confidence. It can also help us adapt to unavoidably difficult situations, losses and events with some mitigation of damage to our ego strengths of hope, will and purpose. The triple aspects of our development – biological, psychological and social – unfold and are strengthened in the rich milieu of appropriately provisioned and protected playtime.

Fostering co-operation

Playing enhances our attachments, from our earliest interchanges and games of 'Peep-bo!' onwards. Shared enjoyment sweetens any effort involved in co-operation, and transfers from play situations into necessary routines and daily events. For example, a game can be made of 'finding' a hand or a foot, as small limbs are guided into sleeves and leggings. As we grow, we are more likely to choose to co-operate if co-operating is associated with sharing its enjoyment, rather than complying with superior power. Play enables our parents to 'get alongside us' so that we gain a 'felt sense' of a co-operation that can enrich relationships for the rest of our lives.

Once we are able to enjoy and co-operate in them, group games, especially those involving action, will increase our skills of co-ordinating effort, and develop in us the possibility of 'teamwork', though natural 'loners' need only as much group encouragement as brings pleasure in co-operation, or will be necessary for practical purposes. These often gifted children can be distinguished from those who may have problems by their otherwise friendly and happier attitudes, and they are usually able to co-operate in a group or team, where they can perceive that this is necessary or desirable. Games also provide experience of 'winning', 'losing' and 'competing', and adult attitudes, example and encouragement potently shape our social choices and ethical judgements in the future.

Playmates

Playmates become our first friends outside our family, and here we encounter individual and family differences, such as the presence of music or family pets, or being vegetarian or liking to play with a ball. Our attitudes to possessions, our own first, emerge and mature, as 'discretionary reservation', 'borrowing', 'lending' and 'sharing' become part of our social repertoire. Words like 'kind' and 'hurt' extend their felt meaning, and with choice and initiative, 'intended' action and 'being careful' are distinguished from 'didn't mean to' and 'didn't realize' as play gets overexuberant or discordant at times.

As well as a growing understanding of individual differences, we absorb a felt pattern of the norms of social behaviour, in practical as well as moral areas. Cross-cultural comparisons provide a fascinating variation of custom, dress, hospitality and 'manners' that quite young children have already ingested, and these can make us aware of how early, cultural and sub-cultural socialization begins. Role-play brings a feeling dimension to our perception of adult roles, and usually portrays fairly faithfully our actual or story-told experience of parents, shopkeepers, doctors, postmen and other community figures from a child's point of view.

Fantasy play is more likely to draw on fictitious or imaginary figures, often given made-up names, and is different in tone from the role-practice play that is part of our early socialization process. Viewing, and especially re-enacting, stories and plays with others, is yet another dimension of fused psychosocial experience that can continue to provide, in later years, the integrating potential of imaginary play.

Through playing with others, we come to know what to expect and what not to expect from them. We also discover what is expected from us and what is unacceptable. In fact, play enables us to discover a great deal about our world, and according to the kind of reasoning we use, to learn how people, objects and substances are likely to behave. The way our reasoning develops as we interact with our environment has been described in detail by Jean Piaget, and we shall now consider a brief outline of some of the main parts of his theory.

JEAN PIAGET (1896–1980)

It is always an advantage to know something of the background and training of any theorist whose work we wish to evaluate and learn from, and the inaugurator of cognitive developmental psychology has a very impressive list of early achievement and a broadly based foundation of experience. Born in Switzerland, Jean Piaget's first published scientific work, on the albino sparrow, was produced when he was ten years old. On the strength of his writing, the Natural History Museum in Geneva offered him a post as curator of their mollusc collection, which he declined as he was still at school. He studied zoology at university, and received a doctorate from Lausanne University when he was twenty-one.

In addition to his main studies in biology, he was deeply interested in philosophy and mathematics, and while still a student, was inspired by the idea that 'God is life' and decided that psychology could help him extend his 'science of life', biology, to an understanding of 'mind'. Accordingly, he studied the theories and methods of Freud and Jung at Bleuler's clinic in Zurich, and trained in clinical interviewing techniques at the Salpêtrière Hospital in Paris. (Clinical interviews are flexible and individually focused in contrast with rigorously standardized research interviews.)

He then spent two years at the Sorbonne in Paris, studying abnormal psychology, the history of science, mathematics and epistemology, during which time he also worked in Alfred Binet's laboratory, carrying out standardization tests for measuring children's Intelligence Quotient (IQ). (These tests involved only the recording of correct answers, without any opportunity to stray from the list of set questions.)

Following his work for Binet, Piaget continued to visit the school, carrying out his own 'clinical interviews' in which he was exploring the kind of reasoning children were using in giving answers to his questions. He published four papers based on his findings, and as a result, he was asked to become the Director of Research at the Rousseau Institute in Geneva. He also became a professor at Geneva University. Later, he observed his own three children, daughters Jacqueline and Lucienne and son Laurent, and it was during this period that he produced much of his writing about play and dreams, and about a child's concepts of grouping.

The third phase of his work included research with colleagues into children's acquisition of mathematical concepts and into 'genetic epistemology' (the development of knowledge about the environment through interaction with it). His interest in international education led to his association with the United Nations Educational, Scientific and Cultural Organization (UNESCO), and he was still engaged in research when he died at eighty-four years of age. Concentrating on cognitive processes, he left to others the question of environmental influences on their natural growth, 'la question américaine' as he called it. The vital connection he made between play and learning is epitomized in his statement that 'to learn is to invent' (1973).

Adaptation to our environment

As a biologist and an interactionist, Piaget perceived our basic biological drive to be adaptation to our environment. This we accomplish by interacting with it and forming mental representations (schemas or schemata) so that we can literally 're-cognize' repeated features and perceive disparaties. Our earliest representations are formed by our repeated reflex actions such as sucking, grasping or random kicking. These 'action schemas' form the nuclei of additional sensory impressions gathered as we suck at our mother's breast, grasp a finger or kick out in our bath-water, and we begin to recognize repeated experiences.

Piaget further distinguished our mental processing as, first, 'assimilation', whereby we repeatedly interact according to existing schematic patterns. This is followed by 'accommodation', whereby we adjust our existing schemas to take in new information. 'Equilibration' (sometimes translated 'Equilibrium') has thus been reached, and is now the basis for further assimilation and accommodation in a continuing progression. Piaget identified four different stages of our overall adaptation process, lasting from birth to adulthood, and his brilliant, long and very detailed descriptions of our Sensorimotor, Pre-operational, Concrete Operational and Formal Operational stages will be very briefly simplified next.

Sensorimotor stage

Our sensorimotor action schemas gradually gather enough information for us to acquire 'object constancy', so that we can perceive that a particular, constant collection of sensory impressions, which include smell, taste, feel, sound and appearance, really *is* constant and represents 'mother'. Other preverbal 'object' identifications follow, so that our mental representations allow us to recognize separate objects around us that continue to exist when out of sight. Early 'Peep-bo!' games, in which we come to expect reappearance, aid and illustrate, this achievement.

We begin to associate the sounds we can hear with people and objects, for example, the bell on a favourite toy, or our mother's voice in the next room. Thus we are building towards '*symbolic* representation', where the sound of a word can come to symbolize a person or object. Many of these word recognitions are evident before we are able to say our own first word, and form the cognitive part of our language development process. Through symbolic representation, we also become able to substitute one object for another in play, such as when a small box becomes all manner of other objects, in different games.

By this time, our primary schematic sensorimotor, or 'felt', pre-verbal patterns are in place, according to the kind of care and stimulation we have received, and our 'felt' understanding of language will continue to be closely associated with experience. Piaget believed that our schematic concepts must be in place before we can understand and use words. This can be illustrated by our 'trying to find the right words' to express our meaning. (See **Texts** for a fuller description of language acquisition and for discussions of the relationship between thought and language.)

Through our increasing accommodation of motor information, gained during our movements and interactions, we gradually achieve voluntary control over our bodies, learning to sit, walk and feed ourselves. Motor skills and dexterity continue to develop as an increasing amount of time is spent exercising them in play. Piaget called our early play 'mastery' or 'practice' play, and we shall return to his play theory shortly.

Pre-operational stage

During the second, Pre-operational, stage, roughly between two and four years old, our schemas continue to develop rapidly, and we begin to link them together, not always accurately. For example, if we, and perhaps a frequent playmate, both have a big sister, we perhaps assume that all the children we meet have a big sister as well. Or, we may attribute a causal relationship to simultaneously occurring events, such as a birthday in the family and a public festival. Piaget called this kind of contingent thinking 'pre-logical reasoning.'

He also thought that, at this stage, we are incapable of simultaneously perceiving more than one perspective, and therefore cannot envisage the possibility of any viewpoint other than our own. We are 'egocentric' in our perception, and gradually have to overcome this limitation in order to reach the next, Operational stage. More recent research has modified this view, and it seems that we begin to perceive a different perspective, depending on the context of the test used, earlier than was first believed.

Because the term is applied to perception, in Piaget's theory, 'egocentric' is not the same thing as 'selfish', as in common usage of the word. An example of unselfish egocentrism is given by a little boy, who was good at drawing, and at this time was fascinated by drains. Asked if he would draw a picture for his aunt's birthday card, of 'something Auntie likes', he willingly produced a pencil drawing of an elaborate, decorated drain, quite sure that this was what Auntie would like best! Egocentrism is also responsible for a child's belief that invisibility is acquired by hiding one's eyes.

Concrete operational stage

Around the age of four or five, the Operational stage is ushered in by our emerging ability to link our schemas together logically, and to use them to carry out 'operations' (calculations), in our reasoning about the world around us. At first we can only perform these operations in regard to 'concrete' objects, and this period, lasting until about eleven or twelve, Piaget called the 'Concrete Operational' stage. It begins as we become able to perceive that two oranges (one set of schemas) and three oranges (another set of schemas) can be combined to make five oranges. To start with, we need to see the objects, or at least their pictures, to be able to calculate, but later on we can do this by substituting our fingers or by making a mental image of the concrete items. Still later we recognize familiar number combinations, such as that nine plus six always add up to fifteen.

Our new ability to consider logically, more than one set of schemas at the same time enables 'conservation' to develop. This operation involves comparing and working out continuities and changes in quantity, volume and mass, usually in that order. Thus we can now perceive that a spaced out row of sweets or buttons has the same number of items in it as a row where they have been placed very close together – we can consider the spaces in between as well as the length of the row. The well-known three-beaker test enables us to demonstrate simultaneous consideration of height and width, whereby we perceive that a 'taller and narrower' amount of water has the same volume as a 'shorter and wider' amount. Likewise we can see that a long, thin sausage of dough has the same mass as when it is rolled up into a ball, though it now looks different.

Play that includes the provision of materials such as small bricks and countable objects, water and sand play, and dough or clay is therefore invaluable experience during which we develop the links between our groups of schemas and, through trial and error, discover a consistent logic in the way that materials behave. Piaget identified this kind of logic as 'inductive logic', which means that experience comes first, and out of it, logical consistency is perceived and accommodated as an organizing set of cognitive 'rules'.

Piaget emphasized that each child 'invents' this system of logic, and other kinds of relationship or facets of reality, in the 'cognitive space' between existing schematic patterning and incoming sensory information. Electroencephalograghic (EEG) research suggests that this takes place in our 'association' cortex, active as we process information. Individual variation in our patterns of understanding are thus accounted for in considerable detail.

Formal operational stage

Provided that our environment and experience have been sufficient, and continue to be so, the Concrete Operational stage is gradually transformed into the Formal Operational stage, as we become capable of abstract thought. Drawing on the schematic patterns laid down by inductive logic, we are now able to deduce logically what is likely in new circumstances, to formulate hypotheses and to test them out.

We have been using trial and error exploration since our early days, but our success rate is increased dramatically as our cognitive base of schematic programming becomes sufficient and well enough interlinked to allow the kind of reasoning in our 'cognitive space' that Piaget identified as 'deductive logic'.

An example of deductive reasoning is when a scientist, inventor or educator is inspired by a new possibility or method, and then uses this formal, deductive process to work out how to test it, and then how to put it into practice. Hypotheses and logic can now be applied *before* the experience of testing, and outcomes depend upon both earlier-accommodated schemata, and upon individual capacity for 'invention'. (EEG and other research evidence shows that left and right hemispheres of the brain contribute to analytical and global reasoning respectively, both essential to deductive reasoning in the context of broader realities.)

Eclectically, we know that practice, modelling and encouragement enhance both logical skills and open-minded consideration. *La question américaine*, concerning environmental provision, is therefore an important supplement to our consideration of Piaget's insights and investigations into the development of our cognitive processes.

Accumulated research findings (e.g. Flavell, 1977; Neimark, 1975; see

*Texts) have shown that only a part of our world population, even in developed countries, achieves this capacity to reason beyond concrete actualities, and to consider, deductively, new possibilities, though they may be aware of these as aspirations. Short-sighted thinking is therefore very prevalent, and actions based on feeling often lack the balance of formal consideration. Without this balance, even well-motivated actions are prone to excesses when it comes to the practicalities of carrying them out, or of daily living. This progression through concrete to formal operational thinking is also very relevant to moral reasoning, as we shall see later in the chapter. First, we return to Piaget's play theory.

Play: mastery, make-believe and rule-governed play

Figure 6.1 *Make-believe. These little girls are trying out their future roles and exploring their own unfolding initiatives and peer comments*

Piaget showed how our play both brings about and is shaped by our cognitive development, and he distinguished three kinds. The first to emerge is 'mastery' or 'practice' play, characterized by repetition and trial and error acquisition of skills. Thus our early repetitive banging movements become more co-ordinated as we achieve voluntary motor control by means of our developing action schemas. Combining these growing abilities with schemas composed of information gathered through our visual senses, we recognize a toy or interesting object and reach for it. As our control develops, we begin to manipulate objects as well as exploring them with our mouths.

Mastery practice continues throughout life, as we learn new skills through trial and error and repetition, and we are closest to the child's eager activity when the skill is one that we enjoy for its own sake. The early sounds of language are similarly practised, and our basic drive to explore our environment and to develop our own adaptiveness maintains our childlike curiosity and enjoyment of mastery play.

As we develop symbolic representation, a new dimension of imaginary play opens for us, bringing with it increasing understanding and use of language. Piaget calls this 'ludic' or 'make-believe' play. At first, our pretending that one object is another involves only ourselves, though we may permit a privileged carer to enter our imagined scene and later request that they do so. 'I'm a little cat' or 'Let's play rabbits' might be among our earliest invitations.

Gradually we begin to involve other children in our games instead of only playing alongside them, and our imaginary role-play can now include other participants. 'Mummies and Daddies', shopkeeping, or driving and riding in a train enrich our repertoire, and we can take part in nursery nativity and other plays, as well as inventing our own scenes and action.

Symbolic play, also, has a life-long potential, not only serving us emotionally and recreationally, as already described in the previous chapter, but also assisting our cognitive understanding beyond our actual experience, by extending our range of schemas and by establishing extra links between them. For this reason, role-play is frequently used in supplementary training sessions, both in business and professional courses. It can also exercise our imagination, so that we become better able to consider new possibilities in our formal operational thinking.

The third kind of play that Piaget found in his studies of playing children was 'rule-governed' play. In addition to observing his own children from an early age, he traced changes in the way children played marbles. The first games to emerge with rules are early rituals, such as always jumping from the second step, placing bed-time toys precisely, not walking on lines in a pavement, or other invented solitary games. It seems that we need to lay down cognitively, as well as emotionally, experience of making rules for ourselves before we can progress to an understanding acceptance of rules generally.

In games of follow-my-leader, the first child will often establish an arbitrary sequence of actions that constitutes the 'rules' for the others to follow, and this sequence may be repeated several times. In this way, we come to 'accommodate' schemas about *voluntarily* accepting, or not joining in, rules laid down by others, so valuable to leaders and followers in various projects and organizations later in life.

When we begin to play rule-governed games with others, we often modify the rules. Sometimes exceptions are made for younger children, by being given a start for example, or agreement is made permitting an extra 'go' for some or all of the participants. Penalties, such as being 'out', may be altered by common consent, or by the accepted dictates of a leader, or the method of scoring may be changed.

This *social* experience of rule-making appears to be an essential transition to the willing acceptance of *coded*, universal rules, of the uncertainties of chance, and of the existence of varying individual capabilities. In turn, established rules are the precursors of inductively derived *principles*, be they ethical or intrinsic to the nature of the activity, sport or game that they serve.

As adults, the structured arena of rule-governed games, whether they be played as a team, in a group or as an individual, is anathema to some. In others, such structures release a zest that spills over into other areas of their lives, enabling them to recapture a youthful sense of challenge, and to sublimate any excess aggression into socially accepted competitiveness, as recommended by Anthony Storr (1968). As spectator pastimes, these games affect people similarly with aversion, indifference or keen enthusiasm.

Cognitively, rule-governed games serve both to model ordered procedures, and to provide structures for social activity. Many people derive reassurance from these prescriptions, as they exercise their mastery of physical or computational skills, and encounter the sometimes all-or-nothing interventions of chance within a securely contained area. 'Fair Play' is a concept from rule-governed games that is echoed in moral judgements, and we shall next consider how each stage of cognitive development affects the kinds of moral judgement we are able to make.

Moral judgements

Piaget found that, until about seven years of age, children perceived moral authority as coming from outside themselves, either from parents and adults generally, or from God or some mysterious, absolute, moral standard existing in the outside world. For this reason, he called his early stage 'heteronomous', and observed that it was characterized by 'moral realism' and was 'authoritarian' in nature.

Moral realism occurs because we have difficulty in weighing up more than one aspect of an action. In our focus on the amount of damage done, we may fail to consider the intention behind an action, or the circumstances in which it occurred. Authority embodies knowledge of right and wrong, and therefore obedience to it is regarded as a moral imperative.

Only gradually do we begin to compare the relative values of intention, amount of damage and degree of circumstantial responsibility in a particular accidental or purposeful action, and so become capable of 'moral relativism'. We also begin to perceive moral value in peer concerns and agreements, and, depending on our social experience in this direction, become more 'democratic' in our judging. It is not until the age of about twelve that our own capacity for moral judgement can responsibly replace our former blind, obedience-oriented standards and we can enter what Piaget describes as the 'autonomous' stage.

We have thus passed from the limitations of egocentrism, through operational, socializing experience of 'what works', to the stage where more abstract concepts contribute to the establishment of our own guiding values. Formal operational thinking enables us to consider the relationship between actual choices and underlying universal ethics. Piaget believed that we first practise moral behaviour, and then come to a 'conscious realization' of moral precepts. On the basis of our experience, we can then reason autonomously, and make moral judgements of our own.

We can compare Piaget's description of this cognitively registered internal value system with Erikson's psychoanalytic model of the superego and ego-ideal, and his recognition of the adolescent proneness to project personal values into ideologies, religious or otherwise. (Ego-ideal is our *individually determined* set of positive values, maturing as our ego overcomes dependencies and develops qualities and strengths.) Both these theories can be useful to our own understanding of moral development, not forgetting a consideration of Social Learning Theory and of the insights offered by research into child-rearing methods.

Kohlberg's levels of moral judgement

Lawrence Kohlberg examined these varied psychological approaches, and decided to focus his own research on the cognitive development of a child's sense of justice and moral principle, 'the child as a moral philosopher', as he termed it. Accordingly, from 1955 onwards, he began to carry out studies based on Piaget's stage theory of moral reasoning, like him, posing 'moral dilemma' questions, then probing the reasoning behind the answers given by the subjects. His research, often with colleagues, continued throughout the 1960s and 1970s, providing both longitudinal and cross-cultural evidence about our socio-moral maturing process (see *Texts).

In this way, he developed his own, more elaborated, description of what he termed the 'Pre-conventional, Conventional and Post-conventional' levels of moral reasoning. He labelled his subjects as having reached a particular stage, when they made fifty per cent or more of their judgements in accordance with that stage of reasoning, thus recognizing that we vary in our level of reasoning according to different circumstances. We may make very ethical professional judgements at a high level, and later in the same day, unfairly commandeer the bathroom, or obey someone's inconsiderate behest solely to avoid displeasing them.

Each level has two stages, and the Pre-conventional level begins as we realize that some of our actions have unpleasant consequences and are therefore 'wrong' in some way, and to be avoided. The second stage is when we add to this a recogniton of 'right' actions that bring need satisfaction, first of our own needs, and then the needs of those close to us. We begin to develop a pragmatic and rudimentary recognition of 'fairness', and can understand 'fair exchange' and the reciprocal benefits of co-operation, as we play our way into operational thinking. The essential routines of family life are also part of the living 'aliment' (Piaget's concept of food for our cognitive processes), which we accommodate to form our basic moral schemas.

The second, Conventional, level is reached as we become familiar with our increasing potential for 'helpfulness' and for gaining approval, which characterizes stage three. Social esteem is vital to our self-esteem, and re-assurance that we are 'nice' and 'good' is especially valued. Intention also assumes importance during this third stage, as our own intentions are recognized and taken into account, and we cope with the accidents of our well-meant helpfulness, or find that we can understand and forgive the ignorance or accidents of well-intentioned others.

Stage four begins as inductive logic derives *implicit*, moral rules from our experience. More readily accommodated than explicit prescriptions, but strengthened by explicit repetition, implicit patterns of 'right' and 'wrong' are laid down for reference. Rule-keeping becomes a moral obligation, a 'duty' now understood to be necessary to the maintenance of social order. Unfairness is strongly resented. 'It isn't fair!' is a frequently heard protest that accompanies this fourth stage.

Concrete operational thinking, inductive logic, and the rules that are derived from them constitute the Conventional stage, and this is the highest stage of moral reasoning to be reached by about two-thirds of our world population, who fail to achieve the capacity for formal operational reasoning and Post-conventional moral judgements. This is not to suppose that only formal operational thinkers are capable of high ideals and inspirations, only that the practical considerations necessary for their application may well elude those less able thinkers.

The Post-conventional level is reached as stage five judgements emerge from a code of principles that considers individual rights as well as circumstances and social justice, as opposed to a more impersonal, automatic and rigid set of rules. Thus a manager may deal more justly with our complaint than an assistant dealing with it 'by rule'. Kohlberg found that many professional judgements were made at this level. However, later research showed that so few people made fifty per cent or more of their judgements at stage six, where code gives way to principles based on ethical values alone, that a sixth stage could hardly be included in a typology (list of types) of normal development.

Moral behaviour

Kohlberg's research also supported Piaget's belief that it is both the practical experience we have of rules, contract and principles, and the stage of reasoning we have reached when we encounter this experience, that determine how well we express our moral judgement in our own behaviour. Our moral schemas develop as they register the advantages of restraint, co-operative exchange, approval and the need for some regulation of play and other social activity. They are consolidated by the practice of familiar habits of behaviour, inextricably a part of our family relationships, neighbourhood customs, school and social life. We all learn the 'norms', whatever these may be for us.

Formal operational thinking can enable us to formulate contracts, procedures and agreements, realistic and workable because they are based on a fuller range of facts and probabilities. From these experiences and their results, we can use our capacity for abstract thinking to understand and uphold, not just aspire to, basic ethical values. These, already tested out in practice, constitute stage six ethical reasoning. Stage four is usually adequate for most of our socially regulated behaviour (for example, car parks) and stage five for contracted agreements (for example, dental treatment), but most of us encounter situations not covered by rule or code, and must struggle with 'grey areas' as best we can for the 'right' solution. Many of us try to include stage six reasoning.

Formal, more comprehensive, reasoning allows us to bridge the practical gap between our own moral rules and habits and our formerly unattainable ideals that involve the ethical co-operation of others. Kohlberg and his colleagues found that reasoning and discussion alone could raise the level of judgement, but had little effect on behaviour unless discussion was rooted in practical, participant situations. Their research confirmed that each stage is a necessary precursor for the next, just as we need to establish basic foundations in all learning. There is much we can derive from this approach that is valuable in education and in remedial training.

This chapter overlaps considerably, both with the last chapter and with the next, in which we shall focus on the remaining years of childhood and adolescence. It is our daily experience in home, school and neighbourhood during these years that prepares us, more or less well, for adulthood. The kind of understanding we have acquired in our interactions with whatever environment raises us from infancy, will potently shape decisions we shall make, our failures in perception of alternatives and choice, and our recreational and moral attitudes.

Piaget did not deny the importance of emotional factors in the direction of our motivation to explore, but he focused on the way we lay down, cognitively, information about all our experience and use this 'schematic processing' in future interactions (see *Texts). We turn now to Erikson's 'triple book-keeping' description of his fourth and fifth stages of psychosocial development, to help 'round out' our own understanding.

SCHOOL AGE AND ADOLESCENCE

7

SCHOOL AGE: INDUSTRY V. INFERIORITY

Erikson described the onset of this fourth stage as a turning from preoccupation with play, personal relationships and concerns in the home to an outward focus on production, which involves the learning of skills. Freud called this post-Oedipal period the 'Latency' stage, when libidinous urges become quiescent, and Erikson added his own observations, '..✳The child must forget past hopes and wishes, while his exuberant imagination is tamed and harnessed to the laws of impersonal things ...'. Whatever our cultural background, we apply ourselves to the learning of skills, both for the satisfaction of already achievable production, and as a conscious preparation for our adult working and providing life.

We develop a sense of industry, as our aim of bringing a productive situation to completion 'gradually supersedes the whims and wishes of play'. Steady attention and perseverance become associated with a sense of achievement, and our capacity for 'felt' work satisfaction is established. We are submitted to systematic instruction, of whatever kind our culture provides, including the teaching of practical skills and usually literacy and numeracy. To this modern societies are adding computer literacy as one of the fundamental 'tools' of modern technology.

In whatever way it is presented to us, in different cultures, we continue to be instructed variously in 'the story of our people' (religion, history) and in 'features of the world we live in' (geography, environmental studies, science). Many cultures teach art awareness and skills in music, dance, painting, modelling, drama and especially narrative and literature. We are fortunate if this communicating, integrating experience is ours, for its rich, deep level of 'feeling' communication extends our sense of belonging and can fill some of the gaps in our family experience. Shared appreciation has a significant bonding effect, as well as the enjoyment it brings.

The more complex our society, the greater the role of specialist teachers, but we learn also from parents and older children, and any skilled adult with the patience to teach us. Those people we meet who have the skills we admire become important to us, especially if they are willing to help us develop our own. Our peers are increasingly influential, as we co-operate in learning and play projects, compare their attributes, skills and achievements

Figure 7.1 *Cultural education. Story-telling, symbol and custom portray cultural experience and values that are being brought alive for these children in their classroom*

with our own, seek their esteem and give and receive support. Our capacity for friendship develops, depending on our earlier experience of trusting, choosing and co-operating, and on the compatibility of our companions.

When our skills let us down, failing to achieve our productive aims or comparing unfavourably with those of our peers, we experience a sense of inferiority. This is not necessarily the negative phenomena its discomfort might suggest. Like mistrust, shame and guilt in earlier stages, it can help guide our choices.

Competence and constriction or inertia

Perhaps we need to persevere with careful practice in our deficient skill, but it could be that our efforts would be better directed into alternative areas where we have greater aptitudes, even gifts. With a 'favourable ratio' of industry and inferiority, a sense of 'competence' is the ego quality that Erikson said develops at this stage. We recognize what we are good at and where our weaker areas lie, and although we are heavily influenced by parents, teachers and peers in our choices, and must apply ourselves to the practice of skills deemed essential, we begin to select where our persevering efforts shall be concentrated.

Individual differences of temperament, reflective or impulsive tendencies, physical and intellectual potentials and family attitudes, together with our earlier experience and opportunities, all shape our inclinations and industri-ousness at this and later stages. Our size, appearance, dress, manner of speech and possessions all make an initial impression on our peers; this can be longer lasting, so that through our satisfying or otherwise peer relation-ships, our school work is enhanced or hindered. Similarly, however much we would wish to deny it, neighbourhood relationships are likely to be influ-enced in the same way, and one of the invaluable social skills we can learn at this time is to look beneath obvious differences, and to establish relation-ships on the basis of common values and interests.

A school ethos and presentation of learning experience can inculcate care or compliance, encouragement or censure, interest in 'finding out' or un-motivated performance of requirements. A secure framework will leave us free to apply our efforts to the acquisition of skills, and we shall also take in the values that shape it. We may give up in despair on skills and values if there is punitiveness instead of guidance and correction, or if there is a *laissez-faire* laxity instead of communicated, mutual understanding.

Our schooling can reinforce a sense of self-worth and responsibility, re-gard for others, hope for the future, and even remedy some of these residual deficiencies, or it can, for whatever reason of over- or under-action, fail us and leave our natural inclination for the industrious learning of skills to focus on 'survival' or 'get what you can' lessons. Reinforcement of whatever our schooling spells out to us is provided by our increasingly important peers. In cultures where the 'schoolroom' is mainly field, jungle, family busi-ness or city street, our capacity to learn will feed on *whatever is adaptive to our surroundings*.

Much will depend on family and social values, as to whether feelings of inferiority become a useful indicator for well-directed effort, or become a pathological 'inhibiting' characteristic leading to inertia. Inferiority feelings may give rise to a reactive, defensive necessity for superiority, which can often include 'putting others down'. Such feelings may also prolong dependencies.

Erikson observed that pathology at this stage includes not only 'inhi-bition' of industry and despair of achieving 'tool' competence accompanied by inertia, but a 'constriction' of horizons, where work may become the only criterion of worthwhileness. Thus a child can become a 'conformist and thoughtless slave of his technology and of those who are in a position to exploit it', and may develop a pattern of 'doormat' relationships.

Social institution: technical ordering

The social element associated with this stage is the technical ordering of a society, that is, the ways in which we carry out our economic activity and the frameworks in which we can earn our living. The terms 'technology' and 'tools', here, include skills and knowledge as well as methods and structures of production and distribution. Erikson's studies of American Indians showed a direct relationship between their means of livelihood, governed by their ecological base of riverside or grassy plains, and the social values and kinds of teaching given to their children (1963). The skills valued by a society and the way that their application is organized will provide the pat-terns for our learning at this School Age, and changes in value, working re-quirements and organization will be reflected in schooling.

We need to remember that both desirable and undesirable skills and 'felt' attitudes are inculcated during this extremely fertile learning period, as the values expressed in the technical ordering of our society add their direct weight, in school and neighbourhood, to our earlier psychosocial foundations laid down in our home. Our society's technological organization is functional, not only in shaping our schooling and neighbourhood ethos, but in forming the milieu in which parents earn a family living and make whatever kind of home that their own education, competence and resources allow.

Erikson's School Age corresponds in approximate age with Piaget's Concrete Operational stage, and we can gain from the insights in both theories. Piaget visited Erikson during the 1960s, and during their discussions, stated that he saw no contradictions between their different approaches. Schooling, in many societies, continues 'systematic instruction' into adolescence and provides for the development of 'Formal Operational thinking' for some members, and sometimes for the continued training in 'Concrete Operational' and practical skills of others.

Remedial principles

Residual problems from stage four are frequently compounded by earlier residues, and these need to be considered in any remedial attempt. For example, as we explore the world beyond our home, and even before that, reality often faces us with necessities which govern some of our choices. If we operate only from 'having to', a negative attitude to 'industry' is likely to pervade our schooldays. We may not like the practice that is necessary to acquire some skills, but if we have a goal of *our own* in mind, we can choose to work at the difficulties involved with willingness. A sense of choice based on realistic, available alternatives is necessary if motivation is to aid the development of competence in the wide range of skills we are capable of acquiring at this highly critical period.

Provided that underlying residues are catered for, the acquisition of deficient skills can proceed as appropriate, and remedy may involve literacy or numeracy classes, subject instruction or social skills experience. Older children and adolescents need good family, foster or therapist support as they re-work their earlier schooldays, just as all children need the warm support and encouragement of their families to make the most of their learning opportunities. A residual sense of inferiority may be at the root of later hampering attitudes, and competence may be slow in emerging.

Adults who have missed out on support or opportunities as children may find the needed warmth and encouragement in their partners or friends, or may need the support of a therapist or counsellor until their own self-reparenting skills have sufficiently developed, and their ordinary relationships are able to encompass these needs. Emotional needs in remedial work mirror those of the 'first-time-round' process, and ignoring them would impede progress. Adults with deficient School Age experience usually find that their Adolescence has also been affected, and we will now trace the usual pattern of development, beginning around puberty.

Adolescence: identity v. role confusion

Basic biological changes in size, strength, appearance and genital maturity precipitate us into what is for some, adulthood, or for others a recognized change-over period known as 'adolescence'. Freud's psychosexual description of Genital maturity, his fifth and last stage, includes both the emotional capacity for relationship with the opposite sex, emerging at the end of this stage, around the age of eighteen, and the productive capacity to support this which may well take longer to achieve. *'Lieben und Arbeiten'* (to love and to work) was his summary of what he considered necessary for mature adulthood, and Erikson endorsed this statement, explaining that love includes both genital love and a quality of 'being loving generally', from which work-productiveness flows (1963).

Again incorporating Freud's basic theory of a biologically unfolding psychosexual process, Erikson extends beyond it with his own description of adolescence and its psychosocial events, tracing the changes in our sense of 'identity' from child to adult. The more varied and complex our society, the greater our 'role-confusion' as we work our way through the doubts and decisions involved in becoming grown-up, assuming adult roles, and establishing an occupation.

Erikson describes our conscious sense of ego identity as a 'sense of inner sameness and continuity of one's meaning for others'. During adolescence, we adjust this self-image to accommodate our biological, psychological and social changes, often reworking conflicts from earlier years. Our developing size, strength, genital maturity and appearance, and our rate of change compared with our peers, not only bring new abilities, awarenesses and feelings to ourselves, but changes in the way that others feel and behave towards us.

Sometimes people who know us well, especially our family, may fail to accommodate changes in us and continue behaving towards us as before, so that we can feel lonely and misunderstood by them. Sometimes new expectations of us and our own inconsistent feelings are more than we can handle, and we become moody. Hormonal changes affect us generally with bouts of extra energy or lassitude, and more specifically, with increased interest in individuals of the opposite sex or concerns about our own sexual orientation. Our desires generally and sexually are felt in surges, and our ego now has to work extra hard balancing out our basic values and motivations with our current inclinations and opportunities, while at the same time carrying out a major re-evaluation of childhood maxims and guidelines.

Adolescent questioning

This 'moratorium' (discussion to the point of conclusion) that we hold with ourselves, and usually our close peers, is a sign that a healthy search for our own identity is under way. Erikson and James Marcia, who researched this process during the 1960s, found that some adolescents 'foreclose' on the outcome, and prematurely identify with existing or conventional values, thus avoiding the discomfort of uncertainties that accompany genuine questioning. Foreclosure limits the choices open to an adolescent, so that over-conformity and 'tunnel-mindedness' are likely. Childhood values that have stood up to honest questioning, on the other hand, will be released into a fuller potential, just as a pot-bound plant can achieve better growth when planted out and given space.

The roots of our motivation, throughout life, are the values that matter most to us, consciously and unconsciously. These include basic biological survival needs, and aspirations for comfort and convenience. They are usually lumped together as 'economic necessities' which may also include objects we 'cannot do without' and intangibles such as education, health care, leisure or other opportunities that depend on economic factors, and involve earning, or getting by some other form of acquisition. Material and other consumer values will be carefully weighed with psychosocial needs that include peer regard, satisfying communications and mental stimulation, or at least occupation, to which are now added urges to explore sexual relationships. Priorities jostle for position.

Incomplete emotional tasks from earlier stages often complicate adolescence still further, throwing up immature feelings and values that, given acceptance and understanding, can be resolved. 'Childish' games, for example, may allow more mature expectations and perspectives to emerge, as conflicts producing the ego qualities of hope, self-control and direction are reworked. When they have served their remedial purpose, these games will be replaced by more pressing interests. Dependencies often linger, and we may alternate between fond, affectionate feelings for our parents and siblings, and dismay at the thought of 'moving out' from them, and furiously critical impatience with them, when 'getting away' cannot come too soon. The greater our residual dependencies, the more likely we are to disrupt and rebel in order to achieve separation.

Comfort and protectiveness are likewise hard to break away from, and caring parents may need to be perceived as unreasonable, restrictive and out-of-touch by the adolescent struggling for the courage to become independent. Relinquishment of home comforts and parental provision is most easily achieved in young adulthood, when positive, if more demanding, motivations supersede, such as training courses, flat sharing, or work abroad or in a different part of the country.

Obnoxious behaviour may externalize inner turmoil, ensure separation, or be a cry for attention and reassurance. Paradoxically, it may be motivated by all three, or be part of a health imbalance or drug problem, and outside help is often of great benefit, especially in providing the support needed by both parents and adolescent during a stressful separating out period. Fortunately, although disruptions are common, many adolescents and their families can enjoy this time of exciting development, and adult friendship begins to bless the departure of childhood.

In contrast, homes may partially or entirely fail to provide caring support at this crucial time. Immature parents and step-parents, changing partnerships, illness, inability to cope with the pressures of unemployment, job demands, loneliness, overcrowding or neighbourhood problems may make impossible an adolescent's natural unfolding and moratorium, often repeating the inadequate parent or parents' own distressing experience. Without a 'good-enough' internalized pattern to follow, parents are bound to be at a loss unless this has been remedied, even where they still feel parental concern. The situation is often complicated by residues from earlier traumas and lack of 'good-enough' care in Infancy, Early Childhood, the Play Age and Schooldays.

'Good-enough' care does not all come from parents, and sometimes a youngster, even with these compounded hindrances, is able to 'make good' by building on good or adequate experience with others, and by finding support from adequate peers and others. Otherwise he or she must survive as best possible, when parents, home and society have all shown clearly that he or she is an unwanted burden of little or no worth. Despair, resentment, 'grab what you can get, by force if necessary', and ignorance of anything better are surely to be expected. Michael Rutter's work on privation and deprivation has given us the awareness we need to prevent and drastically reduce these tragedies, but we still await democratic will for action, by whatever political principle we choose.

Social institution: ideological worldview

The social element associated with this stage, Erikson said, is an 'ideological worldview', arrived at as an ideal by the adolescent, and manifest worldwide, expressed in behaviour between people and in our use of our environment. We still await sufficient general motivation and specific co-operation to apply more widely the knowledge and skills that we already have, in the promotion of independent, sustainable living, and the rescue and rehabilitation of the human and environmental casualties of our carelessness. An example of an adolescent 'ideological worldview' matured into expression and linked with the real ideology in the world is a poster advocating that we 'Stop Wasting People!'

In whatever culture or conditions, especially in complex societies, each generation of adolescents is motivated to take part in whatever is the 'in' experience, be it sex, drugs (including tobacco and alcohol), sport, warfare, vandalism, tribal ritual, mechanical skill, meditation or music making. These activities variously incorporate needs for rebellion, reaction to frustration, pleasure, self-exploration and testing, but above all, of belonging to the new generation. 'Keeping up with the Jones's' is an adolescent remnant that sometimes remains in adulthood, but as more mature adults, we also tend towards common peer interests.

Aesthetic and spiritual values emerge, unless these have been drowned in an environment of ugliness, substitutes and materialism. Ideals are recognized, inspired or formulated, and religious, intellectual, political or artistic ideologies all provide structures whereby, as adolescents, we may identify our own particular value priorities, and therefore our own psychosocial identity and ideological worldview.

Erikson said that we may also experience, if fleetingly, a kind of core 'existential identity' that can mature and gradually transcend the psychosocial 'ego identity', especially in old age. He thus distinguishes between 'self' and 'ego'. During adolescence, and often persisting, there is a gap to be bridged between core ideals (from 'self') and our personal ways of putting them into practice (ego function). Sometimes these ideals will be projected into 'gurus' or 'idols', who will then be followed, often fanatically, according to the 'pull' of the gap in the immature sense of ego identity and core purpose. Symbol and ritual may be similarly helpful as a bridge or stepping stone towards the realization of a more integrated identity.

Fidelity

Formal Operational thinking is an obvious advantage in the moratorium process, but there are many personal ideals and other aspects of identity that can be at least partially expressed in simple, concrete concepts and applied in our living. We do not have to understand in detail everything we perceive to have value for us and practise 'because it works', though understanding is obviously useful when adapting to change. Whatever the cognitive capacity or culture of an individual, Erikson said that a 'favourable ratio' between a sense of identity and acceptance of the range of possible roles produces the ego strength of 'fidelity'. Thus we can make choices that enable us to be 'true to ourselves' and our identified, 'felt' values, be these pro- or anti-social.

Role acceptance or repudiation

New personal goals and likely roles arise according to our awareness of possibility and our confidence in our ability to carry them out. We draw heavily on our sense of competence here, and if this is deficient, will be seriously at a loss. We may cover up with defensiveness or aberrant alternative, or react with helplessness or resentment, or we may take advantage of a well-presented 'second chance' such as a college of further education or other suitable opportunity to recover our missing skills.

The pathology that Erikson identifies is 'role repudiation', when it extends beyond the rejection of roles that conflict with our values and desired self-image. It may emerge as diffidence or defiance, and complete 'drop-out' may occur from persistent feelings of inferiority, or from real or perceived absence of acceptable roles.

Our adolescent dreams of our future mingle with emerging ideals and ethics, and are of *whatever kind our experience has spelt out to us as desirable*. Our views of personal happiness and social ethos will differ enormously according to our cultural and environmental background and our childhood experiences, so that we may variously perceive the desirability of living, both personally and socially, by inspired idealism made practical, by the exercise of skills and integrity, by tribal custom, by artistic presentation, by unrealistic romantic projection, by wits, deceit and ruthlessness, or by stealth, force or violence.

During adolescence, our peers become and remain our most influential arbiters, and we will seek out those who best represent our own perceptions, aims and fears. Belonging to, and being approved by, our peer group, eases our final steps towards adult independence and commitments, and we will continue to incline towards those who are 'like us' and to value their opinion above that of others.

Whether our society permits, especially with higher education, a lengthy moratorium period and choice of roles, or precipitates us, at puberty or soon after, into adult responsibilities, perhaps marriage, with little or no choice of role, the pre-adult stage is usually a time for emotional preparation.

The consideration of adult values and the learning of adult skills is aided by mentors, adopted by individuals or appointed by society, and any society which leaves to chance this critical opportunity to synchronize biological needs and urges and psychosocial needs, emotions and evaluations with the social role-opportunities it offers its emerging young adults, is likely to have many disrupted, and therefore disruptively inadequate, members of its adult population. This disaster can be seen both in the sickness and crime rates of modern civilizations, and in undeveloped societies brought into contact with technologically advanced people and hitherto unknown industrial and economic possibilities and ethical issues. Societies may err in the opposite direction, religiously or ideologically, by over-prescribing rules and roles so that an imposed 'foreclosure' restricts many of its members.

Coping with change

The successful accomplishment of these adolescent tasks lays down a useful pattern for coping with changes throughout adulthood. Partnership, parenthood, job changes, moves, emigration, retirement, bereavement or other precipitating events, all require the review of at least some aspects of our identity and the possibilities and requirements of any new role or circumstances. It follows that one of the common residues of this stage is difficulty in coping with change. Alternatively, we may deal with change in a way that limits its potential outcome.

Remedially, we may need to learn how to review even long-held priorities of value and practice, and to discover how to behave in new roles and situations. We may also need to clarify, and to avoid as unsuitable for us, roles, or ways of filling them, that mismatch our actual and *updated* identity. We can then move forward, less hampered by residual or immature habits of thinking and behaving, to renew our valued relationships and enjoy our commitments to the people and issues we care about.

Apart from shaping our entry into adulthood, adolescence is a valuable pre-run for later changes and choices, and we can beneficially allow ourselves an adequate moratorium for whatever changes our lives bring. Invaluably, we can apply the same openness to the changes that are taking place in those close to us, discussing and accommodating *before* differences become rifts.

Adolescence merges with what Erikson describes as 'Young Adulthood', and this continued process of self-discovery and progress towards maturity is examined in the next chapter. It is useful to compare Erikson's stage theory with the Humanistic approach of Carl Rogers and of Abraham Maslow (first published 1954), who describes a hierarchy of motivation based on need priorities, progressing, where circumstances allow, to self-realization. Rogers' theory, and Maslow's, will be described more fully in a later chapter (see chapter 13).

Missing from this discussion of our schooldays, which include adolescence, is the vital element of teaching methods most suited to different ages and subject matter. Piagetian theory underlies discovery learning, including guided experience, and Behaviourist theory has produced widely used programmed learning, which is based on reinforcement, but specialist educational texts provide a wealth of detail which is not, for reasons of continuity and space, included here. This text is intended rather to provide a background understanding of psychosocial development during schooldays, with emphasis on how we acquire our 'felt knowledge', and how our feelings emerge and mature. It should complement a variety of other literature on language acquisition, cognitive skills, social development, presentation of learning material, and the general management skills needed by parents and teachers.

YOUNG ADULTHOOD AND ADULTHOOD

YOUNG ADULTHOOD: INTIMACY V. ISOLATION

With the achievement of a sense of adult identity, adult life begins. Erikson was the first psychologist to suggest three stages of adulthood, and the earliest of these is stage six of his life cycle theory, when the ego's main developmental task is to achieve a favourable ratio between 'intimacy' and 'isolation'. Its emergence corresponds with the end of Freud's psychosexual stages, in his concept of achieved genitality, the capacity 'to love and to work'. The commitment to adult responsibilities involved may be precipitated early, around fifteen or so, the adolescent 'testing-out' period curtailed by custom or circumstances, or it may be delayed into the early twenties by extended educational opportunity, at least so far as choice of livelihood is concerned.

Commitment

Based on 'fidelity' to our identified values and self-image is the emerging adult capacity for practical 'commitment' to the affiliations and partnerships that best represent our adolescent ideological aspirations. Thus we will commit ourselves to, or continue a search for, a lasting sexual partnership, and to training, work experience or entrepreneurial projects in accordance with our chosen priorities and available opportunities.

The level of satisfaction we find in our work is a fair measure of correspondence to our achieved identity and values. Thus we may enjoy achieving order and efficiency in administration, perceiving benefit to our clients in caring, education and service occupations, nurturing growth in plants or animals, or using our physical strength and mechanical skills to produce tangible and concrete satisfactions in building, manufacturing and maintenance industries.

Alternatively, we may have identified with values of personal power, money, and material comfort and status, in which case we might commit ourselves to achieving a position of power, or the highest bank balance we can in the shortest possible time, by whatever means we find available and acceptable to us.

Our personal relationships undergo the stresses of adjustment to the changing patterns of our need of privacy and personal space. We may need solitude for temporary purposes or longer-term needs, for study, skill-improvement, uninterrupted thinking or spiritual development. At other times, we may have temporary or longer-term needs for specific kinds of companionship, or for company with others generally.

Alongside the patterns we develop from the necessities and contingencies of life, are our personal inclinations for time alone, time alone with our partner, and time, with or without our partner, spent with other people. It is the pattern of these personal inclinations that can make or mar a close relationship and affect our capacity for working alone or with others, and our corresponding working stress levels.

Love and exclusion

Central to ego development at this stage is our striving for a more mature tolerance and flexibility, and a capacity to accompany or allow space to another, while mindful of the needs of our own spirit and creative potential. Young adulthood is a testing time, when our basic temperamental pattern and residual insecurities shape our preferences. We work towards independent strength, flexibility and time-management skills to cope with valued relationships and activities, and with work demands. We develop the ethical strength necessary for sacrifices and compromises involved in our various commitments, and, out of our own experience, sensitivity to the needs and preferences of others.

Erikson said that, although some 'exclusion' is necessary in selection, commitment and feasibility of our love and work, too much exclusiveness is pathological, as it involves denial of parts of our own creative potential. In order to be able to 'fuse' our identity productively in affiliations with others, we first need to have our self-image firmly established. 'I' can only become a comfortable 'we' when we perceive that our values and purposes are being shared, so that we must first be aware of them, and choose our affiliations accordingly. Our 'style' develops, and 'social solidarities of style' emerge. If pathologically excessive, styles and solidarities can become unproductively 'elitist', operating towards exclusion, and losing touch with the functional values around which our original choices gave rise to them.

Emotional residues from earlier stages may have shaped a self-image characterized by withdrawal, compulsion, inhibition or inferiority, and these can lead to isolation and a shrinking from intimacy. Our initial sense of separateness and worthwhileness, and a capacity to relate co-operatively may have to be reworked before progress towards a favourable ratio of intimacy and isolation can begin.

Fear of loss of identity, or of being swamped in the identity of others, may also result in too much isolation, and adolescent strivings to discover our own firmly held values, and to establish the roles that we can best fulfil in relation to others, may have to be prolonged before we can overcome our sense of isolation. A weak or threatened sense of identity may alternatively lead to dependency on finding it in others, so that we can constantly seek a suffocating kind of intimacy and feel depleted when alone.

Intimacy between people with a healthy sense of identity to express, on the other hand, has an enriching and developmental effect, enabling creative co-operation. Sexual intimacy has its best potential between two people who have the capacity for the mutual regulation not only of orgasm, but of procreation, productive work and recreation as well. Erikson said that orgasm 'takes the edges off' the differences and antagonisms inherently arising in other aspects of the relationship, and thus has a binding and consummating effect. He emphasized that this comprehensive kind of relationship between parents is the soundest basis for ensuring the successful nurturance of the childhood stages of the next generation and for maximizing their own satisfactions.

Social institution: patterns of co-operation and competition

The social element that Erikson associated with this stage lies in the cultural patterns of co-operation and competition and of selection processes, marriage and work organization that can help or hinder the achievement of this full 'genitality'. Among the most harmfully far-reaching residues, resulting from inadequate social norms and unachieved individual maturity, are premature parenthood and a lack of opportunity, aptitude or motivation in the consolidation of productive earning skills that are socially valued (and therefore relatively secure). Triple bookkeeping of biological, psychological and social elements is patently essential if young adulthood is to lead successfully, without overload, stunting or distortion, into the 'love and work' of full adulthood.

Erikson is not the only theorist to point out links between the collective values and stage of maturity of a given society, and the kind of ego qualities and sense of personal identity that its members will develop. Freud and Jung were very aware of the social attitudes that led to the pathologies of so many of their patients, especially perceptions of authority and of the role of women. Maslow perceived that society itself has the same hierarchy of needs as an individual, and can only develop towards self-realization accordingly. The founder of modern sociology, Auguste Comte, described the important function of different social institutions, as they arose from collective social values, and social psychologists describe for us the pervasive effects of social influence and group pressures.

Erikson holds out hope of a society's growth towards maturity, in the capacity of some individuals in each generation of adults, to re-inspire social values, organization and institutions. Young adulthood is a time when choices are made and when directions are established, for good or ill. These patterns will be at their most energetically potent during this and the next stage, and may bring advance in quality of life and social attitudes, or may perpetuate degenerate trends affecting the next generation's growth. Examples of these changes are found, beneficially, in at least a proportion of our population, in better-informed parenting and the growth of our environmental caring, and detrimentally, in our rising crime rates and trends, unemployment and increasing poverty and destitution. In all these, individual values and 'social solidarities of style' are easily identified.

ADULTHOOD: GENERATIVITY V. STAGNATION

Somewhere around the mid or later twenties, styles, directions and often partnerships established, we progress into what Erikson describes as 'Adulthood'. Our effectiveness and responsibilities increase, often including marriage and parenthood. Our capacity to balance our inclinations for intimacy and isolation will have shaped our loving relationships, and will now be even more tested and developed as our family demands increase, and working progress extends our influence, or conditions curtail our scope. We become the 'cutting edge' of all that we aspired to and committed and trained ourselves for as we emerged from childhood. We will now look at how the 'love' of young adulthood becomes the 'care' of adulthood.

'Generativity' encompasses, according to Erikson's description of his seventh stage, 'procreativity, productivity and creativity, and thus the generation of new beings as well as of new products and new ideas, including a kind of self-generation concerned with further identity development' (1982).

Where 'generativity' becomes inactivated, a sense of 'stagnation' either provides respite for renewal of inspiration and energy, or may overwhelm those whose generative outlets are frustrated or non-functional. From the balancing of these two opposite 'sensings', we develop our ego strength of loving perseverance in the 'taking care' of what we 'cared about' and committed ourselves to, in the previous stage.

Taking care and careless rejection

Whether or not we have our own children as part of our generativity, we form what Erikson called the 'generational link', passing on to the next generation our fruits, our failures and our example. As we strive to fulfil this Atlas-like responsibility, he points out that we need every one of the strengths arising from our development in earlier stages: hope and will, purpose and skill, fidelity and love. Our libidinous investment and satisfaction, in addition to procreation, now embraces our joining relationships, and whatever we are joined in taking care of.

Our newly developing ego strength, the capacity to take care, extends its practical application as it grows, and includes not only nurturance and provision where needed, but effort towards the development of others into their own care-taking adulthood. We also become the prototypes for the next generation, the mums and dads, train drivers, teachers, tradespeople or doctors that children play at being and adolescents take as role models. The pathology of this stage is likewise doubly potent. 'Rejectivity', as Erikson identifies it, not only limits our own generative potential, but powerfully contributes to the careless norms of our own society, and in turn, to careless world ideologies and practical policies, through its shaping effect on new generations.

Erikson acknowledges that there are practical limitations to what any adult or group of adults might attempt without detriment to well-being and to existing active care, and as in earlier stages, choices and selection among priorities have to be made. Pathology creeps in when our *perception becomes bent* in the service of justifying our refusal to take care, and our attitudes harden into rejection, even aggression.

Thus we are over-ready to blame others for their own misfortunes and poor upbringing, to decide that they do not deserve our care or help, to condemn their differences from ourselves, and to ignore their human potential for development and independent, generative living. Erikson's own childhood and early adult experience made him a very informed commentator on this particular pathology, as a Jew of Danish appearance during the rise of German Nazism.

Social institution: education and tradition

The social element that Erikson identified with this stage is composed of the current trends in education and tradition, and he said that 'ethics, law and insight must define the bearable measure of rejectivity in any given group, even as religious and ideological belief systems must continue to advocate a more universal principle of care in specified wider units of communities' (1982). He thus defines the relationship between individual and smaller group norms of caring practice, and larger unit responsibility for maintaining the ethical principle and practice of 'universal caritas'. Without the firm establishment of this principle, there is nothing to counter the rejectivity that can lead to warfare and cruelty at individual, family, community and national levels.

Erikson's theory provides a description of how feelings of rejectivity need to be superseded by wise recognition of the limitation of time, energy and material resources, and still wiser recognition of the longer-term effects of our choices. It is a significant contribution to our understanding of the causes of all levels of conflict. The triple bookkeeping of this psychosocial approach shows that current trends in education and tradition can only be as ethical as the people who instigate them and carry them through, and our individual accounting at this adult stage is the most vital of all, in its effects on ourselves and on others, including future generations, for now *we are* the 'cutting edge'.

Personal and circumstantial limitations

As individuals, therefore, our grappling with the easily overwhelming demands of our many commitments and would-be commitments requires a realistic acknowledgement of personal and circumstantial limitations, together with a generative concern for our own grappling capacity. This is the crucial area of ego development in adulthood, with its repercussions on the advancement of mankind. Only from this personal point of experience can we address the personal and circumstantial limitations of others, and exercise a generative concern for their grappling capacity and development.

Crucial at this time of our lives is our ability to co-operate, and to facilitate the contribution of others, within what Erikson (1982) describes as our 'division of labour' and 'shared household' structures. This ability, along with our attitudes towards competition, depends on both our childhood experience and on the social ordering of Young Adulthood. Erikson's writing reflects his strong Jewish sense of family, shared by a high proportion of our world population, but his concepts apply equally to those of us who, willingly or not, live alone or within a different kind of group. Whereas in Young Adulthood we worked out personal boundaries and the ratio of privacy and being together that best facilitate comfort and potential for us and for those close to us, we now address ourselves to the practical tasks involved in our work and in the maintenance of our domestic arrangements.

We learn to accommodate the differences in the performance of tasks by others, from the way we prefer to perform them ourselves, discovering strengths and inadequacies, in ourselves and others, that make division of labour such an advantage in human living. We allow for the poorer performances of learners, in the interests of increasing the pool of skills available, and, hopefully, we learn the delicate art of facilitating the smooth running of our co-operative units, 'oiling the wheels' with sensitivity and good communication.

Competitiveness is present in the aspirations and needs of individuals, and sometimes in organizational structure. One chance of promotion, or one bathroom, for six people will equally need ingenious and careful management, with a focus on alternative scope for individual potential, or on timing and supplementary washing arrangements. Otherwise aggressive attitudes and the erosion of co-operative energies will be the result. We learn to cultivate a sense of corporate interest, and to realize how dependent this is on taking thought for the responsible well-being of each individual, overlooked at some cost to the whole group.

Competition based on aspirations and needs is also present between various groups of people, and where this leads to improved performance and use of potential and resources, all groups may benefit from advances made. But unless this ingenuity is matched with careful consideration and some co-ordination, the potentially productive co-operativeness or creative diversification of other groups will be damaged or lost, and acrimony will erode the health and ethics of many individuals throughout affected populations, inevitably affecting the whole.

We can best empower our human generativity by understanding the long-term effects of responsible co-operativeness and of the aggression that is aroused by uncaring competitiveness. By learning the necessary management and administrative skills, and by making properly balanced choices, at individual as well as at corporate levels, we can maximize the potential of co-operative attitudes and well-harnessed competitiveness. We learn these skills, and the destructive, sometimes delayed, effects of their absence, at a very personal level indeed and *we are* the most potent part of our prevailing social institutions, affecting the shape of what is to come.

Adult stress

Adult stresses may arise from 'too much' concern, arising from family anxieties, work intensity or poor health, or from 'too little' satisfying involvement caused by loss, displacement, unemployment, lack of family or friendly support, involuntary childlessness or residual emotional problems. Ways of handling stress as it arises, and especially of recognizing when a 'general adaptation syndrome' (Selye, 1956, 1979) is eating away at our resilience, are vital personal resources (see chapters 2 and 9). As discussed earlier, in the context of parenthood (see chapter 4), a 'vital faith' can bring a restorative confidence in all areas of our adult living, and provide a basic philosophy that inspires and supports our adult generativity and our later years.

It is during Adulthood that the older generation may begin to need more help, and this can be an added burden, however willingly it is undertaken. The balancing task of the ego may indeed be formidable, and we are fortunate if our parents and other role models have provided us with useful examples of how to cope and extend our capacity, or even how to survive, in the torrents and deserts of life. Each generation must also pioneer ways of handling its own newly arising contingencies.

Erikson claimed that social 'ritualization', that is 'the way we do things', has 'adaptive value for all participants, and for their group living', and that it guides our 'instinctual investment in the social process'. He compared this human social adaptation with the 'instinctive fit into a section of nature' of an animal species. This pattern of social norms and expectations can certainly act as a guide, but each new generation of human adults can also act upon the norms to bring adaptive changes.

Stress management skills

Necessary skills for adult function therefore include these essentials: ways of determining our priorities, time management and negotiation, communications and relationship development, and methods of stress management. Self-awareness is vital if wise choices are to be made, though methods of acquiring it do not always assist with adjustments in existing close relationships. Unless we give attention to self-maintenance and to our close relationships, we shall be of little value to others, and we may find that strategies we have used before are now inadequate. Detailed guides to assist in our various 'deficiency areas' are available through libraries, bookshops, other media, or counselling services, but a few general pointers are outlined here.

Anniversaries, birthdays – especially those marking a decade or half of one – and new-year transitions are all likely to evoke review, and if we are consciously seeking self-awareness and development, we need more frequent monitoring of our progress than this may provide. Whether we are motivated by a sense of problem or deficiency, or from a desire for growth and development, the process is much the same. Priorities need examining, and may require temporary or longer-term adjustment. Basic values may also need to become deeper in order to accommodate recent insights, and long-held assumptions questioned.

For example, young parenthood or early career pressures may impose their own priorities which will need to be reviewed as time passes. Family relationships and customs may need adjustment, and dominant figures, whether parent, boss, religious leader, teacher or other respected person, may need to be assigned a less influential role in our lives. The identification of residual gaps, distortions and dependencies will be invaluable in indicating beneficial growth to aim for, and Erikson's, Berne's or Rogers' guidelines describe how this may be achieved. Thus we might cultivate a sense of self-worth (the basic principle of assertiveness courses), a capacity for perceiving choice or a change in our feelings about responsibility.

To discuss priorities and basic values, aspects of the growth process, and to listen to and exchange confidences, advice, skills and strategies, someone else who shares our central values and aims can add an almost indispensable dimension to our understanding and capacity for generativity. Unless we are under time pressures, this peer discussion occurs naturally, but many such opportunities have been squeezed out of modern schedules. In some situations, as in times past, ignorance and values arising from overriding priorities, such as poverty, war or authoritarian stricture, may negate or distort this natural opportunity for exchange of personal insights in a context of mutual support and encouragement.

We may therefore need to seek out a trusted friend or group, or a professional person, and to set aside regular time for nurturing our own growth. Journal-keeping may aid clarification for personal or discussion purposes, and even when entries are brief, provided they record relevant feelings, behaviour and comments, can be valuable in aiding insight, and monitoring progress.

Later chapters will draw other useful ideas from the theories of Rogers,

Maslow, Argyle and others, all of whom have addressed different aspects of personal development. Whether we live in harsh economic conditions, which impose their own kinds of stress, or in affluence, where 'rat-race' pressures and our own appetites for goods, pleasure and status embroil us, we are all subject, in varying degrees, to what psychologists call 'stressors'. Stress-management skills are therefore vital in maintaining resilience, and in mitigating individually distressing events, and the sometimes inevitable, concurrent over-loading that arises in our different areas of commitment.

The balancing function of our ego is often stretched to full capacity, sometimes beyond, in which situation healthy temporary defences, or pathological adaptations (less often breakdown) may occur. Stress management can therefore protect the health of our nervous system (see chapter 2) and reduce the pressures on our ego so that it can function more effectively. Recreational patterns need to be monitored for their 're-creational' effects, and physical health reviewed before symptoms become troublesome. If they are not already in place, communicating and negotiating skills may need attention, and improvement in the tone, adequacy and sensitivity of these, in family, neighbourhood and working relationships, can considerably reduce stress for all concerned (see chapter 12).

Balancing competing needs

Perhaps the most difficult ego-balancing task of adulthood is the conflict we must resolve between the competing needs of those to whose care we are committed. At work, giving more time, resources and attention to some people or aspects of our responsibilities means that less is available for others. The same is true in our family life, and the nurturing needs of the young can often clash distressingly with declining health in the elderly or a partner, or with special opportunities in our work. Many adults solve this

Figure 8.1 *Balancing family needs. Young and old both need care and support, but what of the carer's own needs and aspirations?*

difficult equation by postponing their own satisfactions in some or several areas of living, but where there is no end in sight, this is a hazardous solution. A sense of stagnation may cause some to give up in despair, or to rule out from consideration their own needs and wishes, often with disastrous consequences.

Before deciding on the allocation of time and resources, the needs and aspirations of each person involved can be listed and thus validated. The solution will not be helped by denial of their existence. Where can the burden of compromise best be borne? What alternative provision can become available? What generative growth might each person contribute to the solution? Realistic answers are essential, and sensitive, meaningful communication even more so. Gradually, generative answers will emerge, and where an unsatisfactory emergency solution is already in place, a better one can be substituted. Inevitable feelings of disappointment are best acknowledged with appropriate sympathy, and mutual support given for necessary adjustments.

It is the rejectivity in unfeeling demands and unsatisfactorily explained denials that cause the deepest hurt, the most aggression and the least co-operation. Compassion and realism will achieve much more than 'oughts', 'rights' and competitive power wielding.

Examples of these dilemmas arise in work situations, marriage relationships, health or disablement problems of our own, or those arising in our family, care of the young and the elderly, community or neighbourhood relations. Or it can even be all of these, for one set of problems often has a domino effect, setting others in motion. Each of us can only start to seek solutions *from where we are* (state of maturity and available or possible resources), building on strengths which may lie buried. We need to be realistic about our own capacity for growth, and that of others involved, *from where they are*.

Our ego works with what information it has, and this can often be usefully supplemented by extra information from others, including those involved, especially when the important consideration of consequences and available alternatives is undertaken. 'Why didn't I think of that?' or 'If only I had realized!' is a frequent outcome of insufficient ego balancing, which is the crucial focus for formal or informal counselling.

It may turn out more potentially generative to stick with a situation and work towards adjustment and re-allocation of priorities. It may be possible to gain co-operation and achieve crucial changes, or it may be that, even if rejectivity is overcome, the possibility of change is too remote to contemplate. Emotionally, and often physically, we may need to withdraw from an intractably destructive situation, adjust our attitudes and contact with it, and relocate and reinvest our generative capacities.

Coping with loss, rejection or failure

Unemployment, all forms of redundancy and the void caused by rejection or disablement are also injurious, depriving our ego of its generative prospect. The no man's land of grief for loss, even loss of hope of ever getting started, is bleak and painful, and small shoots of generativity that might naturally arise are easily bruised or bulldozed by further failure or rejection.

As in bereavement, basic ego strengths of hope and will are needed to precede renewed purpose and skill before fidelity and love can blossom, or blossom again, in generativity. Where these early strengths are insufficiently developed, at least the void can become a space for their cultivation. Just as young children benefit from a familiar structure within which to grow, disrupted patterns can be replaced by new routines, adjusted as recovery proceeds. Small, everyday enjoyments will bring comfort and aid the return of a sense of well-being. 'Gently forward' is a phrase we can use to encourage ourselves with, in times of pressure or distress.

Basic self-worth can be in danger in experiences of failure or rejection, and may need nursing back to health. It is important to seek 'enough' affirmative company, especially where loss is permanent, for instance after a death, or a permanently disabling accident, or where self-esteem has been low even before recent injury. Erikson's developmental guidelines spell out the order of recovery, and make much easier our adult tasks of rehabilitation, change and readjustment.

Ego development and 'self'

Our ego develops and matures naturally by means of the constant decision-making of adulthood, and also by the re-working we may undertake in areas of residual inadequacy. Increasingly during these years, we are likely to become aware of our core 'existential identity', if we have not already so progressed, embodying our ideal principles and faith. Our ego is the 'executive' through which these are put into practice, as far as possible, in our psychosocial living.

As we move into our later thirties and forties, we may experience this central 'self' as a sense of 'something missing', especially if we have been unable to fulfil at least some of our core values (see chapter 9). Deficiencies, and especially distortions, in ego development may have caused more superficial values to hijack generative energies into materialistic and hedonistic channels with little regard for the quality and depth of our relationships. We may therefore lack the capacity for 'listening into' the dimension of living, in which 'self'-discovery is likely to occur. Alternatively, we may have searched too hard in what are, for us, sterile places.

Mid-life adjustments

Whatever the level of our generative achievement, it is our unfulfilled aspirations, beginning to emerge in feelings of 'time running out', that may precipitate a 'mid-life crisis' or major changes in direction. To the extent that our ego is sufficiently mature and principled to balance out factors involved realistically and generatively, greater fulfilment is likely to follow such changes. To the extent that our ego is still governed by the values of residual dependencies and distortions, our changes, or clinging resistance to change, both of them powered by the wilfulness of immature emotions, are most likely to bring stagnation, deterioration or disaster.

As in Young Adulthood, residues from this stage may include the consequences of immature decisions, the trauma of tragic events or the stunting effect of stagnation, however caused. Rejectivity or inertia may have become established characteristics, or we may have so channelled our generative energies that we are left with little other developed potential when our 'mainstream' runs out, or no longer needs us. Over-identification, in parenting, partnerships or working role, is manifested in possessiveness and in the crippling of our capacity for adjustment to loss.

These are painful residues indeed, and their resolution lies in the discovery of possible remaining genuine outlets, and in often difficult adjustments, for in old age, when adult residues are felt, adaptation requires much more effort. Professional occupational therapy has skills that can help this process, but is in short supply for the elderly. The training of carers often includes ways of expressing the warmth and wisdom indispensable for progress, and understanding friends can encourage and support appropriately. However, only our own efforts can produce actual growth in ego capacity. It is well to remember that generativity can take many, many different forms, detectable by its fruits, and can therefore be achieved in small ways and continue indefinitely. (For further discussion of ego development in Old Age and of bereavement see chapter 10.)

Forty may seem a very young age for Erikson to identify as the approximate beginning of his eighth and last stage, and he explains this as the time when a search for the next developmental ego quality can begin to assume some dominance and to precipitate the 'crisis' of such a shift in priorities. Menopausal symptoms and the approaching end of the child-bearing years have increased a sense of crisis for some women, but where changes are gradual or well accommodated, many people would not describe their mid-life experience as a crisis. Others would describe a series of crises rather than one major occurrence.

Adulthood has hopefully brought us a favourable ratio of active generativity and patient use of stagnation, and may well extend a high level of care-taking for some, well past the time when others are adjusting to declining capacities and loss of roles. Nevertheless, at some time in our forties, we may begin to relinquish some of our earlier ambitions, and to realize that time and opportunity are getting shorter. Parenthood changes as a family grows, and the birth of grandchildren and the death of older relatives mark a generational shift. Greater responsibility and more senior and powerful positions may become ours, and we may realize that we are at our peak in our working ability, or past it if our skill is dependent on physical strength, speed and stamina.

Erikson observed that we begin a search for 'wisdom', a 'getting it all together', to make sense of our lives and to look ahead more soberly at our remaining active years and the realities of ageing now on the horizon. This mid-life 'crisis' marks a change in our approach to life, and sometimes a new urgency for some aspect of generative achievement. During these and earlier, especially eventful years, we can find it useful to give particular thought to our own functioning and development. Other psychological theories that may help us deepen our understanding and make wiser decisions will be included in later chapters, and in the next chapter we shall look at some of the ideas of another psychoanalytic theorist, Carl Jung, who placed considerable emphasis on mid-life changes.

MID-LIFE CRISIS: JUNG'S ANALYTICAL PSYCHOLOGY

9

Mid-life brings significant changes to many of us, some of them arising from work achievement or failure, from fortuitous or unfortunate events, or from the blossoming or falling-apart of our different relationships, marriage, friendships or social involvements. But the most crucial changes are internal, and indeed are often the cause of other changes, especially relational ones. Jung describes these changes as a turning from our ego's prime concern during the first half of adult life for the establishment of a necessary economic and social, probably family framework, to focus our attention on the expression of the core values of the 'self' through a process he calls 'Individuation'.

Jung's theory, like others, arose out of his own experience and training, and a brief biographical outline will help us understand how his way of thinking developed. At first very interested in Freud's theory, he came to disagree with it, mainly regarding the nature of libido, which he perceived as generally creative (as Erikson's concept of generativity), not only sexually. He believed that we are primarily spiritual as well as biological beings, and also that morality is a core personal value, the superego representing only the conventional and social part of our conscience.

He is regarded as the initiator (1917) in Europe of what has become known as the Transpersonal approach in psychology, and many of his concepts, with those of his contemporary Roberto Assagioli (psychosynthesis), form the basis of transpersonal therapies, which all recognize the importance of our spiritual needs and resources, and our central 'higher self' (see chapter 13). Modern analytical psychologists have modified some of Jung's ideas, but his concept of individuation (described later in this chapter) remains as a valued guide to practice.

CARL GUSTAV JUNG (1875–1961)

Jung was the son of a Calvinist country pastor of the Swiss Reformed Church, and an only child until he was nine years old, when his sister was born. His father was a classical and oriental scholar, which meant that young Carl had access to books and learned discussion on these subjects during his formative years. He also had no less than eight uncles who were pastors, and was able to supplement his income by lecturing in theology, when he was impoverished by his father's death while still a medical student at Basle University.

When he was three, his mother was hospitalized for a period, during which time he developed eczema. Later he attributed her illness to marriage problems, including the repression of what he perceived as her 'other personality'. She had creative writing gifts which she had conventionally set aside, as the wife of a busy pastor, and Jung's theory reflects his early sensitization to the importance of individual creative expression.

Born at Keswil, his earliest memories were of Laufen, where the family moved when he was four, and include vivid dreams and childhood games. He was a very intelligent boy, popular locally, but also needing time to follow his own pursuits, and two years after the family moved to Klein-Huningen, near Basle, he entered the Basle Gymnasium (High School). While there, he wrestled with considerable religious doubts, and when waiting for a friend in the cathedral square, had a vision of God causing the roof of Basle Cathedral to disintegrate, and felt a vocation to resolve the apparent conflict between his own experience and various discordant traditional religious views.

He believed that it was his father's own unadmitted religious doubts that hastened the latter's death a few years later, while Jung was still a medical student, and a substantial area of his later research and his self-exploration led him to develop concepts of our 'collective unconscious' and of 'archetypes'. This part of his theory encompasses all the different ways in which mankind expresses spirituality, and the religious symbols and formulations that have arisen in different times and places to accommodate the spiritual and psychological aspects of our existence. The theory has become a major contribution to our understanding of an underlying unity in which spirituality, psychology, theology and religion can all be discussed.

Jung's decision to make his career in psychiatry was made only during his final examinations in medicine, and on qualifying, he obtained a post at the Bergholzi Mental Hospital under Eugen Bleuler. In addition to his work there, during the next six years he married, was appointed as a lecturer in psychiatry at Zurich University, became interested in Freud's theories, and in 1906, published a psychoanalytic approach to schizophrenia. As a result of this, he was invited to meet Freud, and there followed several years' close collaboration, which included lecture tours in the USA. In 1913, their increasingly strained relationship ended in disagreement, and Jung began to develop his own major theory of 'Analytical Psychology'. His earlier work had included a study of personality distinctions, in particular between *introvert* and *extrovert* tendencies (Jung, 1964), but during the next few years, while World War I raged in Europe, Jung made his own lone journey into the unconscious, undergoing a series of personal crises as he made sense of his own dreams and visionary experience, developing the 'art' of analysis. His wife, Emma, and their five children helped him to keep his feet on the ground during this demanding time.

He developed a method of working with patients using their paintings as well as dreams, helping them to release their own kind of creative potential (generativity as well as craft or art) into their lives, at the same time increasing his own insights. His principles of nurturing individuation were passed on to others whom he trained as analysts, including his wife.

The collective unconscious and the archetypes

Jung also spent painstaking years travelling and making investigations into religious experience, symbols and myths, consulting anthropologists of particular experience to supplement his own. He developed his conviction that we not only have consciousness and a personal unconscious, but that we are also, at a deeper level, part of a 'collective unconscious' which he perceived as a field of spiritual energy containing 'archetypes'.

These are inherited mental 'shapes', incorporating potentials for disharmony and destructiveness as well as for compassion and creativity. They are universally encountered in dreams, art, myths and religions, striving towards expression in individuals. (Examples are a hero figure, a villain, a wise old man or woman or, at a deeper level, a candle, a bowl, a still pool or flowing water.) It is the *qualities* of these archetypal shapes that may be lived out as qualities in individuals. Hence their potency as role models or symbols (see chapter 13).

Figure 9.1 *A symbol of wholeness. This Hindu and Buddhist Mandala represents cosmic completeness in perfect balance and also our own* potential *for balanced wholeness; Jung described it as an archetype, an expression of our 'self' as well as of cosmic harmonies*

The 'self'

Jung described the 'self' as the central archetype of our unique individual potential. He wrote [translated] that 'The self is not only the centre but also the whole circumference, which embraces both consciousness and unconsciousness; it is the centre of the totality, just as the ego is the centre of the conscious mind' (1943). Our modern equivalent language might be 'wholeness of person' or 'personhood' (c.f. Assagioli's model in chapter 13).

The self represents our wholeness in two ways: firstly, centrally present at birth, as our life's goals, a life plan of our individuality, guiding and renewing our energies, and having the capacity to heal and unify our opposites;

secondly, perceived in our emerging capacity and awareness, as we integrate our potential and outwardly express it in our whole personality.

Self can be portrayed in different archetypal shapes such as a growing tree or vine, as an unfolding rose or lotus, a mandala or a star, and as a young child, and we can see how the essential qualities of these universally known metaphor shapes correspond with potential-releasing functions of the self.

Some modern analytical psychologists have recognized that, despite Jung's original brilliance of insight, his logical thinking was hampered by his contemporary conceptual habit of emphasis on opposites. This dialectic of conflict, classically expressed as thesis, antithesis and synthesis, can now give way to perception of a range of appropriate qualities and available responses.

For example, there is a wide sweep of practical and just possibilities between greed and generosity – self-interest and concern for others do not have to clash unless they are polarized. We still use concepts of these opposites to delineate the *extent* of our range, but can now be freed from their *polarizing* effects and much of the resulting conflict (Samuels, Shorter & Plaut, 1986).

Good and evil

Likewise, Jung's perception of self as our innate god-image (a 'picture' of God's existence limited by our own human conceptual boundaries), which ran into such opposition because it contained the opposites of good and evil, can be resolved by this alternative concept (see chapter 13). Namely, we can see that the *self* incarnates a god-image of creative appropriateness, and that evil arises in the form of too much or too little appropriate *ego* interpretation, response and activity. Evil also arises in this way collectively, expressed in malevolent or treacherous archetypes such as a tyrant, Satan, or a wolf in sheep's clothing.

Philosophically, evil is reduced to existing, individually and collectively, where there is too much, or too little, of what is *potentially good* if beneficially practised. Furthermore, the two kinds of evil often co-exist where there is imbalance or polarization, as when too much time and resources are given to some form of activity, be it work or recreation, accompanied by too little spent in other vital areas, or in our relationships, again manifest individually and collectively. It is the task of the ego, with reference to the core values discovered in the self, to perform its balancing function of deciding appropriately where is the most productive point for response along a range of possible alternatives.

It is unfortunate that the term 'self' has also been used by religious teachers and by others to denote 'selfish' and 'narcissistic' (too much emphasis on us, too little on others or our surroundings) aspects of our ego-centred personalities. This has led to tragic confusion, including the misrepresentation of a commandment to love our God, and our neighbour as ourself.

Individuation

In a synonymous way, the spiritual and practical process of 'individuation' involves the inwardly focused efforts of our ego to become aware of and to *serve* our deeper level potential and then to express this *outwardly* in our relationships. Our residual dependencies are thus gradually left behind, giving way to the self's more mature priorities. In this way, we may experience an enriching change in emphasis, even if we remain in the same circumstances, although where ego immaturities or traumas remain unrecognized, they may continue to exert a distorting influence on our behaviour.

During the 'inner listening' and analysis of the individuation process, an ego that has not developed sufficient balancing capacity may fail to distinguish the source of immature, distorted or short-sighted qualities and urges, so that resulting changes, perceived as an expression of 'self', may in fact be egocentric, impulsive and hazardous, if not disastrous. A sufficiently aware analyst might mitigate this by pointing out the dangers evident in the presenting symbols and dream images, which will unfailingly be present in some form, or in a significant *absence* of form or quality.

Jung regarded individuation as the pursuit of the fairly mature person aiming to integrate his or her spiritual nature so that it could be better expressed. In his view, the full process requires an already achieved level of ego capacity sufficient to cope with the sometimes unwelcome perceptions involved, and to distinguish between our self's core values and our egocentric concerns. It is useful to compare other approaches to spiritual or personal growth, many of which beneficially nurture a learning process, and include prescribed exercises and group support, relying less on achieved levels of maturity, but whose structure of understanding may *impress upon*, rather than release, core values, and may foster dependency and conformity. This risk applies to some psychological belief systems as much as to religious movements.

Whether or not we attempt a deliberate 'individuation' process, mid-life marks many milestones to which we are likely to give much thought. We may already have achieved a considerable level of spiritual and practical integration which may flow smoothly through the middle years, or which may need to be released from an earlier-established rut. It is useful to supplement a psychoanalytic approach with other, more outwardly focused descriptions of the improved functioning we may achieve, especially at this middle-age period, as we take time to consider what is happening in the passing years. Later chapters describe some different examples.

Mid-life changes

Some mid-life changes are imperceptible, while others may suddenly blow our lives apart. Whatever our individual situation at this time of life, many of us will be concerned with making the most of the active years that no longer stretch limitlessly ahead. It is like coming to Wednesday, when Thursday and Friday suddenly seem too short a time to fit in all we had hoped. We are likely to pause, and to do at least a little re-planning, perhaps realizing that we need to gain new skills or knowledge in some area.

As in earlier years, we tend to compare our situation and our capacities with those of our peers. It often seems that 'nearly everyone else' is now well-situated and coping admirably with any problems they have encountered, and have successful children, co-operative families and generally correspond with the 'happy family' advertisements. Conversely, it may seem that 'everyone else' is divorced, or considering it, made redundant, or concerned about the behaviour of family members.

Now more than ever, it is important that we work out *for ourselves* the best way forward for our own development, or the solutions to our own problematic circumstances, in our own particular situation. We may have problems of health, economic provision, or family needs, with their accompanying stress-levels, or we may, through earlier choices or misfortune find ourselves distressingly, or with a sense of opportunity, alone.

Our efforts will naturally focus primarily in these areas and there are many organizations and a considerable amount of advisory literature to help us with most of the commonly occurring practical concerns we may have. Many of these help our specific understanding about some subject, but we often feel a need for a deeper-level understanding of ourselves than we have hitherto had time or interest enough to develop, and this is where the theories and research of a range of psychologists can be useful to us. Some widely used examples are discussed in later chapters, and we shall look now at some of the skills we shall need for any reorganization we may decide is necessary.

It is always useful to discuss our concerns with others who like and encourage us, but this is no substitute for an unhurried 'stock-taking' and future projection of our own, to be included in any significant discussion. An initial time slot must be carved out to consider our condition now, how we would like to be, and how we might move in the direction we want to go.

Until we see it written in front of us, we may be amazed at the difference between how we actually spend our time, and how we think we spend it. This will become evident if we make a time-slotted diary for a typical month, and add in the actual 'extras' as they come. Listing priorities comes next, and it is useful to write a list of basic, longer term priorities and of shorter term necessities, such as our work demands or our children's current and later needs, not forgetting our own restorative needs of recreation. Are all these satisfactorily reflected in our use of time?

We may happily discover that our day-to-day living does in fact fulfil our principles without the need for any further planning; but we are more likely to want changes, if we can only work out how to achieve them. Sometimes 'clutter' can be identified, and the principle of beauty or usefulness we might apply to clearing the clutter of our physical surroundings can help in time as well as space allocation.

Some valued activities can be spread more thinly, moving from weekly to fortnightly or monthly frequency, and social contact may need to be reduced or increased, or to be carefully maintained and allowed for. Review of all contacts and commitments is essential, and this moratorium will need enough time reserved for the process. Keep priorities firmly in mind, questioning them and their relative importance as new recognitions emerge.

Flexibility can be achieved by making interchangeable 'slots' wherever fixed appointments are not involved; thus we may change our 'study' slot to accommodate a visiting friend we particularly want to see, provided that we say a firm 'No, sorry, otherwise engaged' to provide for our study purpose in one of our 'social' slots. It is this capacity to say a firm and pleasant 'No, otherwise engaged' that can protect time set aside for particular relationships, and also for that so often neglected necessity, *time alone*. The secret is to put 'time engaged' lines in our diaries instead of leaving them blank and vulnerable to all comers.

Improving communication

Broadly speaking, in the light of our considered priorities, where we find 'too much' on our month's survey, we need to plan for 'less', and where we find 'too little' we need to plan for 'more'. It may take a little while to put desired changes into practice, and where others are affected, they may need time to get used to our new approach. For both men and women, it is especially important for partnerships and families to have their needs included in discussion, and to have time to consider and adjust, if co-operation is to be gained. Their point of view needs to be at least understood, and accommodated in a way they can manage, during the planning stage.

Perhaps they, too, can benefit from changes, or perhaps they find their work all-demanding, and may resist disturbance of their own 'survival package'. As with the intimacy v. isolation negotiations of Young Adulthood, the general principles of regard for self and others, of independent co-operation and of give and take can resolve most incompatibilities, if the process is not rushed.

The time of recognition of middle-age varies enormously between about forty and sixty-five years of age, and by then we have a range of skills that will continue to serve us well. These may include good communication and effective stress management, but improvements in these areas are well worth the investment of precious time.

Our communication may have impoverished areas due to a habit of making basic assumptions about ourselves and others of which we are unaware. We can learn to check out what *actual* feelings underlie our attitudes, and what our attitudes *convey* to others. Likewise, we may need to look behind our assumptions to discover what other people *really* feel about all kinds of everyday, or less frequently occurring, events.

For example, we may underestimate our actual abilities, because we are still operating on assumptions laid down by early experience at home or at school that we rarely meet required standards. We may assume the opposition, or the support of others, based on experience which led to defensive attitudes or to dependent habits which we have continued to present successfully.

In our moral attitudes, we may well have a whole string of assumed 'oughts', some valid on examination because they serve our most honoured principles, others based on outdated, dependent expediency. Our assumptions about 'what other people think or expect' will equally require sifting and evaluating. The quality of our relationships depends very much on the attitudes we communicate, and how we perceive others, and as we approach our declining years, it will matter increasingly what people *actually* feel towards us and what we feel about them. Our well-being will more than ever depend on our capacity for friendship and an understanding respect for and realistic expectation of others. The content of what we communicate and perceive can be greatly enriched if we give it some attention.

Social networks

Awareness and a range of verbal, non-verbal and especially timing skills combine with content in good communication (see chapter 12), and we also need to review the social network that our interactions construct and operate. Our communication network is the context for our relationships, beginning with our partner, family or those we live with or nearest to, our locality, our working organization and our wider community. For many of us, this means our region or nearest urban centres and perhaps our country generally; but our business, family or other connections may mean that we include our own and other continents world-wide in our sense of concern based on our involvement in wider 'community' networks of communication.

There is therefore immense variation in the kind of network each of us may have, and of the personal priorities and professional or concern-oriented involvements at home, locally or at global levels. We may have friends everywhere, and yet experience loneliness in some areas of our lives, or we may have a few close relationships and a strong personal need for time spent alone.

Our stress levels will be closely related to whether or not our own particular social network and our pattern of involvement in it support and enhance our needs and our sense of fulfilment, or whether it merely drains our energy. In handling stress, we therefore need to look carefully both at where we are, regarding our network, and at where we are heading on a very individual basis. In middle age, we also need to allow for present and future changes in energy levels.

Life changes, even chosen and positive ones, have their own stress factors, and while a bit of challenge and pressure can be very productive for us, our general health is likely to suffer if large or multiple changes increase the pressures beyond our individual resiliency level. Researchers T. H. Holmes and R. H. Rahe (1967) produced a now widely used list of stress ratings covering social readjustments and demonstrated the relationship of high ratings with subsequent illness. Items on the list range from death of a spouse, divorce, injury, loss of a family member and moving house, to marriage, job changes, gaining a new family member, financial changes (even a substantial improvement requires some adjustment) and busy events, such as Christmas.

It has been found that we are more likely to find changes stressful, and to suffer physical health problems and some pathological psychological reactions, such as depression, if we perceive ourselves as having little or no control over events, and as lacking the capacity and skills to cope with them (Brown, 1985). We may therefore be able to reduce stress by examining our perception of events, by developing new attitudes and by increasing our understanding and practical skills.

General adaptation syndrome

We may also need to counteract physiological changes, preferably before ill health results. A 'general adaptation syndrome' has been described by Selye (1956, 1979), which distinguishes between the stresses with which our normal resilience and recreational pattern can cope, and those for which we need to provide longer recovery periods. The syndrome begins with the normal 'alarm' reaction involving increased sympathetic ANS activity (see chapter 2), increasing blood sugar, heart rate and blood pressure. The adrenal medulla (see chapter 2 and biology *Texts) produces more adrenaline and noradrenaline, which maintains sympathetic ANS arousal for a period after the stressor is removed, and can produce a self-perpetuating 'closed loop' effect.

If stress continues, 'resistance' sets in, and there is a decrease in sympathetic activity. The adrenal cortex (outer part of adrenal gland) increases in productivity and size, stimulated by adrenocorticotrophic hormone (ACTH) released into the bloodstream by the pituitary, under the control of the hypothalamus. The hormonal releases of the adrenal cortex restore blood sugar, heart rate and blood pressure to normal levels, but the immune response is impaired, increasing the likelihood of invasive infection, sexual function and pregnancy may be affected, and body resources become depleted. 'Exhaustion', the final stage of adaptation, brings a drop in blood sugar, psychosomatic disorders, such as high blood pressure, heart disease, asthma, ulcers, and an increasing number of now recognized stress-related ailments.

Well before this final stage, we need to recognize our physiological requirements, and where this is possible, take an adequate and restorative break, or at least change our pattern as far as circumstances permit. Understanding the way our nervous system functions and how our minds and bodies influence the homeostatic balancing of our hypothalamus can help us to plan the best way of coping with our own particular stresses, and especially to recognize the kind and length of recovery periods after unavoidable pressures that we and others may need. Our ANS function needs a balanced pattern of rest and activity (as gentle as necessary) during recovery, both mentally and physically, and knowing the things we normally enjoy and that have a replenishing effect will also help us to plan our well-being and generativity.

Strategies for coping with stress include avoidance and seeking assistance as well as self-development, and all are beneficial, used appropriately. Temporary avoidance of a situation to allow some recovery of resilience, to consider the best approach and to develop increased coping capacity may be wiser than grim confrontation, and after careful consideration, indefinite or permanent avoidance may emerge as the wisest solution under the circumstances. Thus we may have to admit that our reaction times are now slower, whether from eyesight or other deterioration, and that driving at high speed on the motorway is better avoided; or that some of our regular current commitments are becoming stereotyped and unproductive, a common cause of stress.

Temporary avoidance of the perception of pain, danger or unbearable truth may sometimes allow necessary action to be taken, on which survival or high priority may depend. We need to be aware of the 'bearing-level' of others, in their apparent avoidance, and to exercise the same compassion for ourselves as we focus on developing realistic strengths and strategies to meet our unique experience of stress. If we know that we can be merciful to ourselves if we need to be, not condemning ourselves for feeling negatively, we are less likely to use avoidance in a pathological way.

Seeking assistance can have many advantages. Actual loading may be reduced, or at least sympathetic support may help us to feel less inadequate and therefore less stressed. Assumptions that 'so-and-so doesn't care' that 'no one cares, can spare time or is able to assist' may have some reality, but often it is our own assumptions, or our unwillingness to admit our own humanly real or imagined inadequacy that prevent us attempting to find, or to use successfully whatever help or support may be possible. Pathological dependence on the help of others is another example of 'too much' of a good thing.

Cultivating serenity   Stress management through self-development involves self-awareness and honesty, attention to health and individual recreational balance and the improvement of appropriate personal and productive skills, including time management. Perhaps the most obvious way of handling stress, and for some of us the most difficult, is the cultivation and practice of serenity. This quality is evident in a few people, no matter how hectic a situation, and involves a lot more than just staying calm. Some of us achieve a spontaneous sense of peaceful well-being in relaxation after satisfying activity, or can become immersed in the beauty of art, music or nature, and experience a re-tuning akin to the benefits of meditation.

For those for whom relaxation, let alone meditation and serenity, is difficult, it will be easier if an individually suited method, preferably with skilled instruction, is adopted. A self-help, by-the-book method is better than nothing, but the support of others and experienced guidance facilitates progress. If we know that we are, alongside our internal focus, dealing with the practical issues in our lives, progressing step-by-step from where we are, those of us who are practically minded can more readily allow ourselves time to find a personal way of experiencing serenity. We find that the cultivation of inner space, that many would call spiritual growth, no longer appears as a futile escape into unreality, but rather enhances reality itself, and enables stressful events to be perceived and acted upon differently.

Finally, in a discussion about stress management that has focused on ways of achieving change, we may have problems about accepting things we cannot change, in the shadow of which the cultivation of serenity or spirituality may seem meaningless. Here, it will greatly help us to discover that our own fallible humanity is an adequate tool for us to work with. We do not have to abandon our ideals, but just as we would not expect another person to act beyond his or her own capacity, we need to climb down from our perfectionist high horse of righteous, and often justifiable, resentment or outrage, and start a positive process from our present position of injured or frustrated helplessness.

We can positively cultivate the wisdom to recognize what may be changed and what may not without necessarily giving up hope of change in the future, but acceptance of the present facts is the first step, as it is with irreversible events. Paradoxically, this will set us free to promote the development of a practical way forward, as we mourn, and so heal, our loss and disappointment, and gradually make what adaptations our human nature is able to achieve. This is how we may 'make the best of it'. Thus we need not deny our anger at bereavement, disability or devastating accident, or the impossibly high demands on us that we sometimes encounter, but can allow ourselves to develop and act where we can, and grow into adaptation where we cannot. Serenity need not remain out of reach, a gift for only a few.

Middle-age, therefore, is a time when we get together a working philosophy and a package of different kinds of skill that will enable us to maximize our achievement and see us through into old age. In the next chapter, we shall consider Erikson's description of our continued development towards the completion of our life cycle.

LATER YEARS: INTEGRITY V. DESPAIR

10

Erikson updated his comments regarding his eighth and completing stage during his own last few years, in an overview of his psychosocial stage theory, *The Life Cycle Completed*. This was published posthumously in 1982 (Erikson died in 1979), and in it he recognized the changes that had occurred since his earlier observations, contained in *Childhood and Society* (1950, 1963). He also noted the change in perception we undergo as we ourselves enter these later years. He observed that, during his middle years, 'One could still think in terms of "elders", the few wise men and women who quietly lived up to their stage-appropriate assignment and knew how to die with some dignity' and that only a few decades later, '... old age is represented by a quite numerous, fast increasing and reasonably well-preserved group of mere "elderlies"'. He noted that a ripe old age was soon to become 'averagely expectable'.

Wisdom, disgust and disdain

Erikson reiterated his earlier-chosen terminology, and discussed the task of ego development as that of forming a favourable ratio between 'integrity' and 'despair', forging out of our experience the quality of 'wisdom', and defeating the pathologies of too much 'disgust' and 'disdain'. As middle years become later years, Erikson said, we have an increasing need for a philosophy that can encompass losses and despair, and maintain for us the qualities of hope, trust and faith in the face of bereavement and our own now apparent mortality and approaching death. Libido, he believed, is generalized as the emotional investments of our more energetic years decrease. This allows the emergence of enjoyment in still accessible outlets, and a richer appreciation of the smaller details in our lives, that can emotionally warm these years and brighten their darker aspects.

Social institution: wisdom of sages

Socially, Erikson describes a 'style of integrity' beyond, though a part of, individual integrity, and a similar kind of social wisdom which might be described as the culturally honoured sayings of the sages. Erikson had in mind the deeper wisdom that liberates a mature person, in no matter what culture or socio-economic level, and which includes in it a sense of belonging. In practice, this ancient wisdom is often blended with current discoveries and trends of thinking.

Some of these trends become established culturally, whether for the general benefit or not, while others have great influence as 'modern wisdom' for a while only, for example the 'isms' of political and religious convictions. Unless we have enough perception, deeper wisdom and ego integrity, our need for belonging is likely to draw us into swimming with the tide of currently predominant beliefs, and we may thus miss out on the deeper levels of tranquillity imparted by changeless wisdom.

The social aspect of old age includes the various attitudes different societies have towards their elderly members, and the amount of social involvement and independence they are expected, permitted or wish to have. Each of us, as we grow older, becomes familiar with our own society's stereotypic norm of old age, perhaps confident that we shall 'not be like that' when our turn comes, or perhaps looking forward to the freedoms that these years seem to offer. When our turn does come, our perspective has changed and, consciously or otherwise, we update our sense of identity and adjust to the kind of social roles possible in our own society and individual circumstances.

Identity v. role confusion accompanies any major change in our lives, not least retirement, and any of the other adaptations we need as old age advances. We encompass biological changes affecting appearance and energy levels, and sometimes have to grapple with our own reactions when passing aches and pains become more major aches and pains, and can quickly bore and irritate others, and sometimes drive away casual friends and acquaintances just when we most need them. Thus our 'triple bookkeeping' is brought up to date, often making very high demands on our ego's balancing skills as the moratorium proceeds.

AGEING

Social psychologists as well as personality researchers have investigated patterns of ageing, and Robert Havighurst (1968) combined these approaches in a prominent American study. He identified four main personality types, which he described as 'integrated', 'armoured-defended' (constricted or holding-on), 'passive-dependent' (succourance-seeking or apathetic) and 'unintegrated' (disorganized). The integrated group he further distinguished as 'reorganizers', 'focused' or 'disengaged', all with high rates of measured 'life satisfaction', but the reorganizers had a high level of rated 'role activity', the focused a medium level, and the disengaged a low level.

These results demonstrate the importance of individual differences when levels of activity and social involvement, in our later years, are being considered. 'Activity' theory (Havighurst, 1968 and other gerontological studies), which suggests that maintaining a high level of activity is the best way to retain life satisfaction, is shown to apply usefully to only some elderly people, represented by the 'reorganizers'. In contrast, 'Social Disengagement' theory (Cumming & Henry, 1961), which describes a mutual withdrawal of society from the individual, and of the individual from society, may explain the satisfaction of the 'disengaged' group, and more generally, the dissatisfaction of those who suffer from loneliness. 'Social Exchange' theory (Dowd, 1975; Dyson, 1980 – see Hayes, 1984 and Gross, 1992); which regards adjustment to retirement and ageing as a kind of contract between the individual and society, is a more flexible and widely practical approach that has emerged from gerontological research. Within the range of social practicability, individual personality is thus perceived as the crucial element in adjustment to an appropriate lifestyle, and central to guidelines for socially organized provision, whether privately or communally funded. The wider interests and attitudes of society as a whole constitute the framework of this theory and practice, spelling out the range of possibilities.

Social beliefs and social expediency can easily distort what is advocated as 'good for old people' generally, and may overlook needs associated with an earlier or later than usual onset of decline, as well as other individual differences.

Decline of faculties

Faculties that are used decline less quickly than those unused, but there will still be wide variation in the personal capacity to keep on using them, dependent on circumstances and health, as well as on past experience, perception and personality pattern. A community's failure to recognize the difficulties and needs of some older people, or the lack of deterioration and therefore retained potential and need of outlet in others, can lead to some very unhappy older members.

Statistics concerning deterioration of faculties can be misleading. Graphs are usually based on average scores for progressively older 'cohorts' (age groups, e.g. sixty to seventy, seventy to eighty). Since most of us actually decline, at least a little, in various faculty functions during our final year or few years, there is, in each progressive cohort, an increasing proportion of those who have reached their last years. Their lower rates of performance drag down the tail of the graph in a way that does not affect individuals who have not yet reached their final years. Individually therefore, unless there are damaging health problems, the decline of our different faculties is much less steep than these graphs suggest.

An earlier study than Havighurst's also related personality patterns to the degree of 'adjustment' (similar to life satisfaction and coping capacity), and is useful in our discussion of the ego qualities and psychosocial adjustments that we especially need in later years. In 1962, Reichard, Livson and Petersen (1961) produced five types of personality based on clusters of rated personality variables (see *Texts). A weakness of the study was its biased sample: all eighty-seven subjects were working men, drawn from an area of San Francisco, but this need not affect its value for discussion or in prompting further research, such as Havighurst's.

High on adjustment in this investigation were the 'mature', 'rocking-chair' and 'armoured' groups, while low adjusters were named 'angry' and 'self-hating'. We can immediately call to mind older people of our own acquaintance who would fit each of these categories, or can recognize them in TV soap characters, though we do well to be cautious about this stereotypic kind of labelling, and notice also the individual variations that constitute any person.

The San Francisco study's 'self-haters' openly rejected themselves, blamed themselves for their own failures, and tended to be depressed. They perceived death as a welcome release from their unhappy life. The 'angry' men were generally hostile to the world and blamed others when things went wrong. They had tended to be downwardly mobile socio-economically, to resent their wives, and especially to fear death. It is small wonder that all these men were found to be 'low on adjustment', and Erikson's disdain and disgust were clearly predominant.

These subjects' personality problems can also readily be described in terms of Erikson's residual deficiencies from earlier stages, and this approach can provide very practical guidelines as to how best to respond to these immaturities. For example, as do children, all of us with some degree of these residues need empathy concerning our sense of failure, appreciation of our efforts and achievements where possible, and some opportunity to salvage and develop even just a little self-esteem; or empathy with angry feelings, opportunity to express them verbally or in some form of art, and especially, support in identifying and focusing on positive and personally valued aims, and socially acceptable ways of promoting them.

As we grow older, we are less able to change our long-held attitudes, especially where these are intrinsic to maintaining our self-image, however poor this is; but small, less threatening changes can sometimes be achieved, and at least the damage caused to relationships by depression and cantankerousness can be eased by empathetic understanding, and by the wider community support and encouragement of those near to us, who are affected by our afflictions and deficiencies. Many of those who care for elderly people have these skills, and there appears neither valid nor insurmountable reason why this awareness and practice should not become more widespread in any society, nor why attention may not be given, by some chosen means and alongside other high, educational priorities, to prevention and remedy at a much earlier age. Until this is achieved, the number of 'low adjusters' seems likely to go on increasing.

'High adjusters' in the study included the 'armoured' who defended themselves against any dependency or idleness, and avoided retirement where possible. Ill health or decline was, therefore, much harder to bear in this group than in others, and their satisfaction was much dependent on their being able to maintain a high level of activity. The 'rocking-chair' group, in contrast, welcomed the chance to relax and depend on others. Their enjoyment of taking life easily made them pleasant to be with, and they adapted well to the changes of old age. The 'mature' group approached life changes constructively rather than impulsively or defensively and were less dependent than the 'rocking-chair' group. In a more active manner, they, too, adapted well and were content with their lives.

Critical evaluation

We should note that of the sixty men who were rated either high or low on adjustment (those with medium ratings were left out of the final analysis), twenty-three did *not* fit into any of the personality clusters that were categorized and named. Similarly, Havighurst's 1968 investigation had nine, out of the fifty-nine men and women between seventy and seventy-nine that he studied, whose personality ratings did not include them in any of the eight patterns of ageing he identified.

These unclassifiable subjects provide an important balance in evaluating research of this kind. While findings can support or refute traditional or popular beliefs, or uncover unsuspected new evidence, and convenient labels can greatly aid discussion, we are each of us a unique mix of qualities and needs, and do best to follow the lifestyle that matches our individuality within the options available to us.

We turn now from this discussion of some of the overall personal patterns of ageing and their inseparable social context, to a consideration of some of the major events that shape our later years, starting with retirement.

RETIREMENT

Retirement from work is an individual and cultural variable that for some happens gradually or not at all in a recognized form, and for others, in business or employment, is sudden, complete and often marked by a 'rite of passage' retirement celebration, with formal presentations and tributes to achievement. In some cultures, there may be formal or informal elevation to becoming an 'elder', and this status may occur under varying titles or none. Many of us look forward to and greatly enjoy a new lease of freedom, whether for active pursuit, contemplative opportunity or both. For large numbers, however, there may be a very significant loss of social role, status and esteem, and an even more significant loss of self-esteem, especially if we now feel useless.

Means of livelihood, including whether a personal pension is part of cultural custom, governs how far and at what age retirement can become possible and be anticipated. World-wide, and even in developed countries, there are many who continue to carry out as much work as possible, employed or otherwise, for as long as possible, whether this be from economic necessity, cultural expectation, the dependencies of those who need constant and unremitting care, or from the frequent intermix of all three causes. There are also some of us who cannot bear to give up the work satisfaction of a business, profession or trade who likewise keep working for as long as possible, or exchange it for an equally high level of alternative work commitment, often voluntarily undertaken. Thus there are many for whom retirement from work is never a reality.

Gradual retirement, or the lessening of work load as stamina decreases, allows time for adjustments to be made, and those of us who can follow this pattern will minimize discomfort. The availability and use of leisure time during our working years will also affect our adaptability to work changes, retirement or to the health problems that sometimes precipitate them. Even if we, mostly women, have never worked outside our home, we shall be affected by the retirement and necessary adjustments of those who share our home with us.

Sudden retirement, especially if it occurs involuntarily, often earlier than anticipated, through accident or redundancy, can be very difficult indeed to accommodate. Sometimes our work has been totally demanding, especially as our energy supply decreased, and we have been unable to picture realistically how we may feel when retired, or what our needs and inclinations might be; or we can discover that we have anticipated wrongly. We may have worked and lived abroad for many years and face home and culture changes as well, often finding that when we return to our own country, our memories and dreams of home are barely recognizable because of the changes that have come about since we left. If our main occupation has consisted of caring for someone close who dies, personal grief is added to the changes precipitated by their death. All these sudden events, radically altering several areas of our life, can be very traumatic, and disorientation will add considerably to the time we shall need for readjustments.

Even if we have given thought to, and have in place ready for ourselves, an expansion of our genuine interests and a new mode of living, we must live through the process of change. This can be unexpectedly uncomfortable, however much we welcome many of the changes involved and the increased time available for so much that has been set aside or not yet discovered. Alongside any discomforts, and as guidelines into a new future, we need to keep firmly in mind these dawning possibilities and choices ahead, which can do so much to restore our happy participation in perhaps a very different kind of life. This principle is invaluable at any time, not only in our later years, but also in instances such as incapacity through accident or a health problem, or family change or exile, or any of the events that can end the past as it has been for us.

The more of ourselves we have put into our work, whether from pressure or choice, the longer it is likely to take to adjust to retirement. However, there is much we can do to help ourselves through the process, once we understand what is happening to us. In a few instances, the discomforts may have become so intense that they constitute a depression or 'breakdown', and this can occasionally be complicated by the emergence of repressed 'leftovers' from earlier years. For example, a resentment or grief from long ago, pushed aside at the time, may reimpose its patterns of feeling now that other pressures are lifted. Professional help may be necessary, but again there is much we can do to prevent or mitigate depression or breakdown, or to work through our left-over emotions.

Major change

The basic process of any major change begins with recognition of what has happened, and our retirement from demanding full-time work has many implications not at first apparent. Acceptance may take a while, and 'helping out' or 'a little part-time work' may be a useful bridge for us, or an unrealistic hope we cling to until we can face the final fact that we are no longer needed, and that the past is indeed the past. We are then free to develop new involvements, gradually becoming apparent in the space created.

Self-esteem, hitherto upheld by work satisfaction, may take a severe knock, especially if alternative self-affirming satisfactions have been crowded out by heavy work loads. Erikson said that we now learn to face 'not being any more' in the strength of 'having been', and that this becomes a part of our changing identity and our new sense of integrity. This includes the consequences of our retirement as well as other significant losses of close relationships or health.

Passing through the nadir

'Despair' at whatever irretrievable losses we now experience is the nadir from which recognition of endings and a willingness to look towards new possibilities enables us to rise. Even with lesser feelings of loss, we need to become conscious of whatever we are losing, to mourn an appropriate amount and to release ourselves into a new direction. This is what Erikson meant by a favourable ratio of integrity and despair. If we try to bypass any loss without recognition and a sifting of its implications, we are likely to experience discomfort from any repressed sadness, and this can very often be the root of a depression in the post-retirement period or later.

We need to give ourselves time and space to reminisce, to feel sad where we have a sense of loss and to be patient during the time when our habitual patterns of motivation, thought and action are going through the necessary changes. We usually experience a kind of no man's land before our motivation and enjoyment re-emerge into our new, even carefully prepared directions, and puzzlement about this flatness can contribute to feelings of discomfort or depression.

If we consider the neuronal connections in our brain that form the pathways of our habitual mental processes, we can readily understand how new ones that can become dominant and automatic will take time to establish, and how our existing patterns can be responsible for a sense of strangeness, even significant disorientation, until this has happened. It is helpful to adopt a supportive structure of small routines, which can be as temporary as the emergence of new directions indicate, and it is important to include small comforts, at least until new satisfactions are in full flow. It is also helpful to 'keep scanning' during flat periods for openings around us that correspond to our sense of values, side by side with the sifting and the treasuring or leaving behind that constitutes the acceptance process in any change or loss.

Remembering that our autonomic nervous system works best when we balance our active and relaxed periods, and that our brain cells and thinking processes also benefit from change and rest, we can beneficially monitor our pondering and occupation patterns. The complex experience we call emotion (see chapter 12) is likewise most healthy and resilient when we give it time and space to function, but also enough change and rest. With any

Figure 10.1 *Grand-generativity. A well-loved hobby can be continued, modified as necessary, into active retirement; here there is the added bonus of sharing time together*

major life change, new alternating rhythms of activity, rest and recreation need to be carefully considered and adjusted around our own central and new priorities.

Our focus, in these last paragraphs, on the discomforts and sometimes 'despair' aspects of change, and ways of mitigating them, should not cause us to overlook the outward-looking approaches to retirement and other changes, which enable so many of us to adjust well and enjoy our later years. Open and explorative scanning and considering of life around us will increase our awareness and range of choice, and lead to investment of interest and involvement according to our personality. Involvement may include direct social contact for those of us who are more extroverted, such as playing whist, fund raising or visiting the house-bound, or it may mean activity mainly carried out in solitude, but within some social context, such as various arts and crafts, listening and viewing, writing or studying. Unless we are very extroverted, or fond of solitude, we shall probably choose a mixture of types of involvement.

First learned in infancy, this sequence of sensory interaction and response is indispensable to the maintenance of the 'integrity' side of Erikson's formulation. Together with the processes that help develop our capacity to handle 'despair', also begun in infancy, our sensory and considered interactions will provide our ego with the experience wherein may mature our felt sense of 'wisdom'. Our practical decisions, comments, advice and our underlying philosophy will all resonate the degree of wisdom we are thus able to make our own.

Besides the leaving behind of our former work role, other losses we shall increasingly encounter in later years are the friends whose company we have so enjoyed, and sooner or later, if we have been married and outlive our partner, our husband or wife. If we have not already lost our parents, this, too, is more than likely to happen to us, perhaps after a period of caring has brought them very close. Bereavement is a special kind of loss, and we will consider next how wisdom may help us to approach, comfort and bear it when it happens to us.

BEREAVEMENT

The loss through death of a partner, close family member or friend adds a focused personal poignancy, constituting an extra, sharply painful dimension to the sense of loss we experience through other deprivations or changes. Grief (from a word meaning 'injury') is our natural reaction to any overwhelming loss, especially bereavement, and mourning (from a word meaning 'anxiety') is the expression of our grief. Between the initial state of shock and numbness, and the achievements of recovery, there are many reactions, perceptions and emotions that are our natural responses when someone close to us dies.

Apart from the closeness of relationship, circumstances that add to our grief include whether the person who dies is unexpectedly young, how suddenly death occurs and the manner of dying. In addition, the absence of a body, when this has been unlocated, irretrievable or buried in a distant, unknown place, can make recognition and accommodation of the fact of death a more difficult process. Irrational hope, whether conscious or not, can then obstruct the necessary 'bottom of the nadir' changes that open the way to recovery.

We are also variously affected by the degree of our dependent attachments to the lost person, and whether these are in areas where we have never developed a capacity to cope, or whether we have handed over parts of our independent initiative in some areas, in the mutual exchanges of division of labour or in close sharing. Two variables, in particular, influence how intensely we experience our grief: firstly, how much the person we have lost represented to us a part of ourselves, so that we did not need to live these parts for ourselves but could gain satisfaction from his or her living of them instead; secondly, how much he or she was indispensably complementary to us, enabling us to live out our own qualities and roles.

Thus, as a husband or wife who has been immersed in a lost partner's career or creative output, or as a parent of a young child who dies, even if we still have others, we lose so much of our own personal hopes and satisfaction without our partner, or our own parenthood of this particular, precious child. In addition to the kind of emotional investments we have in those dear to us, our different residual vulnerabilities will make different aspects of loss especially painful to some of us.

These paragraphs address the experience of major bereavement, but the loss of someone whose friendship and regard we have valued, even if our lives are not significantly disrupted, will still constitute a sadness that we will need to pass through and accommodate. Each loss is the loss of someone with whom to share some or many of the unique aspects of our living, of 'someone to tell' who has cared and been genuinely interested, and whose news and welfare has concerned us personally.

Common experiences of grief

Allowing for the many differences, there are still several common experiences of grief, and since our society (for reasons probably associated with this century's heavy losses in two World Wars) has only recently begun to give them any attention, we can easily be dismayed by our own reactions, or at a loss in coping with the grief of others. (N.B. Many of the descriptions of handling our feelings and of the processes of accommodating change and making readjustments that appear in other chapters, and earlier in this one, can be usefully applied during bereavement.)

Colin Murray Parkes (Parkes, 1972, 1986) has recorded the mourning of men and women from a range of ages and circumstances, and has described three main stages that he observed before recovery was established. Initial 'shock' usually brings numbness, a sense of unreality and a disorganization of thinking processes lasting from a few minutes to a few weeks. Physical symptoms may accompany these reactions, and health is more at risk than usual during the first six stressful months, due to a depleted immune system, after which the extra risk gradually declines. Feelings of illness are common, with or without organic cause.

Numbness gives way to 'pining', a strong sense of absence and a tendency to search for the lost person both in actual places and in memory, accompanied by deep sorrow and often tears. These feelings usually occur in waves, with less painful patches in between, often triggered by some object or reminder of the person. Our eyes seem unconsciously to search among groups of people, and if we glimpse someone with any resemblance to the familiar figure, our grief can spill over in waves of dismay and sorrow.

This searching, which verifies and familiarizes our loss, and the waves of sorrow that accompany our dismay and despair and carry us through the nadirs that we need to pass through in the different aspects of our bereavement, constitute the main and most sharply painful process of mourning. The waves of sorrow are often followed by a comforting sense of release, as our desire for each familiar element of the person we have lost accommodates its own impossibility and begins to change its expectations and open towards a return to reality, rising from the nadir of our despair.

Those of us whose faith teaches, 'Blessed are they that mourn, for they shall be comforted' can find its truth substantiated in this process, but even if we have no particular faith to explain them, our natural processes of mourning incorporate this merciful release. We find in our searching, the memories we can treasure, a source of joy once we have mourned their passing, and build up a picture of wholeness of the life lost to us, not just the person as he or she was most recently. Since no close relationship is without discordant flaws, these we can leave behind.

Depression

Sometimes, however, the process is held up, and what Parkes describes as a third stage, 'depression', listlessness and cold, grey, iron despair, may predominate for a while. This may occur earlier, during the second stage, in the months following the loss, preventing the release of sorrow and tears, in however much of the mourning there remains to be undertaken.

Depression may also occur after the acute mourning period, as we face what seems a cold, empty future with dread. Reassurance that this is a very common element of bereavement, and usually passes spontaneously may be of some comfort, but new skills of dealing with loss and grief feelings may need to be developed by working through some of the depressive elements. Alongside this working-*through*, a focus on adjustments and expectations of recovery will help forward scanning begin to find the pathway *out* of the iron imprisonment of the depression.

A more apathetic kind of depression may accompany the no man's land of the disintegration-reintegration process of change described earlier in this chapter, when varying degrees of bleakness may be present, either in patches, or pervasively. 'Moving gently forward' is the way to emerge from it. Making a cup of tea, taking a walk, telephoning or writing to a friend, or getting on with some small manageable task or leisure interest, has brought many of us gently through such trying terrain onto firmer ground, where we can more easily consider our overall direction, and move gently forward into it.

Sometimes where survival is at stake, or where, for example, the pressing needs of young children overload a bereaved parent, mourning may be repressed for stronger priorities. Bereaved children, in particular, may need help in understanding, as well as time and emotional space, to mourn effectively and overcome grief satisfactorily. Persistent depression occurring at any time of life has been linked by psychoanalysts to the inability to mourn in earlier bereavement, or to deal in a similar way with other deprivations.

Guilt, anger, irritability and anxiety

Emotions that are extremely common in bereavement include guilt, anger and irritability. Guilt can be especially painful. However much we may have done for the person we have lost, we will almost certainly wish that we had done more, or had kept in closer contact. Where there are *actual* causes for regret, in ill feelings, quarrels or neglect, guilt may be very burdensome until we can resolve it with a sincere acceptance of our own regret, and some compassion for our human fallibility, and for the other person's part in the failure.

It often helps to imagine how we would regard someone else in our situation: when feeling personally guilty, it is much easier to forgive someone else's failings than to forgive our own, and to perceive that the most useful thing to do is to put them behind us, and try to become kinder and wiser in future. The self-forgiving process might take time, especially if imagined or real guilt is too painful to acknowledge readily, perhaps hedged around by often very real reasons or excuses, but it can be a comfort to know that it is in progress.

Anger is another natural reaction to any injury, and is sometimes directed at someone we feel is responsible for our loss, by action or default, or perhaps, along with a sense of our own guilt, our anger is directed at ourselves. In the exceptional instances where human fallibility, carelessness or destructiveness is partly or wholly to blame for our loss, anger can be especially bitter, and sometimes guilt at our own bitterness can add to the burden of it. Unresolved past bitterness and resentment can also add to our unhappiness. We may become deeply angry with God, or with life generally and its unfairness, wondering why we should be the one to suffer a perhaps premature or avoidable loss.

More frequently, anger may burst out of us in exaggerated proportion to an incident evoking it, or arise in a way that seems, even as we feel it, to be irrational. For example, we may feel generally angry with everybody, aware of our reason or not, simply because they are not the person we have lost, and never can be.

Irritability can persist in patches for several months, or longer, until our soreness begins to heal and we become less generally hyper-reactive. Rather than be unpleasant to those who would try and comfort us, we may avoid their company. Sometimes the solitude is just what we need for the various parts of our mourning, or to rest and replenish our resources or to look ahead a little; but sometimes, where they are understanding, or willing to understand if we explain, we will do better to accept their compassion and company, and allow their warmth to help in our healing.

Anxiety and waves of fear are at least as common as anger, and are usually fairly pervasive during the mourning period. There can be a variety of causes and effects: fear of losing control of our emotions or our mental processes, confusion in the loss of our familiar role identity, which was perhaps a major part of our whole sense of ourselves as an individual; dread of emptiness ahead of us, or of having to manage things that our lost one formerly did for us, are all producers of anxious tensions. In turn, these can produce a variety of unpleasant symptoms such as aches and pains, sleep disturbances, loss of appetite or excessive comfort eating, digestive disorders and periodic or general exhaustion. Anxieties concerning individual survival after death can also torment some of us.

Comfort and recovery

We may be comforted by a sense of our loved one's presence after death, perhaps very briefly, sometimes more frequently. This does not seem to depend on whether we have faith or belief, though such an experience can confirm an open expectation. We may find that, despite any doubts we have, we can still talk to him or her, though a sense of reply is much less likely to occur. It is usually when we least expect it that this kind of sense of presence or reassurance happens.

Faith can be discovered or strengthened by the very functional support it can give in coping with loss and the painful feelings and anxieties of bereavement, but sometimes, because of the unplumbed depth of the new experience, a previously strongly-held faith may be temporarily, or even permanently, found inadequate or abandoning, and this may constitute an added devastating bereavement for some of us.

A deeper and broader search may restore our inner assurance over time, or the more concrete aspects of reality may become the only basis on which trust can again be ventured. Where faith has mattered much to us, sometimes the circle of concrete and spiritual reality can be completed by our discovery of the underlying unity and balance of all its aspects, however dimly and differently we may perceive it. Some of us will be able to describe it artistically, psychologically, in religious terms or metaphorically in considerable detail, while others may simply find an inner assurance that needs no description. We shall return to this theme in the next chapter.

Recovery begins as each phase of mourning restores to us the functions that were so closely involved in our lost relationship. We begin to separate out what constitutes past joys, and what is now the desolate hunger of our own unmet needs. These may be sexual, sometimes intensified by other unmet potentials (see chapter 3), our need for receiving and giving affection, for support and nurturance in different areas of our life, for stimulation of interest and exchange of ideas, and whatever we have previously shared that has left us with an emptiness.

At first, this seems like a painful void, and although there may be someone or others who can come into this void, we are very susceptible to unwise attachments or commitments in various areas with others who are likewise ameliorating the anxieties of their own variously occurring voids. Sometimes recovery can be achieved alongside each other, but more often, and with long-standing voids, a relationship is distorted by the imploding pressures. It is far wiser to accept the undemanding support of true friends and independent acquaintances, and wait with patient expectation until the void becomes a creative space that can be shared with a sense of freedom and enjoyment.

Thus we need to avoid premature joining of households, moving into a new neighbourhood, falling into a new partnership, or any of the impulsive new refuges or commitments we may feel will resolve our loneliness. Gentle occupation and social contact, and suitable kinds of usefulness to someone else, will help us to recover our self-esteem, but we shall become stronger, sooner, if we wisely monitor and protect our own stressed energy resources, and especially our vulnerabilities.

Recovery is a step-by-step process where we can move gently forward, encouraged that it is a naturally programmed progress. For all of us, time for mourning needs to be as long as it takes us individually and at a pace that we can manage. Our capacity to enjoy our lives gradually builds from small beginnings, and we can gain comfort and encouragement from every step forward that we make, and learn to look out for the treasures along the way.

The realization that we are 'next in line', at the funerals of the older generation of our family and friends, is relentlessly brought home to us as we begin to lose more and more of our contemporaries, and even those younger than we are. Funeral attendance and letters of condolence become increasingly frequent occurrences. Our capacity to enjoy the sweetness of our own later years, is therefore heavily dependent on how well we learn to cope with major bereavement, with the dying and loss of friends, and with the increasingly frequent reminders of our own mortality. We can learn much from those whose wisdom is demonstrated by their example, as they find enjoyment in each day, or despite the discomforts that finally overcome them, find a sure pathway to peace.

The next chapter overlaps in many ways with this one, as we focus on the ego development during these later years that will enable a truly peaceful completion of our life cycle. We will also examine some of the problems, and ways of approaching them, when this underlying peace is not at all apparent until it finally and inevitably occurs when we die.

DYING, PEACE, LIFECYCLE PERSPECTIVE

11

Erikson describes the kind of wisdom we need in our declining years as 'an informed and detached concern with life itself in the face of death itself' (1963, 1982). 'Detached concern' means the absence of anxiety, produced by a capacity to 'let be', accepting our loss of active involvement while retaining informed interest and compassionate perspective. While we can help maintain a sound integration in satisfying and suitably adapted levels of '*grand*-generativity', our ego must also work for our integrity by allowing us to pass through the despair nadirs of bereavement and of other losses brought about by depletion of bodily functions and often a slowing down or deterioration of our mental faculties, in particular, of memory recall. Increasingly, and despite our best efforts, we may have to rely on the help of others, and to relinquish our highly valued practical independence.

Ego resources

Now, more than ever, our ego needs to draw on the strengths and qualities developed in earlier stages. Erikson's epigenetic perspective, whereby all later stages of ego development are present in embryonic form during earlier stages, once more emphasizes the essential foundations of earlier ego achievements, and the impediment of residual deficiencies. Most often, it is in our later years that this particular ego task is presented to us, although we may have met the heavy demands of adjustment to considerable decline and premature loss, through accident or severe misfortune. In the latter case, all the ego qualities we possessed plus new strengths, forged as best we could from the embryonic resources we didn't yet know we had, would have been necessary to get us through.

Thus we shall need to draw from both sides of the antitheses Erikson described. From the directly positive side, we shall need our capacities to trust, to choose from what is possible, to direct our attention and effort, to persevere, to know what is most important to us and what are our strengths and weaknesses, to relate intimately and appropriately and to generate according to our values and skills. For the positive outcome of our negative polarities, we shall need our abilities to register and choose our response to our feelings of mistrust, of doubt and shameful failure, of guilt, of inadequacy and incompetence, of confusion in new roles and situations, of isolation and of the frustrations and inertias of stagnation. Out of these capacities and abilities, and corresponding 'felt senses', will come our understanding and sensitivity to the potential and the limitations of others, and therefore the quality of our relationships.

All these are strengths which we shall only possess in varying degrees, and we shall need to muster and improve on them as best we can, as we affirm the identity and values that maintain our integrity. As we progress along the pathways of growth and allow our ego through the smaller and larger nadirs of despair, we can expect to find, in the new integrations of our maturing wisdom and our appreciation of whatever blessings may be around us, the treasures of old age.

To the demands of living, and adapting to our individually varied experience of decline, is added a personal realization of the coming end of life as we know it. We shall probably have pondered on the mystery of death from time to time, especially when we have lost someone close to us, and this will have shaped our approach to our own dying. In cultures where dying, death and mourning are openly talked about, where privacy and independence are less highly valued, thus allowing communal participation, and in the hospice movement, which is infused with a similar open acceptance, many of the fears experienced by some people in our own culture do not arise. Familiarity with the facts and feelings builds up an acceptance of how dying will probably be.

Dealing with fear

In our own culture and some others, we are particularly likely to fear the possible manner of our dying, and the fact that we could well find ourselves alone and helpless at the time. For example, in a mechanized, short-staffed hospital or between rounds in a nursing home, if we live by ourselves, or in a caring family when carers need to work and, of course, to rest, some of us may fear that we could be in discomfort (or worse), and alone during our final few hours or minutes. With the increasing number of very old people, and the slow growth of arrangements to cover care that may be needed, this is a realistic possibility and often needs to be faced and worked through so that it can be allowed for, even as the outside possibility it is, with greater confidence. Facing the worst will often defeat our fear of it, along with any tendency to dwell on our fear.

Just as we are programmed to take our first breath, it seems that we have natural resources that provide for our last. Many, many of us experience a deepening peacefulness as death draws near, and the endorphins thought to be responsible are also released under conditions of stress. The reports of people who have survived violent, injurious, terrifying struggles for their lives, suggest that pain and fear are either not experienced until later, or experienced only up to the point of unconsciousness. Endorphins (their name is derived from 'endogenous morphines') appear to suppress some elements of normal consciousness, especially pain and fear. Sudden death would therefore rule out re-emergence of this consciousness, and any death struggle might be expected to release our natural endorphins. Longer-term pain is most often controlled medically, and sometimes by a re-focusing form of self-hypnosis.

Resources of a 'vital faith'

Specific fears can be responsible for general anxiety, but perhaps the greatest common dread is fear itself. Erikson links this worst of fears to residual incapacities in dealing with early mistrust, and once again emphasizes the value of a 'vital faith'. We may have an early established or later-discovered faith that has matured with our own personal growth, finding that it is always 'there for us', even in our worst extremity. This does not absolve us from normal fear, but it does give us confidence that we will be able to cope with it.

All is not lost, however, if we have never found an adequate foundation for belief in any underlying truths, or perhaps more distressingly have found earlier beliefs inadequate: for as in infancy, when we were afraid, we were able to draw reassurance from the vital faith and confidence of our parents, so in old age, the vital faith of others can be communicated to us in their confidence, as we come to trust them as friends or carers. As Erikson pointed out, faith is the mature form of the hope kindled in infancy, and the elements of truth by which it is nurtured may be perceived in religious form and teaching, or in the expressed wisdom and compassion of the actions and aspirations of others, and in the natural forms, processes and harmonies of life around us.

Depression and withdrawal

Depression is another common hazard of old age, and we vary in our capacity to work through it. Where losses and discomfort are overwhelming, and the future appears to offer only further decline, death is often looked on as a welcome release, and it is a mature ego indeed that can still arrange space for our life-loving self to approach daily living with interest, and with motivation for even passive participation. This is a very different and more peaceful approach to dying than clinging to life out of fear, or grim, insatiable determination. It is a sad fact that some of us 'keep fighting' to a bitter end, and only then succumb to the underlying peace that is so apparent when we can 'go with' whatever old age brings to us.

Withdrawal may be a feature of general depression or inability to cope with ageing, or a reaction associated with loss, especially if we have to leave our home and familiar surroundings. Sometimes this respite from social interaction gives us the space to uncover deeper resources, although unreality can set in if we cut ourselves off from others too completely, for too long.

A different kind of withdrawal surrounds the enjoyment of solitude, though here again, unreality may result from too much avoidance of social contact, 'too much' being a very individual variable. Unreality itself can take many forms, whether arising from deterioration of our brain cells or from psychological causes.

Senility

Perhaps senility, and fear of it, is one of the most frightening possibilities of ageing. Although we know that most of us do no more than slow down in our mental processes and become forgetful, we cannot be sure that we will not be among those who are affected more seriously by brain-cell deterioration. Here again, well-established ego strengths will mitigate some of the worst effects, and 'gentle' senility is a frequent form of this kind of deterioration. However, since some of the brain-cell loss from senile dementia or stroke damage may affect areas specific to the organization of behaviour, or the inhibition of impulse, bizarre or aggressive behaviour is not uncommon.

Many skills have been developed by those who care for us if we are thus afflicted, the basic principle of which is to try to communicate with whatever ego organization is still functioning, at the level at which it functions.

This means getting to know us as an individual, and finding ways of re-inforcing co-operative and acceptable actions and of providing access for satisfactions enough to maintain some quality of life.

Where seemingly bizarre actions or verbal statements occur, these can often be interpreted as symbolic in the same way that a dream expresses meaning in its symbols. This requires the development of some understanding and sensitivity to archaic metaphor, as described by Jung's theory and others (see chapter 13), but this skill is sometimes developed instinctively by those who care for us when we are senile or mentally ill.

It seems that we all have primitive areas of brain function, thought to be associated with the right hemisphere, where semantic (meaningful) or sensory-linked imagery is formed, as in dreams. This imagery can come to the fore when our usual thinking processes are disrupted, as in senility or mental illness, or superseded, as by creative artists or sensitive carers. We can learn to be in touch with these images, and the images communicated by others, consciously enough to make the verbal linguistic connections and logical sense, as assessed by the left hemisphere (see *Texts). This is achieved by tuning into our own or another's image, or archaic metaphor, and then attempting to clarify it as far as we can verbally. The study of ordinary metaphor is a good beginning.

In practice, we may respond with appropriate action, and using the same metaphoric imagery as the communicator, or with a mixture of action, metaphoric and logical language. A caring person, who is closely 'tuning-in' and attempting to understand another person, can gradually develop the brain connections necessary for interpretation. The logical language connections are needed for communication among carers, for maintaining accountability in caring professions, and for educating the rest of us in the general population.

Thus a comfortably-off old lady who frequently complains of poverty can be understood as complaining about deficiencies of relationship, perhaps of energy or motivation, or of her own vital faith. Imaginary spiders, germs, defective appliances or other troublesome 'presences' portray internal threats and need responses that will also reassure and communicate at the depth of self-image. Thunder or earthquake may represent psychological fears of disruption, or physical events such as incontinence or digestive discomfort. Fears, guilt, or any emotional need or sense of deficiency may be expressed in terms of religious imagery, for example, a fear of the devil or a punitive god (see chapter 13). The loneliness of being misunderstood need not happen to us, nor, for the want of a little effort that will also benefit our own self-understanding, need we condemn others to it in our ignorance.

Aggressive behaviour

Aggressive behaviour is often caused by the frustrations of not being understood, or supported in despair, though it may be linked with cessation of a customary addictive substance, such as a regular 'nightcap' of alcohol, or with residual deficiencies in balancing autonomy with consideration for others. Untamed primitive impulses can emerge when normal social inhibitions weaken due to cell damage or to mental illness. When our own capacities for self-direction and restraint are weakened, like children, we benefit from a warm, firm and secure framework, with reminders of the needs of others around us. Central to this, we need to be assured of respect and regard for our integrity, even if we are having great difficulty in holding it together, and to have this demonstrated in the choices available to us within a realistic framework.

Choices,
preparation and
adjustments

Choices often diminish as age advances, and those that remain are especially precious. Even ownership and position of the chair we choose to sit in can be at stake, and available diet and possible mobility may also considerably narrow our former freedoms.

Our ego is concerned with reality and can adjust to new frameworks for available choice, but there is much we can do to prepare ourselves and to help one another. The task is made easier if we have developed a capacity to attend to the underlying beauties, harmonies and joys of life that do not change. Thus, when active participation is reduced, we can still choose to focus on the beauty of flowers, pictures, people, the harmonies of art, music, poetry and literature, the excitement of watching many different kinds of sport and adventure, and the human interest in drama, short stories and especially the qualities and concerns of those around us.

Our physical limitations are likely to be less if we have remembered to take sufficient exercise, maintained our fitness, and attended to health problems intelligently as they arose. Even if we have lost the battle with weight, we can maintain a more limited mobility if we attend to it. We therefore need, so far as this is possible for us, to develop, earlier in life, the outline of a suitable future structure for ourselves, within which these appreciations and concerns may find provision. Some of our limitations, such as internal discomfort, or the deterioration or loss of sight, hearing or limb movement, can be devastating, and in addition to accepting the help and guidance of experienced others, we need to temper the self-criticism and demands we make on ourselves with compassion.

We also need to cultivate tentative patterns of participation and occupation that will be in place if and when we come to need them. Many of us will find it simple to adjust our patterns during what can most often be an active and enjoyable old age, but some of us may live for a considerable number of years in varying degrees of incapacity when we may need deliberately to adopt patterns that will assist our remaining faculties. Pastimes may get squeezed out of our younger years for very good reasons, but if we can lay down a few genuinely enjoyed foundations, these can be developed as other activities drop away and can significantly help to maintain failing faculties, adapting as we go. There may come a time when very little is possible, and we shall examine that situation later in the chapter.

Our chosen recreational activities are often central to our later interests, and capable of adapting to reduced abilities. Dancing may have to give way to more limited movement to music, but even our perhaps restricted dancing hands and arms can still give us great pleasure. Some of us may paint or write, even if we are not especially good at it. The simple enjoyment of colour, form and words can stay with us even in considerable decrepitude. Arranging flowers, cultivating plants or putting together engines or electronic circuitry will also give us a life-long source of interest and an occupation for as long as we choose and are able. We may be inclined towards craft of some kind, and even if our skills and facilities have decreased, once we have become familiar with the satisfaction of making things, our interest can often be suitably transferred and adapted to less ambitious undertakings.

Solving crosswords or puzzles, letter-writing or tape-making and exchanging, doing jigsaws or quizzes, playing cards, bingo, 'party' games or board games can keep our minds and spirits active and capable of communication and enjoyment. Following particular interests, or radio or TV programmes, and talking to others about them will also keep our social senses active and allow scope for continuing to form and express our personal opinions, for as long as possible. Some intellectual interests may have to be pursued through reading and writing or recording tapes to exchange with others in our field, unless we are fortunate enough to have similarly interested regular visitors or can afford substantial telephone bills. These interests, too, will have to undergo adaptation to our own 'rustiness' and shortage of contacts for discussion, and may give way to other, more accessible interactions.

Many of these suggestions can seem trivial, meaningless and commonplace when we are younger and in the full flow of our adult years, but if old age does bring us reduced faculties and mobility, these occupations can form an unpressured structure within which our principle life-experiences, relationships and satisfactions can continue to function. As Erikson reminded us, we usually begin to look ahead around the age of forty, and can learn much from those already ageing, both about what to cultivate in ourselves and what to avoid.

Pathway to peace

Conversation can become increasingly difficult, especially when deafness or the constant company of similarly incapacitated or withdrawn others makes communication a considerable effort. Like other experiences, confusion can be increased if it is joined with the confusion of others. Under these circumstances, withdrawal is common and understandable, and we may come to depend on passive watching and listening for the input that our minds need to balance our internal musings. As Piaget described, we need 'aliment' to feed our cognitive processes, which will in turn continue to be influenced by the contents of their own processing. We become more and more selective about what we take in, and our horizons may shrink to daily routines of care, meal times and cups of tea. The availability of caring time and input and of visitors is individually very variable, and a realistic balance of needs and availability has to be negotiated, hopefully with resourceful sensitivity.

Sometimes we create for ourselves 'a world of our own' as a refuge, and the nature of it will depend heavily on our earlier developed capacity for creative imagination. Even in these conditions, a formerly well-developed ego can help us experience a sense of integrity and retain enough hold on reality to enable us to communicate and interact with others, although from an observer's perspective we may appear out of touch with some aspects of objective reality. Earlier patterns are very potent in shaping the way we are able to handle the considerable deterioration that a few of us undergo in our final years.

In our deteriorated physical or mental faculties, and in the ill effects on our personality of our residual psychosocial deficiencies, we shall greatly need the wisdom and compassion of our own society, and the skills and sensitivity of those who care for us. Provision for necessary care, and earlier prevention of what is possible to prevent, in forms that assist ego development, however we may wish to organize ourselves, are the measures of our society's quality of compassion and of the level of maturity of our corporate wisdom. Triple bookkeeping is unavoidable.

For some of us, there comes a time when our capacity for participation is minimal. This final phase may be fairly brief, or may last for many months. Our vital faith, or sufficient 'good enough' care, is usually sufficient to make of this time a pathway to peace, and we often sleep or daydream much of the time. The hospice movement has developed a whole range of compassionate skills that can enrich our final decline, from massage, holding and sensory treats of sound, taste or smell, to listening to the differently vibrant levels of silence, gently reassuring us in many ways.

There may occasionally be an apparent physical struggle as our organs fail, but our own endorphins, which can be supplemented by any needed pain-relieving medication, ease our final passing. This sometimes appears to observers to be a visionary or home-coming experience, or at least one of gentle and profound peace.

Jung has described death as 'being taken into a wholeness of nature and spirit in which conflicts and contradictions are resolved' (1961). This, of course, applies to death whatever the manner and circumstances, at any time of life, but accords very well with Erikson's concept of the completion of our

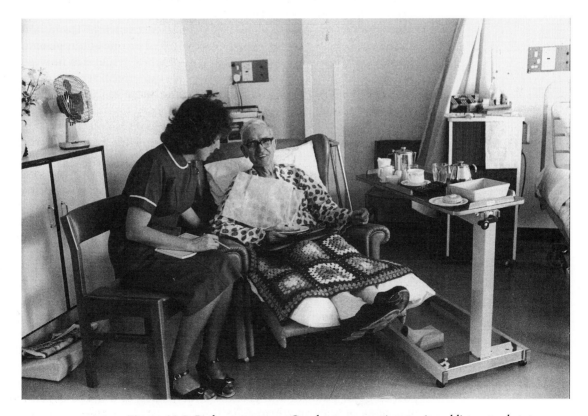

Figure 11.1 *Pathway to peace. Good care means time to sit and listen, to chat, to arrange treats and to support our inner process of accommodation and acceptance, as we live each day during our approach to dying*

life cycle. Erikson perceived this cycle expressed clearly in the quality of trust, defined as 'the assured reliance on another's integrity', and added that 'healthy children will not fear life if their elders have enough integrity not to fear death'. We can turn to artists, poets, mystics and writers of sacred texts for the images and metaphors we use to describe the actuality wherein rest our trust, integrity and 'mature hope', however inadequately and differently from one another we may perceive it (see chapter 13).

EGO AND ETHOS

In his final years, Erikson reviewed his theory (1982), refining many of the basic philosophical perspectives that both shaped and arose from his work. He writes competently, in detail, and we will consider here a few of his emphasized insights and recommendations. Drawing on Freud's psychoanalytic concepts, social insights and statement that 'civilization is a process in the service of Eros, whose purpose is to combine single human individuals, and after that families, then races, peoples and nations, into one great unity, the unity of mankind' (Freud, 1930), Erikson equates communal and collective development with the lifespan psychosocial stages of each of us.

Not only do we individually develop through stages that are progressively moral (right and wrong, rules), ideological (ideals and commitments) and ethical (active practice of ideals and principles, existential awareness), but so do the societies we live in, most closely linked at our adult, generative level (see chapter 8). Moreover, since environmental issues are now commonly and communally raised among many of us, our ethical sense is extending beyond mankind, and we are beginning, in a more mature way, to love our universe, or at least our own planet, as opposed to marvelling at its beauty, and dependently exploiting it. Erikson compares this development with how, as young children, we can learn to love, with regard and respect, the facts and features of life around us, not only our carers.

Already, just as in middle age we begin to consider our own final years, we are becoming aware of our sun's progression towards an eventual state that will no longer support life as we know it. We speculate on what this finite future holds for us and where mankind will go from here? For Erikson, there is an unbroken continuity of existential and cyclical psychosocial and biological interdependence. He pleads for an 'art-and-science of the human mind' with a 'life-historical orientation' as well as an individual 'historic self-awareness', which means that we develop a psychoanalytic understanding of cultures and communities as well as of individuals. He appeals passionately for the insights accumulating in psychoanalytic practice to be added to those of other disciplinary approaches, and concludes that 'only a new kind of cultural history can show how all the details of individual development dovetail with or come to diverge from the grand schemes suggested in the existential cycles of religious belief systems, in the historical postulates of political and economic ideologies, and in the experiential implications of scientific theories'.

Principles of social remedy

With a better understanding of how we develop, dovetail and diverge, our collective ego, of which the ego of each of us is an intrinsic and influential part, may at last be able better to strengthen our ethos, by directing our collective immature, destructive, immoral and amoral id energies into ethical, developmental progress. As with individual remedial work, we can help this progress of our societies with a better comprehension of the stages we are stuck in, our corresponding levels of regressed or fixated emotional response, and the 'next steps' we need to take in the different facets of our development. As with individuals, triple bookkeeping reminds us that our efforts take place within the essential context of our relationships with others. Thus can we ease and resolve our collective conflicts and better inform our collective communal, political and economic attitudes and policies.

Erikson advocated '*generative ethics*', and from that principle derived a simple Golden Rule: '*Do to another what will advance the other's growth even as it advances your own*' (1964, 1982). His lifespan theory has been widely adopted in professional training courses, and has made an invaluable contribution to our understanding about ourselves and others, and what positive steps we may usefully take in a variety of situations.

Others have also provided useful perspectives, as we have seen in earlier chapters, and in the last chapters of this book, we will look more closely at a few that have only been mentioned. In the next chapter, we will consider some of the findings of Michael Argyle concerning social encounters, and the conceptual framework which allows a better handling of our emotions, described by Nico Frijda. We shall also outline the theory of personal constructs developed by George Kelly. All of these theories are relevant to us at most of the stages of our lives, and can usefully complement a developmental approach.

SOCIAL NEEDS, EMOTIONS AND CONSTRUCTS

Social psychologists have concentrated on our interactions with one another, and have provided us with many insights into social processes and influences. Among other topics, they have researched group dynamics, crowd behaviour, prejudice, social facilitation, non-verbal communication, authority and styles of leadership, to name but a few (see *Texts). From this vast field of research literature, much of it American, is selected the approach of Michael Argyle who has led a British research team and has investigated, in particular, social interaction and its wider application to social problems. He has also linked his observations to developmental processes, which makes his work very appropriate for the purposes of this book.

MICHAEL ARGYLE (1925–)

The biographical notes on the author in *The Psychology of Interpersonal Behaviour* (1983) tell us that in addition to his work at Oxford University, Michael Argyle has been a visiting professor at many other universities world-wide. He has included visits to Israel, Belgium, Africa, Australia and Canada, with longer sojourns in different American research centres. Married with four children, his interests in travel and interpersonal behaviour are complemented by 'Scottish country dancing, Utopian speculation, theological disputation and playing the goat'. With this rich background, it is not surprising that his descriptions of the findings of his research take into account wider social and international features of our interpersonal encounters and are also perceptive and penetrating in their detail. As an added bonus, his style of writing is lucid and easy to read.

Drawing on the work of other researchers, including ethologists, and on his own observations and critical discussion with others, Argyle 'provisionally' postulates eight 'roots of social behaviour', the social motivations that cause us to interact socially. He notes that animals lower in the phylogenetic scale have almost entirely instinctive social behaviour, but studies of apes and monkeys have shown partly instinctive, partly open, patterns of social behaviour (DeVore, 1965; see *Texts). Human social behaviour is much less dependent on innate factors, due to our elaborate culture (learned and passed-on behaviour), longer period of socialization and especially our use of verbal language. Nevertheless, innate drives are present in much of our social interaction, and it is well to be aware of them. A drive is defined as a combined relevant, internal state and external stimuli, leading to autonomic arousal and goal-directed behaviour.

Argyle acknowledges that modifications and additions to his list might be desirable, but of pragmatic value are his readily recognized labels that provide pegs' for fruitful discussion. (Before reading further, it can be useful to consider a short list of our own and to compare the social motivations we perceive with those of Argyle and of others.)

1 Biological needs

First on his list, Argyle places our biological needs of eating, drinking, warmth and bodily comfort. Comparing our human behaviour with that of other animals, especially primates, he points out that both co-operative and competitive kinds of behaviour are closely involved in the satisfaction of these basic needs.

In primitive societies, groups are drawn together for co-operative production that directly provides for these biological needs, but in modern societies, work leads less directly to their satisfaction. Nevertheless, they remain an important source of motivation and influence on our behaviour, a fact that Argyle considers can often be overlooked by social psychologists (Graham, Argyle & Furnham, 1980; see *Texts.)

2 Dependent behaviour

Secondly comes our motivation for dependent behaviour. This is derived from dependency needs of care, support, protection and guidance, especially in infancy, or in new or frightening situations, all resulting in submissive behaviour. Dominance is closely related as the opposite of dependence, and alternating styles of submissive behaviour to those in authority and dominance of those of lower rank are the hallmarks of authoritarian personalities. Authoritarians come from homes, Argyle reminds us, 'where parents have been very dominating and strict' (1983).

Dependence is at the heart of early attachment, more short-lived if younger children are born, and earlier independence becomes necessary. It extends from the satisfaction of feeding needs to a lessening of anxiety brought about by physical or visual contact. Later, we can feel secure with a trusted carer close by, and as adults, our anxiety can be alleviated by knowing that a trusted 'someone' is in charge.

3 Affiliation

Third on Argyle's list is affiliation, and this capacity and need for friendship arises out of the meeting of dependency needs by the mother. He cites evidence in support of this link from research in developmental psychology, namely that Harlow's monkeys, when reared in isolation, showed no later affiliative behaviour, and that research into the history of affectionless psychopaths has often found links with earlier maternal deprivation (see *Texts).

Affiliative behaviour can reduce our anxieties and can provide a means of checking our opinions against those of others. This social monitoring helps us to adjust in directions that will add to our social integration, or to develop the strength to maintain our own divergent opinions. Friendly relationships make co-operation easier and inhibit aggression, although task performance may suffer where affiliative needs are high enough to distract the performers. Hence it is of value to a work organization to provide social opportunity separated from working time. Our affiliation needs vary, but Argyle observes that it is usual to seek the company and approval of others, feel unhappy if we are lonely or rejected, and very distressed if isolated.

4 Dominance

Dominance, already mentioned, is the fourth 'root'. Tracing its origin, Argyle again examines animal and primate evolution, the needs of a group for leaders who can keep order and repel enemies, and the prevalence of male dominance, associated with testosterone levels. In addition to our 'nature', the 'nurture' we receive, such as having a dominant parent with whom we identify, helps determine our own level of dominance, which is likely only to be aroused in certain situations such as elections or struggles for power. Established hierarchies significantly reduce dominant behaviour aimed at achieving position.

Argyle observes that dominance is characterized by wanting to talk a lot, to have our ideas attended to and to be influential in decision-making, usually as task leader. There may also be a need for power, to control the behaviour or fate of others, and a need for status and recognition, or to be admired and looked up to by others.

Applying our understanding gained from former chapters, we may question whether a need we may feel for power and status arises from a strongly responsible and generative urge to be effective in our 'caring for' capacity, or whether it represents a craving for personal support arising from a basic, residual sense of insecurity or inferiority. Dominant behaviour may well have elements of both generativity and unconscious inferiority, or it may be a defence against our own dependency, encouraging the dependence or lower status of others, and sometimes despising them for it. Actual stature and our greatest generative effect (use of power in caring, producing or creating) are achieved by self-awareness and provision for our own realistic self-respect and social affirmation, without a dependent reliance on what can easily become an exploitation of others through egocentrically dominating behaviour.

5 Sex

Fifth on Argyle's list comes sex, which he describes as motivation for certain kinds of social interaction and bodily contact usually directed towards members of the opposite sex. Although dependent on in-built physiological systems, sexual behaviour is also affected by childhood socialization and by cultural attitudes and beliefs. Thus there are both internal drive and inhibitions and external expectations and restraints. A complex set of social skills has been built up in all human cultures that includes certain kinds of eye contact and conversation, to enable the negotiation of elaborate rules and customs concerning the meeting and attachment-forming that provide for our sexual activity.

Arousal is produced by non-verbal cues, especially physical attraction in members of the (usually) opposite sex. Certain kinds of touch and smell can arouse us, as can erotic pictures, films, or a wide range of stimuli that have become associated with sex. Human sexual motivation is continual and is personally and socially regulated; Argyle agrees with Freud that humour provides an alternative outlet. We thus have a fairly constant motivation to seek social or partnership interaction extending beyond our affiliation needs, to enjoy mixed company and to take into account the sexual motivations of others.

6 Aggression

Aggression is the sixth social motivation, defined as an intention to harm, and includes both angry and instrumental aggression. Argyle does not regard it as a specific drive which must be satisfied, but as an innate response to frustration and attack, and he says that, in animals, it is biologically useful in defending territory, gaining access to food or (for males) to females. Humans are especially likely to be provoked to aggression by insults, and sexual or other physiological arousal, pain and heat also increase aggressive incidence.

Argyle states that perceived remoteness of the likelihood of being observed, found out or arousing disapproval or punishment lowers inhibition of aggression, which is restrained, controlled and often redirected by social rules. Rejection or lack of warmth in childhood, physical punishment, inconsistency, parental and social modelling, including media models, all increase aggressive behaviour. Actual encouragement to aggressive or violent attitudes and behaviour, by parents especially, and by peers or nationalistic or cult propaganda, also significantly raises levels of aggression.

Argyle reminds us that occasionally the most violent actions are carried out by individuals who have previously been over-restrained in the face of provocation, and we might question whether this rigid, 'too much' inhibition, that eventually 'cracks' arises from early fears of retaliation or anxieties about rejection or loss of love.

Reviewing what we have learned from past chapters, and elsewhere, about early development and remedial attempts, how can we best understand and direct our natural, aggressive reactions, individually and socially? Argyle emphasizes the links with frustration, response to external stimuli and modelling. Other researchers in his field have contributed to our understanding of how social influences act upon our attitudes and behaviour, including our aggression. We can add their evidence to our triple bookkeeping approach, especially when considering how we need to formulate our social policies, and carry them out.

Social norms of acceptability govern social restraints, but Argyle reminds us of conflict analysis, concerning displaced aggression of various kinds towards weaker people, and indirect aggression, for example in observation and fantasy. All of these are part of our overall experience and expression of aggression. Variations in social acceptability and concepts of harmfulness, made up of individual, family child-rearing and adult peer-group evaluations, are readily observable in a variety of social attitudes and outcomes (see *Texts).

7 Self-esteem and ego identity

Self-esteem and ego identity needs appear as the seventh root of social motivation. Argyle suggests that early parental evaluation is accepted, or partly accepted, and that we then continue to seek experience and evaluations consistent with this sense of self-worth. He notes that there are cultural as well as individual differences in our need for self-esteem, 'loss of face' being a more serious matter in the East than in the West.

Individually, we vary from conceit to inferiority, or pathologically from delusions of grandeur and various false pretences to paranoia, but are dependent on the reactions of others, whom we select accordingly for confirmation of the value we place upon ourselves. We tend not to remember or believe higher levels of evaluation than our own estimation of ourselves. For some of us, especially if we feel insecure, affirmative feedback from others is very important and constantly sought, but for some, intent on other priorities and the satisfactory results of our efforts, self-esteem is no great issue. It is when failure or disruption occurs that most of us are glad of the reassurance of others to maintain our confidence in ourselves.

Ego identity emerges from our need for a clear, distinct and consistent reference system, establishing who we are, as a basis for our choices and behaviour. Part of this need is our desire to establish our individual uniqueness, and part is for the consistency essential for personal and social integration. Our self-image has to cope with motivational conflicts, such as work and parenting clashes, or our ideals and our realistic goals. These internal pressures and processes have to be worked out in their often different, social roles and contexts. Argyle also refers to social pressures involved, in particular, for conformity to occupational, class and other roles, in the interests of social consistency and integration.

As with self-esteem, our social behaviour includes attempts to get other people to accept and to bolster up our self-image, and to avoid them, or change our attitude about them, if they do not do so. We may attribute bias or ignorance to them, lowering our estimation of their powers of perception, and seek out a more compatible and perceptive group to provide our affirmation. We may succumb to group pressures and adjust our own self-image, especially if we have no other social support or are high in residual dependencies.

Self-presentation is our means of making a statement, non-verbally as well as by what we say and how we say it. Dress and accessories often form strong impressions, but facial expression, especially eye contact, and general posture are our most potent non-verbal communications. Argyle has researched these social skills in detail, especially our use of eye contact in our interactions, and from his work, therapeutic groups have been developed to remedy defective, earlier social-skills learning. He has also described how we use settings and positioning to influence our social encounters and how the organization of our work affects our performance of it (described in much of his work of the 1960s, 1970s, 1980s, often with collaborating colleagues).

8 Other motivations

Eighth on Argyle's list is a group of other motivations originally included in the first group of biological needs. Critical discussion caused him to acknowledge that our motivations for achievement, money, intellectual and recreational interests and the pursuit of idealistic values frequently go far beyond our biological needs and their direct and indirect satisfaction. Motivation for achievement, which Argyle attributes to high levels of independence, is most often found in first-born children and in those with achieving parents. Research has shown that it is positively correlated with high expectations of success (Weiner, 1974), and highly motivated achievers are usually task oriented and low in affiliation needs.

Achievement motivation is not like a drive that can be satiated, Argyle explains, for when we have achieved our goals, we revise our targets upwards as does a high-jumper. For some kinds of achievement, we have to be willing to risk unpopularity, and this can give rise to 'fear of success'. Argyle writes that this can be found in women, who often need social approval and may fear to deviate from approved forms of female accomplishment.

We may react as we read the last statement and it is useful to consider the social context both in which it was made and in which we react. Cultural values and customary norms, and our common socialization experiences, shape social approval, and, as we saw in our introductions of other major theorists, they also influence our perception as observers, theorists and writers about our human nature. As readers, we need to take account of any cultural, and especially educational, changes that have occurred over time. We can also usefully consider our own reactions as we read the writings. Thus we can enhance our critical faculties, and without wasting energy on impulsive opposition, adopt a more comprehensive perspective, allow for 'shaping' factors, and draw up-dated conclusions.

Argyle emphasizes the predominance of the immediate purpose of any encounter, for example interviewing, teaching or selling, and the development of particularly appropriate social skills, although underlying social motivations will still be present and active. His perspective can make us more aware of what we are seeking in our social encounters, and his brilliantly detailed analysis of social skills can add insights into how and what we are communicating, and how we might improve our skills, our awareness of others, our range of choice and the fruitfulness of our encounters.

Of course, we shall wish to select from what he has offered, as have many management and communications courses, and in the epilogue of his *Psychology of Interpersonal Behaviour*, he outlines the aims and potential applications of his work. First, social skills training is intended for the 'lonely, isolated, miserable or mentally ill' and to 'raise the *quality* of normal social behaviour' resulting in 'help, co-operation and trust rather than rejection, misunderstanding and social barriers'.

Second, the re-design of groups and organizations to avoid 'alienation, frustration and failure of communication' is not an 'optional extra' but may be 'essential if an organization is to survive'. Apart from increasing job satisfaction, the most efficient and productive system is composed of 'small, co-operative teams under democratic and employee-centred supervisors, and ... few levels in the hierarchy, with delegation and representation of junior members'.

Third, resolving conflicts between groups can be achieved both by improving the skills of interaction between people of different groups of 'race, class, age, and even sex'. Quite a short period of training, which could become a normal part of the school curriculum, has been shown to be effective in reducing the misunderstanding of differences, while better negotiating skills bring faster and more effective resolutions of conflicts between different groups.

Possible dangers that new skills can increase the incidence of insincerity, self-consciousness and manipulation are countered by the following arguments: that some 'insincerity' may be desirable in the restraint of the communication of interpersonal feelings, especially aggressive, sexual or disapproving ones; that self-consciousness is only temporarily increased, decreasing again after the training period has established new habitual responses; that social competence brings advantages that, like knowledge, can be used for good or ill. Improving our social skills can help us to avoid being manipulated, and to monitor ourselves more consciously, in our influence on others.

Argyle concludes from his evidence that social scientific research can increase our insights into 'new human goals, and new ways of reaching old ones'. Socially, and spread widely enough, it can 'sensitize public opinion to new ideals and standards as yet unthought of'. Individually, it can promote self-growth, in a 'build-up of skills, control over emotions and elaboration of cognitive constructs'. Like Erikson, Argyle pleads passionately for the inclusion of his findings, and those of other social scientists, in our collective understanding of ourselves and each other.

Two other theorists add to Argyle's social skills their contributions that can assist our self-growth: Nico Frijda is concerned with ways in which we may understand and control our emotions, and his findings are briefly considered next; our cognitive constructs have been the focus of George Kelly's investigations, and a discussion of the basic features of his theory will end this chapter.

NICO FRIJDA

Nico Frijda is Professor of Psychology at the University of Amsterdam, and published his detailed survey of the accumulated research into our emotions, and his own conclusions in *The Emotions* (1986). He links his approach to that of Freud, in its focus on feeling, development and regulation, and to the cognitive appraisal theory of Lazarus (1966) and Lazarus and Folkman (1984). We shall only mention a few of the most significant ideas that have shaped research since psychological investigations began in the late nineteenth century.

Classical theories of emotion

In 1884, William James in the USA, and Carl Lange in Denmark both developed a 'peripheral' theory (involving feedback from the peripheral branch of our nervous system), concluding that it was our bodily responses to stimuli that activated our awareness of emotion: thus we would feel fear because we were running away. Controversy followed, and in 1927, Walter Cannon convincingly argued his 'central' theory (involving the brain, part of the central nervous system): that bodily changes do not happen fast enough to account for felt emotion, and that brain activity, especially in the thalamus, must therefore both produce emotional experience and initiate our response (see *Texts).

More recently, Stanley Schachter and Jerome Singer (1962) concluded that, once aroused, it is how we label stimuli that accounts for the kind and intensity of emotion that we experience, thus emphasizing appraisal and the 'cognitive' production of our emotions. Other research findings have suggested a complex combination of arousal and peripheral (including our own facial expression), central and cognitive feedback that produces our experience of emotion. (see *Texts and Frijda, 1986).

Action readiness

Frijda's own contribution carries us forward by describing our changing states of emotion as changes in 'action readiness', following from a process of assessment of the world and particular stimuli in terms of our own concerns. He explains that we are programmed by nature with certain 'stimulus sensitivities' that provide us with a 'switch on' threshold to prepare our response. In addition, our experience gives us a base for discriminatory regulation and expectancies, enabling us to 'switch off' when a situation is unhopeful or inappropriate. We also have a more basic satiation trigger that operates to 'switch off' our response.

As individuals, we develop our own hierarchy of values according to culture, circumstances, personal influences and genetic tendencies. Animals, who also experience 'action readiness' and regulate their responses according to their own priorities, are much more governed by natural programming than we are. Our range of experience and capacity for appraisal and assessment give us a much higher potential for regulating our 'action readiness' states and selecting our responses.

Frijda describes how our programming switches on our energy flow, and we then 'feel' subjectively accepting or non-accepting of the stimulus. This assessment governs the kind of action readiness that follows, which is further refined by appraisal of the most significant features of the stimulus and the situation. In this way, we learn to operate our 'switch-off' regulator selectively.

Frijda's term 'action readiness' enables us to make regulatory changes more easily, where we consider this desirable. Instead of grappling directly with emotion and trying to change how we feel, we can substitute a new action goal, which will have the effect of changing our state of readiness accordingly, once we have established our chosen priorities and mastered, with practice, the switch-over process.

Figure 12.1 *Action readiness. With her eye on the ball, this tennis player is preparing in body, mind and emotional state for her back-hand stroke; Frijda states that whatever our priority, we thus become ready for action*

Thus, when we are provoked into wanting to 'give someone a piece of our mind', our anger will cool more quickly if we focus on a consideration of alternatives and on how we may make the most effective and suitable communication that may improve rather than worsen a situation. Awareness of our autonomic programming and of our capacity for conscious regulation and direction can greatly increase our sense of freedom of choice, our confidence and our effectiveness. It can also bring us an enriching flow of natural emotional response that we may otherwise be afraid of allowing ourselves to experience.

Frijda uses the term 'feelings' only to refer to the subjectively pleasant or unpleasant registration that is responsible for our general orientation. Sometimes confusing us, other uses of the term, in psychological and other literature, include references to emotional experience as a whole, to intuitive registrations that we cannot easily put into words and to our empathetic sensitivities regarding each other.

By describing the origins and function of feelings (often called 'affect'), and distinguishing them from the cognitive processes, wherein lie both our expectancies and our opportunity for deliberate direction and change, Frijda has combined in his theory the important role of biological programming and early satisfying, and unsatisfying, experience (the Freudian element), with the research findings concerning our cognitive processes and mood changes (the cognitive appraisal element). His term 'action readiness' invites us to move forward with a more precise and usable understanding of ourselves and each other.

The cognitive element contributing to our understanding and our potential for growth is central to George Kelly's theory of personal constructs, and we turn now to consider his approach.

GEORGE KELLY (1905–1966)

George Kelly was an American psychiatrist who developed his 'Personal Construct Theory' out of his awareness of the individually different ways that we 'construe' our world. His 'man-the-scientist' approach suggests that we form hypotheses (sets of ideas) that we test out and modify through our experience. Each of us develops our own system of 'constructs', represented by the way we describe people, events and phenomena in terms of their qualities and functions. A 'tight' construct system means that we are fairly rigid in our outlook, whereas a 'loose' system denotes variation and flexibility. At its extreme, a very loose system, with little relationship between constructs, betokens inconsistency or thought disorder.

Kelly believed that our constructs govern our anticipation, and suggested that the key to problem-solving is to change the way in which we construe events. He devised the first 'repertory grid technique', whereby constructs could be gathered from a person, and the mathematical relationship between constructs could be obtained. This gave a scientific appearance to Kelly's diagnosis of each patient, but he did not rely on this technique alone, believing that a person's constructs could be elicited in conversation, or in a variety of written productions (Bannister and Fransella, 1986).

Self-characterization

In particular, he valued his patient's own view of him or herself, and often asked for a written 'self-characterization', as of a character in a play, written in the third person, as if by a friend who knew (the person's own name) intimately and sympathetically. Kelly also found it useful to explore a patient's set of constructs used in relationship with others, and began his development of the grid technique with a 'Role Construct Repertory Test', which gave a list of twenty to thirty roles such as 'a person you admire' or 'a teacher you dislike(d)'. The names that the person supplied were called 'elements'.

Repertory grid method

The basic method of eliciting constructs by means of this test, is to pick out sets of three elements, and to ask the person to decide in what way two of them are similar to each other, and different from the third. There can be problems in the implied use of bi-polar constructs: for example A and C may be construed as 'cheerful', while B might be perceived as less cheerful, serious, depressed or morose. A system of rating each element on the constructs elicited has been developed to solve the statistical difficulties posed by this, but for most practical purposes, it is sufficient to obtain a mixed list of constructs, to see how they cluster together, and especially to notice the predominant tone, focus and range of adjectives or phrases used. Elements may be people, such as pupils or employees, or objects or events, wherever we might wish to investigate our related constructs.

One such test is no more than a 'hand on the forehead' sample of our system of constructs, and we may come up with very different lists according to the situation we are in and our recent activities. However, constructs that appear repeatedly in our own or others' conversations may reveal how we habitually select and process information. We can then decide where we would like to enrich our conceptual framework, and to think through some new viewpoints to discover if they may be useful to us in our own self-growth, or in our relationships with others.

Because of his concern with individual experience, Kelly's work has often been included in the Humanistic approach in psychology, as well as in the Cognitive field where his focus on perception and information processing also places it. There is a rapidly expanding body of cognitive research findings, and some of us may find it useful and personally effective to explore some of it, or at least to sample it out of general interest (see *Texts). We shall now turn to our closing chapter, in which some of the insights of the 'third force', Humanistic Psychology, will be discussed briefly, and in which the more recent development of a 'fourth force', Transpersonal psychology, will be introduced.

A WAY OF BEING, SELF-ACTUALIZATION AND TRANSPERSONAL PSYCHOLOGY

13

During the first half of the twentieth century, Psychoanalysis and Behaviourism were the two main 'forces' in the scientific study of psychology, often in opposition, since Behaviourism ruled out introspection as a means of gathering valid and reliable data, and Psychoanalysis relied upon this method. Behaviourism dominated the discipline, but there were many who found the study of only observable behaviour an inadequate approach to understanding human beings. Psychoanalysis appeared to them equally unsatisfactory, in its focus on emotional disorder, with little detailed coverage of positive processes until Erikson expanded his stage theory in this direction, around the middle of the century.

By the 1950s, critics of these approaches were arguing for a more 'human' approach based on a phenomenological way of thinking. Thus the Humanistic approach began, and was called the 'third force' by Abraham Maslow (1954). Its central principles are human uniqueness, in contrast with scientific generalizations (idiographic v. nomothetic), and individual meaning, freedom and choice, in contrast with the determinism of Psychoanalytic and Behaviourist theories. Subjective experience and the development of personal qualities is its main working focus, and selfhood, or personhood, is seen as central to our process of development, though because of its guiding principle, it can sometimes be misleadingly perceived only as an eventual goal (Graham, 1986).

Two founding Humanistic psychologists were Carl Rogers and Abraham Maslow, who wrote extensively and described their differently emphasized perspectives in great detail. We shall only consider their perceptions in outline, very briefly, with an indication of how their insights were arrived at, and how they may be useful. Further reading of longer texts is necessary to do them justice (see *Texts).

CARL ROGERS (1902–1987)

After college studies in agriculture and then history, Carl Rogers progressed from theological studies to train in clinical psychology. Early in his career, he worked with children, publishing several papers during the 1930s. He was increasingly criticized for the 'unscientific' personal approach to psychotherapy that he was developing, and devised a method of evaluation using taped recordings of his sessions with his patients that demonstrated the effectiveness of his method (1942). Working with servicemen in their post-combat and service discharge adjustments, Rogers continued his shift towards non-directive, client-centred counselling techniques, and in the teeth of the then current Behaviourist and Psychoanalytic establishments, ventured *Some observations on the organization of personality* (1947).

In 1951, *Client-Centred Therapy* was published, since when it has been translated and spread world-wide, and is still in great demand. Ten years later, from Rogers' increasing need to emphasize his 'starting with self' principle, *On Becoming a Person* (1961) appeared. The book is based on a series of lectures in which he used his inside experience of his own developing self-hood to illustrate the core concepts of his way of working with people, and the theory that he had formulated as a result.

Genuineness, empathy and unconditional positive regard

His emphasis on the personal qualities of the therapist has been found relevant to the effectiveness of therapy based on other approaches as well as his own. Genuineness, empathy and unconditional positive regard are now recognized as essential to good practice in psychotherapy, counselling and student-centred teaching (in which the teacher facilitates students' self-responsible search for information, discussion, example and practice). These qualities create an atmosphere wherein a client (or any of us) feels valued, secure and likely to be understood, and where a sense of self-worth and confidence is nurtured.

Self-image and congruency

Rogers' main focus was on our self-image, and he believed that we all have an inherent tendency towards self-realization (the realization and expression of our self's potential), and that it is our perception of ourselves and the world around us that is crucial to this process. He distinguished between our self-image (who I am, what I am like, what I can do) and our 'ideal' self-concept (what I would like to be or what I think I 'ought' to be), and pointed out that 'incongruencies' (discrepancies) between these inner 'portraits' caused discomfort, conflict or pathology. A feeling of incongruency is even stronger if self-realization is perceived as a goal rather than the process of 'becoming' that can make us feel we are 'on our way'. Likewise, looking outwards, incongruencies between our self-image (how we see ourselves), our social image (how we think others see us) and how they actually do see us can cause problems in our relationships.

Rogers believed that we each need relationships characterized by genuineness, empathy and unconditional positive regard in which to exchange feelings and observations, so that we may develop self-regard, learn to represent ourselves honestly and grow towards self-realization. He discovered that, where these qualities were reasonably established, trust could be placed in the group processes of 'encounter groups' to enhance our individual and collective progress, and his recommendations, based on his long experience, were presented in 1970. Interest in these groups had mushroomed, giving rise to variations and also increasing interest in alternative approaches to group-work (e.g. T-groups: see *Texts). Applying the same three basic principles, in *Becoming Partners* (1972) he advocated that couples relate 'growingly' and adopt as their guideline 'growth for both' (cf. Erikson's Golden Rule).

Revealing qualities
of congruence

Within his framework of open, empathic, unconditional, positive regard, the main focus of Rogers' work was on our actual individual feeling, perceiving and thinking experience, and our capacity to enrich one another in sharing our doubts and dilemmas, our joys and aspirations. He observed that incongruencies in our self, ideal and social images are responsible for self-deception, unrealistic expectations of others, rigidity, vulnerability, dissatisfaction, anxiety and emotional disturbance. In contrast, the characteristics of congruence are honesty and openness with self and others, flexibility, realistic change with new experience, and movement towards self-realization.

Unconditional positive regard for ourselves and for others may seem an impossibly idealistic precept in the face of our human failings, our nastiness and our destructive behaviour. The key to its practice is to separate our potential for self-realization, the 'I', or person's 'I', who can learn to do better, from the attitudes and behaviour that we deplore. In focusing on 'self-potential', we become able to unlock the energies for change.

This approach is not incompatible with the necessity of facing ourselves, or those who offend us, with the consequences of inadequacy, ignorance and offence. It needs to be present alongside a competently handled process of recognition, if there is to be 'good internal experience' against which 'bad doings' may be measured, recognized, regretted and changed. Probation work, and some rehabilitation regimes, provide a range of major examples, both successful and unsuccessful. Less prominent are the examples of personal growth, and the leaving behind of regrettable tendencies as we move in the direction of self-realization, that we can observe in ourselves and in each other.

Rogers came from a close-knit, fundamentally religious family who 'kept apart' from others who did not share their beliefs, and it is easy to see how his necessary later adjustments made him very aware of his own self and social perceptions and of the range of effects brought about by ideals. His courtship of Helen, and their marriage, taught him the possibilities of growth through relationship and sharing, and his group experiences with fellow students and later in his own teaching showed him the potent possibilities of non-directed, growth-oriented group encounters. He also learned from his own mistakes with groups, the paramount importance of establishing, beyond a group's common purpose, a climate of real warmth and understanding based on personal attitudes, *before* growth could be expected.

His 'home-grown brand' of existential philosophy emerged in contrast to his rule-governed upbringing and training, and he was delighted to discover the work of Martin Buber and Sören Kierkegaard which gave him support and comfort in his pioneering endeavours. Described as 'a coda to *On Becoming a Person*, Rogers published *A Way of Being* in 1980, in which he traced the development of his ideas, including his self-perceptions as he grew older, or 'older and growing'. He ended this insightful volume by looking ahead at 'the world and the person of tomorrow', describing a person-centred scenario which he perceived to be already emerging among us.

Rogers is regarded as the founder of the human potential movement, and whether or not we choose to read some, or any, of his books, his ideas have had widespread influence, especially in the field of counselling and psychotherapy. His way of being, feeling and thinking can offer us an optimistic focus as we explore our own potential and nurture each other's.

In a similar spirit of 'self-actualization', Abraham Maslow complemented Rogers' focus on perception, with his emphasis on need and motivation. We turn, now, to consider his contribution.

ABRAHAM MASLOW (1908–1970)

Abraham Maslow's parents were Russian Jewish immigrants who arrived in America around the turn of the century. No doubt their fears and deprivations had influenced his mother's development of a harsh personality, and Maslow had a miserable childhood. His misery was due, also, to his unattractive and awkward appearance, and the anti-Semitism he encountered in Manhattan, where he was born, and he grew up looking for 'something better'. According to Edward Thorndike's tests, applied in adulthood, he found that he had an IQ of 195, which greatly encouraged his confidence. Not surprisingly, he began his work as a psychologist with William Sheldon, who invented 'somatotypes' (types of personality linked with basic bodily shape), and also worked with Harry Harlow who was studying maternal deprivation in Rhesus monkeys (see *Texts).

Hierarchy of needs

His attention turned towards outstanding people who had demonstrated what he called 'self-actualization' (e.g. Albert Einstein, Baruch (Benedictus de) Spinoza, William James, Abraham Lincoln, etc.). Struggling to synthesize their experience and qualities with his own aspirations and experiences during the 1940s, Maslow evolved a hierarchy of needs, from which, he believed, arise all our motivations (Maslow, 1954). We can hear echoes of his childhood in what he called our first four 'survival' or 'deficiency' needs: first, for our basic 'physiological' essentials – water, food, warmth and shelter; second, for our 'safety' requirements, protection, security and familiarity; third, for our sense of 'belonging' – receiving and giving love and affection, and affiliation; fourth, for 'esteem' – the acknowledgement and respect of self and others, and a sense of competence.

Only when these four needs have been adequately satisfied is enough of our motivation freed to give priority to our fifth, 'growth', need for 'self-actualization'. Maslow perceived all these needs to be present simultaneously, but to emerge progressively as priorities, and to be affected by circumstances. Thus deprivation or danger can cause deficiency needs to reassert their importance, and our socialization process can be responsible for 'drowning' or suppressing our urge towards self-actualization that is born in us.

Our first four needs cause us to feel a vacuum-like sense of deficiency if they are not met, whereas our growth needs are experienced in our cognitive and aesthetic urges to explore, discover and appreciate, and a sense of frustration of forward movement if we are unable to pursue our desired progress. As these needs shape our behaviour and begin to bring us some fulfilment, we become aware, on some occasions at least, of a sense of wholeness, or self-actualization, sometimes culminating in what Maslow has described as 'peak experiences'.

Peak experiences and self-actualization

Examples of a peak experience of performance are when an athlete wins an important competition, when a drama company achieves new heights of performance or when any of us become suddenly aware of a full flow of the best within us. Peak experiences of our potential may also occur, bringing us inspiration, when we may be flooded with wonderful ideas of how things could be in the future, and perhaps how to bring them about. Similarly, we may have visionary experiences, in which we become aware of our actualized selves as part of an infinitely greater whole, and which inspire us to try and self-actualize in the nitty-gritty realities of the future, the insights we have gained therein, for ourselves and for others.

Maslow came to place more and more emphasis on the spiritual nature of the self and our capacity for self-actualization, and he made clear, from his observations, the personal qualities that characterize self-actualizers, and gave guidelines about the kinds of behaviour that lead to their development.

Self-actualization becomes gradually apparent, and can be recognized by a number of emerging qualities. We develop an efficient perception of reality, toleration of uncertainty, spontaneity and an acceptance of what our human nature is actually like, in self and in others. Outwardly focused, objective, creative, resistant to cultural pressures and concerned for mankind, we need more time alone and are likely to have just a few, close friends. We come to fully appreciate basic life experiences, as well as the peaks that Maslow observed, and to leaven our observations with a sense of humour.

Behaviour that Maslow identified as leading to self-actualization begins with a childlike approach to life, and includes absorption, concentration, trying out new ways, listening to our own feelings, avoiding pretence and being ready to face unpopularity in the interests of our integrity. We need to identify and give up hampering defences, to work hard and to take responsibility for ourselves and, appropriately, for others. Feeling that we are 'on our way', in a process of 'becoming', can make these ideals less impossibly daunting.

Maslow's hierarchy of needs has proved a useful framework of understanding for personnel and business management, and is widely used on training courses. It is also simple enough to be used in the formation of our social and international policies, as we seek to understand the unconscious and covert, as well as the overt motivations of individuals and collections of people who will form a part of our policies, or at least be affected by them.

Social parallels

In addition to the levels of need and motivation inherent in us as individuals, Maslow believed that our societies have the same hierarchy of needs, including the same growth need for collective cultural actualization, and that our individual progress is hampered when our society has not yet progressed beyond deficiency needs. Pathology arises when individuals, and society generally, fail to progress beyond our maintenance of a social status-quo that is based on only material and social status needs, thus blocking our potentials for self- and cultural-actualization.

Maslow's ideas had their roots and similarities in Rousseau's 'noble savage' concept of human nature, William James's 'spiritual self', Jung's 'individuation' process and the stage theories of developmental psychology. His own Behaviourist beginnings in psychology, though he revolted against their exclusively external focus, were present in his recognition of the 'conditioning' and social discouragement pressures, that hamper our 'healthy' self-actualization and bring about what he called 'the psychopathology of the average'. Although, apart from his hierarchy of needs, his writing is often global and qualitative rather than scientifically precise in nature, Maslow did much to popularize the Humanistic approach and, with Rogers, to ensure its inclusion within the academic discipline of psychology.

Transpersonal psychology: the fourth force

Humanistic psychology, which Maslow had named 'the third force', became to him a transitional preparation for what he called 'the fourth force', Transpersonal psychology. He believed that this new perspective, encompassing different ways of expanding our consciousness, can offer hope for the 'frustrated idealism of many quietly desperate people, especially young people' (1968, 1986). Transpersonal psychology, too, is beginning to find its place in our textbooks (Graham, 1986; Hardy, 1987; Rowan, 1993) and to establish its own literature, and we will conclude our survey of selected approaches with an introductory outline of its emergence and its ways of describing and practising its insights.

Transpersonal psychology is a perspective based on acceptance of the reality of the self as our existential core: we *are* selves (or souls) and *have* personalities. Historically, custodians of approaches to the self have been world religions, schools of mysticism and symbolic systems such as alchemy or astrology, while artists, including poets, have described our spiritual awarenesses (see Appendix I). Psychology has brought into focus various aspects of our experience and behaviour, each approach having a different emphasis, often giving little attention to other significant areas.

The transpersonal viewpoint, which highlights our spiritual as well as our biological and psychosocial aspects, is shared by Carl Jung (*Analytical Psychology*), Roberto Assagioli (*Psychosynthesis*), Viktor Frankl (*Logotherapy*), Abraham Maslow (*Psychology of Being*) and many others, among whom we might include Erik Erikson, though he is better known for his focus on psychosocial development.

During the 1960s in the USA, increasing numbers of humanistic psychologists became interested in self-realization, inward and transcendent experience, ultimate values and practical ways of expanding our consciousness. This interest crystallized, and in 1969 the 'fourth force' was spearheaded by Maslow, thus establishing the transpersonal approach in the USA. In 1973 in the UK, there arose from the grassroots of a series of Transpersonal workshops a London Centre for Training in psychotherapy based on Transpersonal methods. These two similarly inspired and recognized establishments are in contact with one another, exchanging their experiences, and are on a converging course, with off-shoots developing, and increasing interest being shown in this comprehensive way of thinking. It will be interesting to observe its growth and impact.

Carl Jung's insights and theory, presented as Analytical psychology, probably provided the most influential precursors of European Transpersonal psychology (1917), but his less well-known Italian contemporary, Roberto Assagioli, has given us, in Psychosynthesis, a more detailed 'map of a person' and a wider range of psychotherapeutic methods that provide Transpersonal psychologists with a rich source of basic concepts for discussion and practice. We will look briefly at how Assagioli's ideas arose, and how they can help us map out and understand our own processes of personal growth (Hardy, 1987).

ROBERTO ASSAGIOLI (1888–1974)

Born in Venice, Roberto Assagioli had begun his quest, by the time he was twenty, for a conceptual framework in which could be integrated our physical, psychological, social and spiritual aspects. Drawing on his richly artistic, cultural background, his parental theosophic influence and his own education, training, reading, travel and wide experience, he continued to develop his ideas throughout his long life. His early associations with Freud, and especially Jung, enabled him to take part in the early development of mainstream psychoanalysis, and also to differentiate his own perceptions from those of both Freud and Jung.

His model of a person was much akin to Jung's, and included our access to the collective unconscious and the archetypes as our evolved and inherited source of spiritual metaphor and awareness. Assagioli distinguished three levels of our personal unconscious: our 'lower unconscious', our original state which characterizes our childhood, and from which develop our other levels and our consciousness; our 'middle unconscious' (sometimes called the pre-conscious), which is closest to consciousness, and where our impressions and mental and imaginative activities 'gestate' before entering our conscious field; our 'higher unconscious' (or superconscious), which is the field surrounding our 'higher self' and is the source of all that is best in us.

Our 'I' (c.f. Jung's 'ego') is the centre of our consciousness, and has contact with each of our unconscious levels, and very occasionally with our higher self, in our spontaneous responses. For example, we say, or think: 'I want the comforts of life'; 'I think this would be the most effective way to proceed'; 'I am amazed by this wonderfully good idea'; or, with even more amazement and infinite peace, 'This is what I am, and what I am part of'. Our growth consists of expanding our awareness of *all* our levels to form a unitive whole.

Assagioli emphasized that, unless we have developed a firm foundation of awareness of the propensities of our human nature for creative living and for error (associated with our lower unconscious) and a well-established personality, or way of relating to life (associated with our middle unconscious), a disproportionate emphasis on the contents of our superconscious can cause us to distort and topple. Our spiritual penthouse, with its views all around us and of the sky, needs to be supported by a building that is well built and maintained from the cellar upwards, and whose living space in the rooms below is kept steadily warm with use.

Assagioli regarded the role of the 'I' as both a centre of experience and as an observer able to stand back and reflect. Two major differences with Jung's theory are that Jung did not believe it was possible to experience directly our core self, and that he perceived the self as carrying the opposite potentials for good and for evil (see chapter 9). Assagioli taught that our self's potential, always available to us through our superconscious, is essentially good, but that its well-motivated energies become unconsciously distorted by the way we live and by our unskilful reactions to our experiences. Thus our good, natural need for 'enough' becomes 'greed', our needs to maintain our own 'boundaries', for 'self-expression' and for 'satisfying effectiveness', become 'mistrust', a 'lust for power' and a 'trampling over others', or inturned, punitive 'self-destructiveness'.

Sub-personalities

He adopted the concept of 'sub-personalities' to help identify and work with different elements in his patients' personalities. For example, we may have a set of developed tendencies that constitute a student, a traveller, an artist, an opportunist, a victim or a rescuer. Like many others, Assagioli also worked with the collective unconscious figures of myth and fairytale. With this conceptual framework, he made use of a variety of techniques which included Gestalt role-taking (of sub-personalities, dream figures and objects, or significant others), guided imagery and daydream, group psychotherapy, art, music, poetry and meditation (see *Texts).

His theory, which became known early on as Psychosynthesis, has formed an important resource for Transpersonal psychology, and like Assagioli, Transpersonal psychologists are constantly moving forward in their efforts to match their methods to the needs they encounter. They aim to use in their practice an image of the person that is most meaningful and creative for their individual client, and to help him or her to develop an appropriate and balanced access to spiritual superconscious resources, however he or she may prefer to describe them.

Therapeutic use of imagery

For most of us there are many images whose qualities can represent elements of ourselves, or places of refuge and resource. Consider, for example: animals such as a tiger, a lion, a mouse or a rabbit; objects as various as a musical instrument, a dictionary, a ship, a jet plane, a chair or a table; places such as a market place, a meadow, a pool, the seashore, a mountain top or a simple room. It is not hard to perceive the qualities therein and to contemplate how we may relate to, nurture and integrate these qualities in ourselves.

In using these imaginal (based on imagery) techniques, and the metaphor of a 'journey', Transpersonal psychologists explore the meaning of the disturbances that are brought to them. Are the disturbances being experienced a 'breaking down' of overwhelmed, no longer functioning patterns, or are they part of a 'breaking through' process, allowing the emergence of 'something better'? Most often, elements of both are woven together.

This distinction, and the transpersonal precepts of support and caring for the former, and facilitation in the establishment of new patterns in the latter, are insights that we can usefully adopt in our own self-guided journeys through uncomfortable periods of change: we can both care kindly for ourselves, and encourage ourselves towards potentially better openings.

Simple exercises

According to our experience and ways of thinking, we can use the metaphors of symbol, imagery, fantasy or imagined journey to release insights concerning our own nature. For example, if not in human form, what kind of animal, flower, fruit, book, vehicle, hat or shoe would we be? How might these vary at different times, thus indicating a range of qualities? What kind of terrain are we travelling through? What kind of house would best represent us? What kind of images represent our current concerns? What kind of changes would we like to see? Similarly, how do we perceive others and their range of qualities?

In doing these exercises, we can tap into the thought and search processes associated with our intuitive, right-cerebral hemispheres, and so enrich our more usual scientific, left-hemisphere, Western way of understanding. Much of the work of Transpersonal psychologists is aimed at bringing about such a balance, in theory and in practice.

Exercise using imagery

Another exercise we might find useful in opening ourselves to our resources is one based on an individually chosen archetype of the self. (Remember that it is some of the *potential living qualities* residing within our self that are metaphorically represented by these images.) In choosing an image for the focus of our attention, we need also to consider a sense of space in which we may contemplate a 'taking into' ourselves of the image's living qualities. (In so doing, we are actually releasing dormant dynamic potential in the direction of *whatever* values that have guided our choice of images.) A lotus flower, or if we are strongly rooted in Christian tradition, a rose or a vine, are good, simple choices for our main focus, and we can imagine a peaceful place to evoke the open space we need.

Grounding, identifying and tuning

It is important to prepare our ground by first looking around us at our 'down-to-earth', outward reality 'as-it-is', including other people. To this we shall need to return our mental focus at the end of our exercise. Thus 'grounded', we turn our attention to our inward reality, calling to mind a briefly considered self-image, which might be described as a 'just-as-I-am, conscious and unconscious limitations and all' identification. Sometimes, during this stage, we may wish to highlight briefly a particular source of disturbance, but it is important to progress to a whole just-as-I-am concept before going on to the next stage. (Thus our strengths as well as our weaknesses are equally activated.)

The third shaping concept, before approaching the main object of our exercise, constitutes the opening of a 'space' for contemplation and growth within our current circumstances and capabilities of integration. (Hence the importance of the first two stages.) It consists of calling to mind our wish for 'something better from the best within us', *leaving open* the specific form of what we are wishing for. (This will activate our value-system, 'opening the lines' to our deepest guiding values and principles, so that a 'felt sense', as yet unknown to us, may begin to form.) As we do this, letting ourselves feel a wave of wanting for the unspecified 'something better' will tune us into a receptive frame of mind. When the wave begins to level out into a 'may this become so,' we are ready to turn our attention to the main part of the exercise.

This careful preparation is essential. Without it, we could possibly find ourselves grappling with more mental imagery than we could beneficially accommodate, or we could have difficulty in relating our experience to our everyday life. (This is why 'dabbling with the occult' and charismatic cult, or manipulative religious practices and religious mania, have long been recognized as dangerous, since vital mental groundings and links have been ignored, distorted, or bent to a mediator's or leader's often unconsciously dependent or corrupt purposes.) Our own links with down-to-earth reality and other people, our self-awareness and our deepest personal and ethical values are safeguards ignored at our considerable risk, since in an openly focused state, we are open to suggestion and 'programming' from other people.

Grounded, identified and tuned, we may need to imagine ourselves in a peaceful place where we can become still and sense our own inner space, for example beside a pool or the soothing, rippling flow of a spring-fed stream; or we may find that the beauty of our chosen image does this for us when we approach it more directly. Proceeding at our own pace, we allow the potent qualities of the image to imprint themselves within us.

We may imagine ourselves breathing in the delightful perfume; taking in the sweet revitalizing nectar or fruit; being made potent by the pollen's imprint; contemplating the receptive heart with hidden, slowly growing seeds. During our first few practices of this exercise, we may wish to end here, in order to assimilate all the imprinting we have received, but sooner or later, we shall feel ready in our imagination, to follow the seeds through to their fertile seed bed and germination. Thus will drop away the no-longer-needed petals and leaves of our old perceptual defence systems, recycled to nourish new growth. This image, too, can imprint us.

Gently allowing our images to fade, we savour the impressions they have made. If, as can occasionally happen, obstacles or negative elements have intervened, these can be noted for consideration (and interpretation) at another time, but here allowed to drop away so that we can focus on the beneficial impressions of our contemplation. As our savouring also begins to fade, we allow ourselves gently back to outward reality, using a countdown to complete the process (5, 4, 3, 2, 1), if we find it helpful.

Once we feel that changes are emerging and being assimilated into our lives, our contemplation, or self-guided daydream, may need to focus on images associated with replenishment, renewing our direction, monitoring and encouraging our own progress. We may be able to work out suitable images and guided daydreams for ourselves, or may prefer to consult a Transpersonal publication or personal contact.

Positive and negative imagery

Though it is most productive to focus on the 'good' imagery emanating from our higher self, negative images will also arise from time to time to represent our blocks and distortions. These can usefully be interpreted and considered practically, but their resolution is considerably helped by seeking our counteracting, deeper, inner strengths, in the light of positive imagery that represents neither the 'too much', nor the 'too little', of the original urge, before it became blocked or distorted. Positive and negative images will also arise spontaneously in dreams. It is easier and more productive to focus on releasing strengths than on overcoming our defence systems, wherein we may all too easily get bogged down, though it is often helpful initially to identify their origin. A Transpersonal approach would suggest that we need to move forward at our own pace, with self-parenting, compassionate care for our struggles, as well as active self-encouragement of our growing potential.

Social framework

These exercises seek to activate and accelerate the natural healing, replenishing and directing processes present in our dreams. They can also be regarded as an application of the therapeutic potential of visual art and drama or 'felt' qualities and rhythms in music. It is helpful to be in contact with others who understand, or at least have a feeling for these processes, but we must take into account that, in our materialist society, there are some of us who fear practices that we have been conditioned into regarding as superstition, abstract airy-fairyness or dabbling with the paranormal.

Safeguards are certainly wise, as described above, and we may add this social contact guideline, to ensure our necessary outward social balance. Some contact with like-minded others or, if the need is felt, trained Transpersonal psychotherapists, will encourage our progress, together with sufficient ordinary social involvement to ensure our groundedness within a wider social spectrum. We can regard the pathologies of our culture or society as we do our own, and treat them like our own pathological defences, seeking out the deeper, healthy potentials that can replace them, as we release those potentials within ourselves.

Transpersonal psychology encompasses our social ethos both from its Humanistic and its Psychosynthetic roots, and the two strands are coming together to form the 'fourth force', at last becoming accepted as academically respectable. It is still mistrusted by some whose definition of science remains rigidly positivist, though science itself is coming to realize its reliance on the constructs, definitions and models on which its perceptions of reality are founded. The hermeneutic (interpretative) methods of Psychoanalysis, Analytical psychology and Psychosynthesis are still regarded by many as art rather than science, and strictly speaking, the following paragraphs would be classified as outside the *scientific* discipline of psychology.

For this reason, Assagioli kept his own writings on spirituality separate from his papers on Psychosynthesis, but human beings are not so easily compartmentalized, and he and other Transpersonal psychologists found that, in practice, no such division appeared. When we examine and interpret the culturally held images of art, religion and state, and perceive their influence on the psychological processes of individuals, these distinctions indeed seem counterproductive, and we will now briefly trace the 'unscientific' element that provides such a rich source of experience, understanding and collective cohesion in the sharing of commonly known imagery.

Archaic metaphor

Archaic metaphor has been part of human story-telling and religious imagery as far back as we can trace our history; certainly it is evident in the oral traditions passed on to us from pre-literate eras. It appears to be based on associations and images of familiar objects and events that were a part of our evolving mental processes down the ages, and is manifest in the metaphor of our myths, literature and language. The *metaphoric* images we perceive when our normal verbal skills are disrupted or withheld, or that arise spontaneously as we try to describe the nature of some object or event, are an alternative way of expressing our *literal* meaning.

Our conversation is interwoven with unnoticed, commonly adopted metaphoric phrases such as 'delivering the goods', 'the rat race', 'walking on air', 'dipping in a toe', 'sowing a seed', 'spreading our wings' and many more. Likewise, we use qualitative symbols such as 'a tower of strength', 'a bulldozer', 'a leading light' or 'a slowcoach' to describe the predominant personal qualities of people with whom we are acquainted.

If we are still mystified by 'the meaning' of symbols, dream images, allegories and religious and artistic metaphor, the key to understanding them is to ask ourselves what qualities and tendencies they represent. Sometimes these qualities are being lived out, perhaps partially, but more often they are latent in us. They include qualities that will *help* us express the best within us, and those that, unless we consciously monitor them, will *hamper* us or lead us astray.

Like popular drama, dreams often exaggerate these qualities, and we need not be too alarmed or unduly exalted by their vivid portrayals. Even the very worst 'villain' or 'monster' has its underlying origin in an urge that has a natural, good potential that we can find and take into conscious direction. 'Having tea with the queen' is a clear approach to, and imbibing of, qualities residing in the 'palace' of our superconscious. (A queen is one of the archetypes that contain some of our self's ideal qualities.)

Figure 13.1 *Archaic metaphor. The Mundane Tree of Life (Yggdrasill) portrays qualities of our earthly existence – rocky parts, refreshing waterways and a connection from our conscious concept of life to our unconscious sources of replenishment*

When we embark on dream interpretation (as with any programme of Transpersonal meditative exercises using imagery), it is important to remember to maintain our overall balance of interest and activity. We need a well-practised, efficient method of restoring our outward focus, especially if we are fairly introverted by nature. Like watching too much television, it would be easy for our interest to become addictively time-consuming, and we need to be reasonably disciplined in our approach, and to find the level and frequency that is most productive for us in our own daily living. For some of us, an interpretive approach or Transpersonal exercise may be occasional, whilst for others it may be a frequent, routine practice.

Religious imagery may or may not be important to us, but it has been revered because of its potency in representing different parts of our nature, our highest aspirations and perceptions of spiritual and cosmological reality. Although there are some common archetypal images that are important across several different religions, for example candle flames and flowers, there are also symbols, such as the Sikh turban, that have become important only to particular groups. Each religion, arising from its particular cultural history and perceptions, places varying emphases on different facets of our human nature and cosmological origin, and it would be misleading to regard them as approximately similar in inspiration and effect.

However, we can take a Transpersonal perspective and, mindful that we do so from our own culturally shaped concepts and viewpoint, consider the insights about human qualities and potential, and our place in our world and cosmos, that each faith's religious imagery and teaching portrays and encourages. It is only at this deeper level of understanding that antagonistic elements of faith may find a common unity of perception, and therefore a common practical way of living in harmony with one another.

Even the thorny question of belief in God can be resolved by the perception that His reality is way beyond our human cognitive powers of comprehension, whether or not we believe in His existence, and that it is an archetypal *image* of Him mediated through our higher self that is the basis of our human named concept, experience and faith. Where *ultimate* reality of life's 'goodness', or 'God', is concerned, believers and unbelievers are on common, unknown ground, though this does not negate the real functions of a 'vital faith', as advocated by Erik Erikson. Whatever our particular belief, we are all partakers of reality, and benefit from having some working understanding thereof.

Interpretive example: nativity of Christ

The interpretative approach has often been regarded as an attempt to 'explain away' religious values, but can equally be regarded as a confirmation of their spiritual truths, whatever view concerning historical and literal truths we may hold. For example, the traditions surrounding the nativity of Christ provide a constellation of images that portray Transpersonal truths and, in so doing, create a cohesive collective focus for those who share them. We will examine this example in more detail.

An angel represents inspiration from our most revered source, and annunciation is the dawning of a period of preparation and growth towards some forthcoming realization. The 'felt-sense' concept of Christ arises from within our self, and does not depend on the fertilization of another person's equal input. Virginity expresses our pure, natural urges before they become distorted by too much or too little, or become set in a blunted and blinding disregard of others.

Motherhood of a first-born son expresses the most wondrous, joyful, tenderness and caring compassion that our human nature is capable of, and protective, caring fatherhood, beyond a biological gene-investment, reminds us of these tender, generative qualities latent in ourselves, especially if we do not have children of our own to draw them forth in us. Parenthood of our own inner child, and of the child in others, often requires this kind of caring, sensitive parenting.

The child himself has all the qualities of our human potential, all that we might become. In this well-known tableau, he is also recognized as Christ, a part of the Trinity of God, and he therefore evokes a powerful archetypal image of our own higher self with our penthouse view of the heavens. Because he is born in a crudely adequate stable and cradled in a very earthly manger, we are shown the crudities and mundane earthly facets of our own nature, nevertheless capable of holding our higher self.

The shepherds usually mind sheep, and our sheep-like tendencies do need constant minding, but the shepherds have had announced to them a very special birth that will bring joy, peace and goodwill to all people. This news is brought to them by the emissaries of the greatest goodness we can name, but only dimly begin to conceptualize.

Rising to consciousness

Thus is portrayed a rising to our consciousness of the full potential qualities that our human personhood and our earthly relationships might come to embody. As shepherds, we hurry off in search of the baby, carrying our offering of a lamb. The archetypal lamb has the qualities of valued tenderness, and of innocence that may be sacrificed in the mistakes and disillusion of finding out. To act effectively in our world, or to pursue our own spiritual growth, we cannot remain blissfully ignorant of the excesses, deficiencies and distortions, both inside and outside ourselves, that require the changes of redemption and restoration to their proper function.

The star leads the kings on a long and arduous journey, and they run into the danger of asking for direction from an egocentric, hedonistic monarch who rules over many subjects, some of whose children he cruelly has murdered by his soldiers, later in the narrative. The wise man at court knows where the baby may be found, and the kings themselves are often portrayed as wise men, here representing our own wise qualities. The star, like the mandala, is an archetypal image of the full potential, or the wholeness of our personhood, a valuable guide through our life's journey. As wise men, we follow our star and realize that it comes to rest over the place where we find the young child.

The kings portray sovereignty of choice and are rulers of resources and human energies according to their own priorities. Our egocentric priorities sometimes regard spiritual pursuits as a threat, and will then direct energies self-destructively. Though gospel accounts vary here, the baby only returned to his own country when Herod's rule was at an end. The star-led kings offer homage and gifts, which embody the qualities of the respect and resources given to ensure the baby's provision.

The ox is a frequently appearing archetypal image portraying the qualities of our strong animal nature, our warmth and creativity, while the ass image labours and plods, and is sometimes stubborn or stupid. A dove is often included in nativity scenes, and sometimes angels, evoking our sense of spiritual holiness and peace.

Modern additions

In modern times, a variety of animals has appeared around the manger, and these can be understood in the same way as commonly occurring dream images. In dreams and often in allegorical art forms, each animal represents both its level of evolved nature and our associations with it. (Thus monkeys portray our impulsive cleverness, and pigs, our ignorance and sometimes our greed, though we now know the pig to be intelligent and no more greedy than other animals. Birds are our spirit or our intellect, fish inhabit our unconscious and our depths of spirit, while reptiles crawl on earth and represent our evolutionarily archaic, basic, instinctive nature.) Shy animals are usually those portrayed around the manger, but we will end this focus on the Christmas nativity with a story of its enactment by a class in a Dorset infants' school.

> The teacher had involved the children in the choice of animals and the allocation of parts, and one little boy, because he was the smallest, had agreed to become the hind legs of a crocodile, with a suitably long tail. (We can easily recognize feeling like the back, or the front, end of this amphibious reptile on occasion!) His mother, on being informed of his role, expressed disbelief, wondering if there had arisen some confusion with the story of Noah's ark. Her son made the illuminating reply, 'But, Mummy! Didn't you know that *all* the animals come to the manger?'

Examples in other religions

Examples drawn from other religions have similar archaic metaphoric content: the archangel Gabriel (creative inspiration) appeared to Muhammad in a cave (the unconscious); Siddartha Gautama, the Buddha, received his enlightenment sitting under a 'bodhi' tree (tree of life, and for Buddhists, of enlightenment), having finally exhausted all other methods of discovering eternal reality.

Although there are still many working within the separate disciplines and fields of religion and psychology, who regard each other's approach as incompatible if not mistaken, Transpersonal psychologists have no such problem, and continue to gather their evidence of therapeutic and educational benefit from a combination of the different models of understanding. Most recently, John Rowan has made outstanding and lucid contributions in this integrative approach (Rowan, 1993).

Specialization

Critical debate will no doubt continue, but it is useful to remember that, as individuals, we do not have to be tied down to any one approach, although specialists in a particular field often gain a clearer focus on detail by confining their perceptual processes within the framework of a particular discipline. Specialization is very different from earnestly persuading others to adopt a particular approach exclusively, which endeavour frequently arises from a sense of personal vulnerability.

The discipline of psychology now has a greater span than ever, contributing to the array of disciplines by means of which we try to describe and study the various aspects of our individual lives, our social and cultural patterns, our productive and industrial activities, and our immediate and global environment. We are in a better position than ever before to take a truly integrative approach to our own lives, and to our involvement in each others' lives.

Each branch of psychology has its appropriate application, and a selection has been made in these chapters according to a lifespan perspective. Other approaches have been added eclectically, because they enable a more integrative understanding, and because they have been found effective and useful enough to have been adopted in a variety of training courses and therapeutic situations. An earnest attempt has also been made to illustrate by example how some of these theoretical models may be applied in our understanding, or made use of at a practical, personal level.

As has been demonstrated in the brief biographical backgrounds of the theorists whose insights are included in this book, our beliefs, and the perceptions to which we may be open, are heavily influenced by our cultural background, upbringing and education as well as by our inherited tendencies. We each have a different way of thinking imaginatively and of processing information. We have each of us developed preferred focuses for our attention, and a unique perspective.

Choice is ours   As individuals, and in our communities and our world, we therefore benefit from a wide variety of approaches and skills and different fields of activity, some involving conservation, preservation and ordering, others associated with change, exploration and new evolution. In practice, we usually develop within a particular field the skills that arise from our own aptitudes. Sometimes, what may seem to some of us a narrow focus, can be highly productive in its concentration on the nitty-gritty details thus worked upon, while the more globally minded of us contribute to an understanding regard for differences, and to individual and collective cohesion and long-sightedness.

Between these contrasting approaches, each of us needs to discover our own natural propensities and which mixture, of many different possible 'recipes' for understanding, is the most integrative and nurturing for us. We can then choose accordingly, while not losing sight of those alternatives that would help us on occasion. The proof of the pudding is in the eating, and the crucial test for any theory or creed is how it may be lived, and what kind of development may result from it. As our self-awareness and our critical skills increase, we can select more confidently, from the mass of material available, the insights, truths and guidelines that assist us practically in our own lives and work, and in our concerned involvement with each other, our wider community and our world. These chapters have been offered as an invitation to such a lifespan journey.

EPILOGUE

A poem that explains a lifespan journey

The Gates of Heaven

I lay inside my cot,
My bedroom door ajar,
My mother came, I smiled at her,
For she was love.

I waited near the fire,
The door was opened soon,
My father came and read to me,
For he was love.

I played beneath a tree,
And through the garden gate,
My sister came and played with me,
For she was love.

I wandered near the byre,
And from the farmhouse door,
My aunt called out, 'It's time for tea!'
For she was love.

And then I went to school,
The big gates opened wide,
A teacher came and taught us all,
For she was love.

And many friends were made,
Through different doors they came,
Sorrows and joys they shared with me,
For they were love.

So I grew,
Out into the world I went,
A woman now,
The door was to my heart.

One day I heard a knock
That I had waited for,
'May I come in?' my husband said,
For he was love.

Our son was next to knock,
His brother followed soon,
'May we come in?' We welcomed them,
For they were love.

To join our family
A friend and sister came,
She knocked and entered, comfort gave,
For she was love.

Throughout the growing years
The door was never shut,
Sunshine came, and shadows chill,
And there was love.

The family grown, another knock,
The world was at my door,
I opened it, they all came in,
For they were love.

And then I heard the universe
Come knocking at my door,
Life? Intelligence? Come in!
It only can be love.

Then saw I time's dimensions melt,
And with them went my door,
Love free creation's love to know,
My heart was full at last.

And deep within me lies
The need to knock on doors,
That I may come in and share my heart,
For it is love.

APPENDIX I
Historical background and modern psychology

This brief historical background and outline of modern psychology indicates the many origins of our ideas about ourselves and others. It will set the scene if you intend more intensive study, but if the subject is new to you, it may be wise to use supplementary texts alongside it. Please note that A-level students upwards may need more specific references (see *Texts) than are included here, but the outlined perspective can be useful.

HISTORICAL BACKGROUND

Attempts at understanding human nature stretch back into prehistoric ages, and modern approaches in psychology have a long and diverse ancestry. Other disciplines have provided evidence of both differences and continuities in our understanding over time, and we can draw on their findings, as well, with benefit.

Archaeologists have interpreted artefacts and pictorial representations, such as clay figures and cave paintings, and have uncovered evidence ranging from domestic details to burial customs. They give us some idea of the beliefs that both grew from and guided human experience during the many centuries before early writing preserved more precise information about human values, thought and behaviour, and chronicled historical events. **Historians** have studied written records from these earlier ages through to modern times, giving us their interpretation of human motivation and progress and the events that have formed the circumstances of individual experience. We can also study their **primary sources** for ourselves.

Anthropologists, studying mankind from past records and from their own careful observations, help us to trace the development of our personal and social understanding, and our attitudes to our environment. Early ideas that each object, such as a spear or the forest, had its own spirit that required cajoling or placating (known as animism) can still be found in people only recently brought into contact with modern civilizations.

Folklore and ancient customs world-wide also display animistic elements in ritual offerings or actions, while children enjoy anthropomorphic (giving human form) stories and songs depicting, for example, railway engines with faces and personalities, or a sun who puts on his hat to come out and play.

Even closer to home, which of us has not addressed verbally some mechanical object that has 'let us down' or some personal item that is 'hiding' from us? Anthropologists have shown us that it is a long-standing human tendency to relate very personally to our environment as well as to each other.

Philosophers, lovers of wisdom, have shaped our ideas about ourselves and our world with their reasoning and development of earlier ideas. **Philosophy** is the root of all our sciences, and different branches of it inform, with their own kind of knowledge, our modern understanding. From the three medieval branches – natural, moral, metaphysical – we derive **physics, astronomy, chemistry, geography, biology, ethics, sociology** and **psychology**.

Metaphysics includes **theology** and completes the circle, joining psychological self-awareness with questions concerning our being and the ultimate nature of universal being, with the explorations and hypotheses concerning time, space, energy and matter on the frontiers of physics.

Every one of these disciplines enlightens some aspect of our thinking and is relevant to some part of our lives and our environment. However, with only one lifespan, it is evident that, as individuals, we must make do for most of the time with a simplified package of basic general knowledge to shape our beliefs, our values and our behaviour. At best, we may acquire a fuller wisdom in a limited number of disciplines.

Down the ages, **myths**, **religions** and **the arts** have conveyed inspirations and ideas, current in their time, indeed often preparing for or warning of impending events. Image and narrative have portrayed instinctive and inspired perceptions that strike a chord of recognition as some vital human or environmental truth. For example, stories of an ark surviving a great flood may incorporate, as well as an originally **oral historic account,** the instinctive, inspired picture-story of an early seer, portraying in the male and female pairs what we now perceive as the chromasomal inheritance of genetic material at our conception.

Science can now describe in detail, especially in psychology, processes that have previously been felt and expressed in **religious teachings** or **the metaphors of the arts.** However, many of the essential mysteries of metaphysics still require for their expression, especially within the prescriptive frameworks of the differing religions, the new insights of artists and mystics to translate essential truths into the living language, imagery and theology of the present. Both understanding, and the limitations to understanding imposed by fixed conventions, have been handed on to us to become our guiding values, our shared common-sense assumptions and our corporate confusions.

This brief introduction to how we have acquired ideas about ourselves, through thought and inspiration, must leave a great deal to further reading, but a few of the very major influences on Western thinking need a mention. The ideas of Plato and Aristotle (4th century BC), St Augustine of Hippo (354–430 AD) and of St Thomas Aquinas (1225–1274 AD) laid foundations on which was built the rationality of René Descartes (1596–1650) and John Locke (1632–1704). Their examination of 'evidence' ushered in **modern scientific principles**, with the demand that understanding should be based on information acquired only through the senses.

Locke also affirmed that we are born as a 'tabula rasa' (Aristotle's concept of a clean slate), on which our experience writes our understanding and makes us what we are. Jean Jacques Rousseau (1712–1778), on the other hand, argued that man is a 'noble savage' with an innate moral sense, and his **Idealism** inspired the American Constitution. To these last two philosophers are attributed the principles behind the modern **nature–nurture debate** (see below and chapter 1).

The development of **Eastern understanding** has followed a different pathway, though several attempts have been made to infuse some of its wisdom into Western thinking. With less emphasis on scientific sequence and a greater awareness of 'alwaysness', reflected in their language structures, and with their greater acceptance of the balance of opposites, Eastern thinkers have much to offer us. The main chapters in this book highlight the necessity of this balance, and the sensitive range of appropriateness it permits, in the context of **Western psychology**.

With the expansion of **scientific methods of investigation** in the Europe of the seventeenth and eighteenth centuries, a body of clearly observable, testable, concrete facts came to form the body of knowledge that, by the nineteenth century, was regarded by many as the only sound foundation of understanding. Auguste Comte (1798–1857) expounded this philosophy, known as **Positivism**, and in his writings (1830–1842) founded a new science of society, **Sociology**. Sociologists have analysed the complexities of our social structures, some of them according to Positivist principles and methods, but others using intuitive reasoning in a search for social meaning based on our experience. This latter approach is known as **Phenomenalism** and, along with religion, has been heavily criticized as 'unscientific and therefore unsound'. Arguments still abound concerning **validity** (whether a word or description defines its object beyond any doubt) and **reliability** (whether a fact can be demonstrated repeatedly), and have influenced the development of both sociology and psychology. There are many who perceive the value of both Positivism and Phenomenalism (including religion) and who are called **Interactionist** in their approach (see below).

Evolutionist Charles Darwin, in his *Origin of the Species* (1859), notably advanced the debate about our biological humanity and evolved human characteristics. More recently, Richard Dawkins, in his *Blind Watchmaker* (1986), has expanded Darwin's theory of **natural selection** in a positivist manner. Geneticists, building on the work of Gregor Mendel (1822–1884), have informed us further about our inherited features and tendencies, contributing to the nature–nurture debate as we try to fathom the causes of our behaviour and our patterns of thinking.

Ethologists, who study the behaviour of animals, have also shed light on the origin and evolution of our human instincts and behavioural characteristics. Konrad Lorenz, best known for his studies of bonded following behaviour in greylag geese (1930s), and Jane Goodall, who has spent many years filming wild chimpanzees (1970s, 1980s), are two prominent ethologists who have added to our understanding of relationship formation.

Scientist and explorer Francis Galton (1822–1911), a cousin of Charles Darwin (1809–1882), had a great interest in heredity. He developed a **method of measuring** individual traits (characteristics) and also devised a **statistical method of correlation**, by which it is possible to calculate the likelihood (positive correlation) or the unlikelihood (negative correlation) of two traits or events occurring together. This gave a great boost to the scientific respectability of the study of traits, which enabled us to examine critically our understanding of types based on physique. This had begun with the classic sanguine, phlegmatic, choleric and melancholic 'humours' of Hippocrates (4th century BC), and though often inaccurate and unreliable, persisted in our common assumptions made about one another. Galton's work also paved the way for intelligence quotience (IQ) tests, first developed in Paris by Simon and Binet (1905).

More recently, Hans Eysenck and Leon Kamin have contributed to the nature–nurture debate about intelligence (1981), discussing statistical methodology in great detail in their argument. Those who take the middle view in the nature–nurture debate are also known as **Interactionist** (see above). **Nativist–Empiricist** is the more formal name of the nature–nurture argument, but there is a substantial body of Interactionist opinion, believing that we are a complex mixture of what we are born with and what we become through our experience.

During the nineteenth century, discussion that focused on human nature and our behaviour was to be found in the disciplines of **philosophy** and **sociology**. Our pathologies, physical and mental, were studied by **medicine** and **psychiatry**. **Religion** and **the arts** commented on our souls as well as our conditions, and the foundations were there for a new science to emerge, with something to tell us about individuality (known as the **idiographic** approach) and about our common processes of development (**nomothetic** approach).

MODERN PSYCHOLOGY

The word 'psychology' is derived from the Greek 'psyche', which meant, in the 5th century BC, 'the centre of human experience'. This is often translated as 'soul', but with the emphasis on scientific method, it is small wonder that it was in the Leipzig laboratory of Wilhelm Wundt that the modern discipline of psychology recognizes its beginning in 1879.

Wundt was investigating perception, trying to establish the sensory elements, such as 'blueness', 'squareness' or 'softness', from which are constructed our concepts of different objects. Titchener, his student, moved to the United States, where he and his group became known as **Structuralists**.

In the 1890s, the **Reductionist** focus (concerned with basic elements) of the Stucturalists was in contrast to that of a group led by William James, who were known as **Functionalists**. James, who was an artist, doctor, philosopher and Harvard University lecturer, observed and described the 'stream of consciousness', being more interested in the flow and function of thinking than in the separate elements of which it may consist. Both Structuralists and Functionalists used the **introspection** of their subjects to provide their data, and this method was outlawed by John Watson as unscientific.

By 1914, Watson, perhaps best known for **classically conditioning** a fear of white furry animals in an orphanage child, had convinced many that a modern science could only accept observable behaviour as a valid object for study. He and his adherents were therefore known as **Behaviourists**, and succeeded in dominating the new discipline of psychology, though he himself left it quite soon to make a great deal of money in advertising. In the 1930s, Burrhus F. Skinner, with his work on **Operant Conditioning**, ensured that Behaviourism retained a central position well into the 1960s, though other branches of psychology continued to develop.

Meanwhile, in Europe, another approach was gaining ground. Sigmund Freud (1856–1939) had extended his earlier work in neurology and nervous disorders to an investigation of the unconscious mind. During the 1890s, he was using **hypnosis**, but later obtained the data for his theory from his clinical methods of **free association** (wherein the patient on the couch says whatever comes into his or her mind) and **dream interpretation**. **Psychoanalysis**, as Freud called it, quickly gained an international following, his methods becoming especially popular in America for the treatment of a range of disorders and conflicts.

Theoretically, Psychoanalysis has always been under attack for its lack of scientific testability. Though its concepts aid discussion, they are not directly observable, and at best can only be inferred. Nevertheless, Psychoanalysis has survived as a major psychological approach and method of clinical treatment, and has given rise to a variety of therapeutic developments.

The **Humanistic** approach, or 'third force' in psychology, arose in the USA as an alternative to the 'determined by conditioning' nature of Behaviourism and the 'determined by biology and early emotional experience' beliefs of Psychoanalysis. This third approach was initiated by Abraham Maslow and Carl Rogers, who gave central importance to our free will and motivation to change in the direction of self-realization.

Maslow (1954) postulated a hierarchy of needs, with self-realization as our final goal, while Rogers (1959) emphasized the vital role of our self-image and our 'way of being' with each other. Maslow also helped launch the 'fourth force' **Transpersonal psychology**, in 1969, which came into being in America as the interests of Humanistic psychologists concentrated increasingly on our self-realization needs. Because their focus is our inner experience, Humanistic and Transpersonal psychologists are known as **Phenomenalist** in their approach, the term Phenomenalism also being applied to the experiential aspects of Gestalt psychology (see *Texts). Sensitivity training and encounter groupwork are based on Humanistic theory, while Transpersonal theory provides methods of working directly with our right-hemisphere brain functions of self-realization, using **imagery** and **metaphor**.

Social psychologists provide yet another perspective with their studies of social instincts, relationships and groups. Usually dated from William McDougall's social instinct theory (1908), it includes Freud's analysis of groups and cultures, and many studies of social influence, authority and group behaviour. More recently, the work of Michael Argyle has become prominent, focusing on social encounter and interpersonal communication and relationships (1970s, 1980s).

Cognitive psychology investigates perception, information processing, learning and memory. It has overtaken Behaviourism to become the most dominant approach in the discipline of psychology, as we become increasingly aware of the power of thinking, and develop more and more sophisticated methods of observing our thought processes and brain functions. In America, E. C. Tolman's Behaviourist studies of maze-learning in rats suggested 'cognitive maps' (1932), and his work focused on **Gestalt-influenced** awareness of the environment (see Peres, Hefferline and Goodman, 1973 for Gestalt methods and overview), thus initiating one strand of the Cognitive approach.

In Europe, Jean Piaget's **developmental** stage theory described how, from infancy, we build our cognitive capacity as we interact with, and adapt to, our environment. Working in Switzerland during the 1920s onwards, he contributed both to Cognitive and Developmental theory. Although World War II held up the translation and spread of his ideas, they have generated very influential research into children's reasoning and learning processes, by himself and by others. They have also played a significant role in the debate concerning the relationship between thought and language.

In the 1950s, Herbert Simon (later awarded a Nobel prize) and his colleagues showed how computers may be programmed to simulate thought processes, and this led to the development of 'machines that think', or **artificial intelligence**. Opposition to this idea, that a machine, however complex, could validly be compared with a human brain, has generated debate, and many prefer the term 'computer simulation'. Nevertheless, this area of ingenuity remains part of the Cognitive approach. Cognitive psychologists also work in the field of **neurophysiology**, as they investigate brain processes and contribute to the debate concerning the relationship of mind to brain.

Developmental psychologists focus on unfolding and shaping processes over our lifespan, and incorporate theories from other approaches. Originating in Psychoanalysis, the work of John Bowlby put Developmental psychology onto the rigorously scientific map. The foundations he laid down in the 1940s gained widespread international recognition in 1951, through his work with the World Health Organization. Michael Rutter (1970s, 1980s onwards) has expanded on Bowlbys research, and we owe to both of them much of our basic understanding about the essential qualities of parental care.

Comparative psychologists, who study animal behaviour for the purpose of comparing it with human responses, have contributed strong evidence concerning the detrimental effects on later development of maternal deprivation and environmental stress, though there are many ethical and critical arguments surrounding their work (see *Texts).

The Developmental approach is therefore very eclectic (draws from a wide range of different theories), and stage theories include the major contributions of Piaget, Freud and Erikson. In contrast, Behaviourist conditioning theories (Pavlov and Skinner) and Social Learning Theory (Bandura) are also part of Developmental teaching. The study of play, and its role in emotional, social and cognitive development, is especially prominent (Bruner, Sylva, Jolly) and observations of child-rearing practices, socialization, education and cultural influences (Rutter and many others) also form part of the body of research.

From the 1950s, both Social psychology and Developmental psychology have investigated adult development and ageing, so that we now have a more complete coverage of researched evidence over our whole lifespan (Havighurst, Erikson, Jung). 'Ages and stages' is an over simplistic label that the Developmental approach has been given, since the potential of its focus on changes over time, and on environmental influences is to give us more and better-informed choices. We can benefit from these choices as individuals, parents, educators, employers, administrators and politicians, as we unfold our own future.

Since the 1960s, interest in **Transpersonal psychology**, the 'fourth force', has been increasing. In Europe, Transpersonal theory, originally based on the work of Carl Jung and Roberto Assagioli, is extending its influence, and there is increasing convergence with American Transpersonal psychologists. Our existential dimension of experience is at last being accepted by many as a necessary element of applied psychology, and theory progresses as our insights develop and are confirmed by the results of their application.

Different emphases, contrasting views, debate and research continue, in psychology and well beyond, and never before have we had so much carefully observed and researched detail available to us, whatever the area of our special interest. We need to ensure the development of our own maturity and our critical faculties, by means of a sufficiently wide range of sensitive awarenesses, so that we can assess information and choose wisely, individually for ourselves, in our attitudes and behaviour towards others and in our collective institutions. Our understanding, therefore, continues to be informed both by input from the understanding of others *and* by the shaping process of our own priorities, whatever these may be.

This outline has drawn heavily on L. S. Hearnshaw's *The Shaping of Modern Psychology* (RKP, 1987), which is highly recommended as further reading.

APPENDIX II
Suggested exercises and topics for discussion

EXERCISES

The following exercises have two specific purposes: to aid active learning and to stimulate thinking. They are based on this text, and may be useful for general readers as well as for self or tutor assessment. Where appropriate for their purpose, tutors may wish to advise the use of supplementary texts, with the emphasis on the development of *independent study* skills.

A range of varying difficulty is offered, from which to select, according to purpose and level. Exercises may be used for discussion or group work. (The **Discussion subjects** which follow may also offer a suitable focus.) Written answers may be at an optional, tutor-specified length and depth, and may therefore vary in form:

- 'boxes' or cards of information (forming the basis of a Reference system)
- lists
- tables, diagrams (replacing/adding to other answers)
- notes
- two or three written paragraphs
- essay.

Self-assessed answers can be checked with the text, but where personally observed examples are involved, discussion with others may help evaluate application of theory. Often, there are no 'right' answers to this part of the exercise, designed to get you thinking for yourself. Note, however, that when asked to give examples, you should always *disguise identities*.

*Appendix I
(you may have read
this first as an
introduction)*

1 Several outstanding historical events have influenced our current understanding. Cite a few of them and comment on their influence.

2 Modern psychology consists of several approaches. Choose two contrasting examples and describe how they appear to differ.

3 Make a time chart (using left-hand margin as time line) and insert major historical events and developments in psychology that have shaped our current understanding.

Prologue

Illustrate two of the different viewpoints portrayed in the parable by describing two people who have radically contrasting viewpoints about some current issue. How might their different experiences have brought this about?

Chapter 1

1 Taking as an example either musical or sporting talent, describe possible hereditary advantages a person may have and the environmental influences that may help or hinder the development of the talent.

2 Describe the main differences between Classical and Operant Conditioning. Find examples of each, and where both appear to be operating together.

3 Find examples of 'reinforcement' in everyday life and give reasons why 'punishment' is so often unreliable as a deterrent.

4 Drawing on your own experience, give examples of 'observational learning' and comment on its usefulness or ill effects.

5 Konrad Lorenz has said that aggression is the root of caring and love. Explain this paradoxical viewpoint, and briefly apply it as an approach to an everyday situation.

6 Give an example of a concern where a single factor appears of crucial importance, and another where several factors, involving different approaches, need to be considered.

7 Find out what you can about Asperger's syndrome. What has a combination of different approaches got to offer sufferers and their families?

Chapter 2

1 Choose two people of contrasting temperament. List as many differences as you can identify and any similarities, drawing especially on labels used in the text.

2 Explain why researchers use twins in their studies of temperament.

3 From your own observations, give two examples of clustered personality 'traits' that are recognizable as 'types' of personality.

4 Find examples from your own observation of the advantageous use of stereotypes, and of where stereotyping has ill effects. How can we become alert to the difference?

5 Outline the general development and function of our nervous system, including brain lateralization and the main branches of nerve networks.

6 Describe the function of our hypothalamus gland and its role in regulating our behaviour.

7 Describe the role of our ANS as a vital link between inspirational experience and practical living. Give examples.

Chapter 3

1 Describe briefly the main features of Freud's three components of personality.

2 Summarize Freud's five psychosexual stages.

3   What do you understand is meant by the term 'unconscious defence mechanism'? Describe two examples.

4   Briefly describe the Oedipus and Elektra conflicts and show how modern views on the nature of libido can be used to construct new, more productive, models.

5   Describe a healthy superego. How can it combine with ego function to form a healthy conscience?

6   What is Freud's explanation of the moral value of obedience? Give an example of authoritarianism based on his model.

7   What does Erikson mean by 'triple bookkeeping'? Illustrate this concept with examples from everyday life.

8   Apply the concept of 'epigenesis' to a child's progress through school and later education.

9   Explain what Erikson has called a 'favourable ratio' of bi-polar qualities. Think of situations where we need a range of responses that span the opposites.

10   Describe Berne's 'Structural Analysis' and give everyday examples of the three ego-states.

11   In what ways does Berne's approach depart from traditional psycho-analytic theory?

12   Find a simple example of either a 'Child' or a 'Parent' script you would like to re-write. What you would like the new script to be? Can you suggest how this might affect the 'Adult's' repertoire of responses?

Chapter 4

1   Using as your example Erikson's first stage, Infancy (Trust v. Mistrust), explain the difference between Freud's 'zones' and Erikson's 'modes'. Why are Freud's stages termed 'psychosexual',and Erikson's 'psycho-social'?

2   What do you understand by the author's term 'felt knowledge'?

3   Explain the difference between empathic giving, and giving arising from guilt or vicarious need.

4   Describe the change from symbiosis to mutual relationship. What are the essential continuities in early infancy?

5   Outline the main features of Erikson's first stage. State one similarity of his view of the ego with that of Freud, and one difference.

6   How do we learn to hope? Give examples of learning to hope in infancy, and of ways we might attempt remedial learning later.

7   Outline the nurturing qualities of parents that Erikson states are necessary to establish trust in infancy.

8   How does Erikson say that the social institution of religion may best serve individuals, and what are the varying results of the limitations he observes often to be present?

9 How does Erikson suggest that the foundation of our moral sense is laid down?

10 What is the difference between re-parenting and self-parenting? Suggest how these processes might be activated.

11 Outline Bowlby's four phases of attachment. How does a child grow towards independence during the final phase?

12 Describe the Robertsons' Distress Syndrome. What actions are recommended to alleviate distress during maternal separation?

13 How does Rutter describe the essential qualities of parenting and substitute care? In what ways is non-intervention costly?

14 Explain how Rutter has reassessed 'maternal deprivation'.

Chapter 5

1 Outline Erikson's second stage of psychosocial development, briefly including reference to Freud's second psychosexual stage.

2 What kind of 'felt knowledge' do we acquire during the stage Erikson calls Early Childhood?

3 Describe different kinds of saying 'no'. How can we learn to understand and use them appropriately? How is this related to saying 'yes'?

4 How do we learn to choose? Give examples of remedial principles for later learning.

5 What parental nurturing qualities are needed during Erikson's second stage?

6 Summarize the section under the sub-heading 'Boundaries and Limitations'.

7 How might unconscious negativity (see example of what psychoanalysts call a fixated 'hate' of parents) affect our adult autonomy and progress towards fulfilment?

8 Outline Erikson's third stage of psychosocial development, briefly including reference to Freud's third psychosexual stage.

9 Describe a healthy sense of responsibility. Why is feeling forgiven a release from guilt, and a precursor to forgiving others?

10 Why is experience of 'felt good' the foundation of our moral measuring sense?

11 Explain how myths, stories and drama help our Play Age development and continue to enrich us throughout our lives.

12 Why is professional help needed for some remedial processes?

13 How do the creative arts serve individuals and what is their social role?

Chapter 6

1 Explain Erikson's approach to play therapy.

2 Describe the role of adult models during Erikson's third stage.

3   How do we acquire our attitudes to competing, co-operation, sharing and joining in? What influences on child and carers do social expectations have, and how can we learn to handle them?

4   Why is play of such importance in our childhood? How can its benefits be continued into adulthood?

5   Explain Piaget's basic processes of 'adaptation to our environment'. What are 'action schemas'?

6   Outline Piaget's four stages of cognitive development.

7   Explain what is meant by 'pre-verbal concepts', and 'symbolic representation'.

8   Outline Piaget's stages of play. What is the particular value of each stage, and how does imaginative play extend our cognitive development in later years?

9   Outline Piaget's stages of moral development. What is the difference between moral realism and moral relativism? How does formal operational thinking assist the carrying out of moral principles?

10 Outline Kohlberg's levels and stages of moral development. What is the difference between a rule and a principle? Give examples.

11 How might we encourage movement of *behaviour* from Kohlberg's Pre-Conventional to Conventional stages, and from these towards Post-Conventional stages? Use examples of people operating at these different stages to illustrate your answer.

Chapter 7

1   Describe the major change towards focus outside the home that marks the beginning of Erikson's fourth stage. Include cross-cultural examples.

2   Outline Erikson's fourth psychosocial stage of development, briefly including reference to Freud's fourth psychosexual stage. Mention the resolution of the major conflict that Freud said marks entry into the fourth stage.

3   Erikson says that the pathology of the Schooldays stage is a sense of inertia. Give examples of how this may come about, and of how it may be countered or prevented.

4   What role can teachers play in promoting psychosocial development alongside skill-teaching? Include examples of formal and informal teaching outside school, briefly mentioning parental attitudes.

5   How can teachers try to counter deficient parenting and what support and back-up do they need to do this?

6   What residues from Schooldays might make life difficult for an adult, and what kind of remedial approach might be useful?

7   Compare Freud's maxim of *Lieben und Arbeiten* with Erikson's description of the psychosocial tasks of Adolescence.

8   Explain the moratorium process described by Marcia. Give examples of 'identity achievement' and of 'foreclosure'.

9   Outline the adolescent process of Identity versus Role Confusion, described by Erikson. Give examples of adjustments in later life for which this process may be a useful forerunner.

10   Explain why peer friendships are so important in adolescence.

11   Describe, with examples, the earlier experience and current social factors that are likely to result in amoral or antisocial formation of identity during adolescence. How might this be countered? Why do you consider many delinquent adolescents 'grow out of' delinquency?

12   How do we develop and express our 'ego ideals' and 'ideological world-views' in adolescence?

13   Consider a Behaviourist approach to adolescence. On which factors would they focus, and what processes would they emphasize as responsible for our development at this stage?

Chapter 8

1   Explain some of the differences between Adolescent and Young Adult commitments and affiliations. Give examples.

2   Outline the main features of Erikson's sixth stage, and briefly comment on Freud's *Lieben und Arbeiten* maxim. How useful do you consider Erikson's model of Young Adulthood?

3   According to Erikson, what role does sexual intimacy have in Young Adult partnership?

4   Summarize the main potential and pitfalls of Young Adulthood.

5   What are the differences that mark the change from Young Adulthood into Adulthood.

6   Outline the main features of Erikson's seventh stage of psychosocial development. How has the direction of our libido become more mature?

7   Explain the necessity of 'selection, commitment and feasibility' and how the pathology of 'exclusion' affects us individually and socially.

8   How do we acquire 'bent perception' during adulthood? Give examples.

9   What does the author mean by the 'cutting edge' and how does this differ from Erikson's term 'generational link'?

10   Summarize the commonly experienced pressures of our Adulthood stage and ways in which we can learn to manage them.

11   Describe, with examples, good skills of communicating and negotiating. On what principles are they based and why are they so important?

12   How are we affected by loss? What principles will best bring about recovery?

13   What is meant by 'existential identity' and 'self-discovery'? What events

during Adulthood or earlier are likely to precipitate our interest in them?

Chapter 9

1 Give examples of *external* events that constitute changes or crises in mid-life and outline the major *internal* change described by Jung. What were some of his main theoretical disagreements with Freud?

2 What is meant by Jung's terms 'individuation' and 'archetype'? Explain some of the modern criticisms of his basic thinking.

3 Summarize and comment on the reorganization that mid-life often brings. What are the practical skills we require at this time?

4 Outline the 'general adaptation syndrome', and suggest measures that can help to prevent it or aid recovery. Give examples.

5 Why is it often necessary in mid-life or earlier to give special attention to the development of 'wisdom'? Why do you think that Erikson described this predominant shift as the change into a new stage of psychosocial development?

6 What residues from earlier stages can cause problems or discomfort in mid-life, and might benefit from remedial effort?

Chapter 10

1 Outline the main features of Erikson's eighth stage of psychosocial development. Describe one or two examples of 'wise' elderly people who have successfully balanced 'despair' with their capacity for recovering 'integrity'.

2 Erikson identifies the pathologies of old age as 'disdain' and 'disgust'. Explain how they may have their roots in the failures of earlier stages and what might be done to alleviate them.

3 How does culture shape our expectations and experience of old age?

4 Describe some of the personality 'traits' you consider might form clusters corresponding to Havighurst's personality 'types'. Use examples to illustrate your descriptions.

5 Summarize and compare the theories of ageing known as 'Activity' theory, 'Social Disengagement' theory and 'Social Exchange' theory. How important are individual differences as exemplified by Havighurst?

6 What are the advantages and disadvantages of using 'labels' to categorize people, in old age or at any time?

7 Describe, with examples, the wide variation in patterns of 'retirement'. Include examples of its non-occurrence.

8 How could you advise a busy person nearing a set retirement age in western culture to approach and prepare for the event? What advice would you consider useful for a person for whom retirement is a gradual or optional process?

9 Describe the basic processes of mourning including the nadir of despair

and dismay. Suggest ways in which we may 'go with' the stages and develop a capacity to 'move gently forward', whether we are sufferers or empathetic supporters.

10 What are some of the common problems that may occur, affecting some people more than others? How could you encourage yourself or someone else to develop 'creative space'?

11 Why do some of us experience a loss of faith in bereavement? What might be useful general advice then, or if we are without a faith and feeling a need of reassurance?

Chapter 11

1 Give examples of 'grand-generativity' and of how adaptations can be made as energies and faculties decline.

2 Give examples how the ego qualities of earlier stages can serve us in old age, and how important are both our positive responses and our handling of negative feelings. Briefly explain how Erikson's epigenetic perspective helps us to understand this.

3 Describe the common fears surrounding dying, and how these may be alleviated and allowed for.

4 Describe different ways in which 'a vital faith' can comfort us when we are very old.

5 What are the basic principles of communicating with and caring for us should we suffer brain deterioration and exhibit bizarre or aggressive behaviour?

6 What principles can we hope are central to the care and management of us, should we become senile or mentally ill?

7 How can we best ensure that recreation will remain a restorative process for us in our later years?

8 Summarize Erikson's comparison of individual and societal stages of psychosocial development. What is his Golden Rule?

9 What did Erikson mean by 'generative ethics'?

Chapter 12

1 Outline Argyle's eight roots of social motivation. Make a list of your own if you would like to modify his ideas.

2 Compare Argyle's description of aggression as a 'social motivation' with the different views on aggression described in chapter 1.

3 Give examples of commonly observable aggressive behaviour and suggest what measures we, as individuals and as a society, may take to bring about change. Base your suggestions on theories you have studied. What does Argyle recommend?

4 Give examples of non-verbal communication. Why are these skills so important to us?

5 Briefly outline the development of prominent theories of emotion, and

explain how Frijda's theory carries us forward, outlining his description of our emotions.

6   How may Frijda's description of our 'action readiness' enable us to make regulatory changes more easily. What part is played in this process by 'cognitive appraisal'?

7   Outline Kelly's Personal Construct Theory. Give examples of single adjectives or phrases that might constitute 'constructs'.

8   Write a 'self-characterization' in the third person, such as Kelly might have used. What have you learnt from doing this?

9   Choose eight people from different areas of your life as 'elements', and represent them by the letters A to H. Following the instructions near the end of chapter 12, take these groups of three 'elements' and write down the 'constructs' that come to mind as you compare them: ABC, DEF, GHA, ADG, BEH, CFA, ABE, DEH, GHB, AEH, BFG, CDG. (This is only a sample of your range of constructs, but you may learn something about yourself if you take other samples from time to time.)

Chapter 13

1   Why is the Humanistic approach in psychology called the 'third force', and what are its central principles?

2   Describe the three qualities identified by Rogers that have been recognized as essential to good therapeutic practice.

3   In his focus on our self-image, what did Rogers mean by two kinds of 'incongruence'? Describe each, and outline the characteristics that distinguish a congruent person.

4   What did Rogers advocate as guiding principles for partnerships and relationships generally?

5   Outline Maslow's hierarchy of needs, distinguishing between deficiency and growth needs. What do you understand is meant by the term 'self-actualization'?

6   What qualities did Maslow describe as characteristic of a self-actualized person? What kind of behaviour did he believe leads us in this direction?

7   What are the roots of the 'fourth force', Transpersonal psychology? Why did Maslow believe it was necessary to expand our consciousness as well as to progress through deficiency and growth needs?

8   Briefly outline, in words, Assagioli's model of a person. Then, using dotted lines to indicate non-solidity, draw an upright egg shape (this line represents our contact with the collective unconscious). At the top inside edge of the egg shape, draw a very small circle (the higher self, later called the Transpersonal self). Horizontally, across the egg, dividing it approximately into three parts, draw two dotted lines (the top section, in which is the higher self, is the superconscious). In the centre of the middle section, draw another very small circle (the 'I', or personal self), and round it, still inside the middle section, a larger dotted circle

(field of consciousness), leaving the remaining space of the middle section (middle unconscious). The lower section remains (lower unconscious). Draw a dotted line between the transpersonal self and the 'I' (our potential for self-realization). Label your drawing. Compare this egg-shaped model with the author's metaphor of the penthouse.

9 Describe the aims and some of the methods used in Transpersonal psychotherapy. What is the difference between 'breaking down' and 'breaking through'?

10 Explain why grounding, identifying and tuning are necessary if we are attempting to expand our consciousness and increase our self-awareness and personal growth.

11 Describe the origin, value and potential of 'archaic metaphor', giving examples. Consider the impact of some of today's metaphoric images (e.g. Power Rangers and other 'heroes' on Children's TV and films, 'green' ethics, a revived and growing tendency of gardeners to put 'running water' into their gardens).

12 Make a list of images and the qualities you associate with them. Which ones might make you feel better in some way?

13 Choose three of the major theorists whose biographical outline has been given, and show where the theory of each has been shaped by his experience.

14 Review a period of development, either your own or someone you know well, and describe it according to Erikson's theory, and according to the theory of one other psychologist of your choice.

15 Make a collection from the text of the most useful ideas, phrases, perspectives you can find for your own use.

DISCUSSION SUGGESTIONS

These notes are intended for *self-, group- or tutor-guided study*, not as guidelines to encounter or problem-sharing groups. (It is important that skilled advice is available at least to start such a group.)

Discussion can greatly increase enjoyment and comprehension of any subject matter. It also consolidates learning and gives us the benefit of one another's different viewpoint and emphasis. Where discussion is not an option, consideration of what we have read will both increase our understanding and broaden our perspective. Depending on our purpose, appropriate focusing on question or example will structure our discussion or consideration and help us to organize our thinking, our memory storage and the expression of our own ideas. This is especially true when undergoing, or preparing for, training. Suggestions offered can be adapted for specific purposes, for example note-taking during discussion; summarizing afterwards can further improve our recording skills.

Check your findings in the chapters or **Texts** where appropriate. Often there are no 'right' answers, just increased insights. A suggested opening discussion for the first meeting (when preparatory reading may have been patchy) is:

What is intuition? How do you think it arises?

(See page 171 for some ideas on this.)

It is usually the case that practical examples provide the most relevant material for discussions based on a book of this kind. As participants, we may wish to cite our personal experience, if we can do so suitably for the purposes of discussion.

However, possible emotional arousal can cloud clear thinking, so it may be easier to draw examples from our observations of others, bearing in mind that we rarely have full information. We need to avoid making judgemental statements and seek first to *understand*, (a precursor often overlooked when adopting an attitude, recommending or taking action).

Confidentiality is therefore of paramount importance both for personal information and for observed material. This understanding needs to be explicitly established before discussion begins. It helps if conventional research custom is used by the inclusion of deliberately false items of information, so that possible identification is avoided. Inevitably, some confidences will occur and some identifications will slip in, especially of relatives. However, a serious undertaking of the responsibilities of confidentiality needs to precede this kind of person-centred discussion.

Chapter 1

1 Think of examples of behaviour that illustrate the influence of a) heredity and b) environment. Consider briefly what kind of environmental changes might be encouraging (or remedial).

2 Consider examples of behaviour a) where SLT can explain it well; b) where SLT is unsatisfactory as an explanation.

3 Think of an example of observed aggression. How might it be explained by different approaches in psychology?

Chapter 2

1 Consider contrasting examples of temperament. What influence might you attribute to a) sensitivy thresholds and b) other factors?

2 List enjoyable activities that can restore our ANS during stressful periods.

Chapter 3

1 Consider examples of primary and secondary thinking. Where might ideals fit in?

2 Consider examples of Parent, Adult, Child transactions. Taking one example, how might you want to rewrite the script?

Chapter 4

1 List behaviours in later life that indicate residues from infancy. How might trust be relearned?

2 Consider re-parenting. From what sources might 'good-enough' parent-references be derived?

3   What are the advantages of appointing a 'special' carer for a child or sick person? Contrast these advantages with the disadvantages of not doing so. How might the caring load best be shared as necessary?

4   On the basis of Rutter's 'essential qualities', suggest how adult relationships of different kinds may mitigate the ill-effects of earlier deprivation and produce growth.

Chapter 5

1   Consider some of your earliest remembered examples of choosing. What decided your choice? How did you feel afterwards?

2   List examples of planning and carrying out some activity in childhood. How responsible did you feel for the result? Did you feel a sense of achievement if it went well, or guilt if your plans misfired?

3   Consider the advantages of fostering co-operation. How can this best be achieved with a) children and b) adults? How can you best envisage the other's point of view?

4   How might a) role-play or b) watching drama help our education and our relationships? How important is it to develop our imagination?

Chapter 6

1   List examples of play in which you gained some kind of information or understanding. (Include unintended outcomes!)

2   Consider examples of moral judgements made at Kohlberg's Conventional level. In what ways are Post-Conventional levels more productive, and how might this advancement of level be encouraged?

Chapter 7

1   List skills that you learnt as a child that a) you were obliged to learn and b) you wanted to learn. What were you good at? What were you not very good at? How did you feel about these different skills or deficiencies?

2   In what ways are peers especially important during adolescence?

Chapter 8

1   How important is privacy during young adulthood? Consider examples of how it may be negotiated.

2   On the basis that residual deficiencies from earlier stages may be responsible for 'too much' or 'too little' generativity and an 'unfavourable ratio' between generativity and stagnation during full adulthood, find at least one example and consider how adjustments might be made.

Chapter 9

1   From your own observations or experience, how far do you consider that Jung's view of middle-age change is generally accurate?

2   List a few examples of adult stressors and suggest possible strategies and ways of stress management for each.

3   Consider examples of major change that are a) welcome and b) unwelcome from your experience or observation, and trace the adaptation process involved.

Chapter 10

1   List changes often associated with retirement. What preparations can be useful?

2   Trace the process of recovery in two or three examples of bereavement that you have observed. What do you consider most helped each of the people concerned?

3   Do you consider that social attitudes to bereavement are changing? What further changes would you like to see?

Chapter 11

1   What do you consider to be the most commonly found attitudes towards dying? How would you account for the peace that many people experience surrounding their own or another's death?

2   Find examples of people whom you consider have 'grown old gracefully.' How have they accomplished this?

3   What do you consider to be the components of an art-science approach to human understanding?

4   Looking back over the lifespan cycle, how far do you think that the development of a culture parallels the development of its member individuals? Find cross-cultural examples from your experience or learning.

Chapter 12

1   Find examples of social interaction, and describe the motivations of the participants according to Argyle's eight 'roots'? Do the categories roughly correspond with your own observations?

2   List ways in which communications are made non-verbally. How far is this conscious and intended?

3   Consider a few 'action readinesses' you might like either to encourage or to change. Using Frijda's model, how might you attempt this?

4   Basing this exercise on Kelly's Personal Construct method, either a) write a self-characterization in the third person, or b) choose four male and four female fairy-tale characters as 'elements', and using the method described towards the end of chapter 12, take twelve different combinations of three elements, and describe similarites and contrasts using bi-polar 'constructs'. Do you think you might have used different constructs on another occasion? (See exercise 12: 9.)

Chapter 13

1   How might a person's self-image differ from their ideal self, or from their social image? How would these 'incongruencies' produce the characteristic qualities given in chapter 13?

2   How would the three essential qualities described by Rogers – genuineness, empathy and unconditional positive regard – assist changes in another person's self-image? (Think of people known to you who have these qualities in some measure, and of their effect on others.)

3   Find examples of individuals and social groups whom you might describe as having need priorities according to Maslow's hierarchy. How far do you consider that there are individual and social parallels?

4   Make a list of images and the qualities you associate with them. Which ones might make you feel better in some way?

Some ideas for the preliminary discussion

Psychologists regard intuition as:

- a level of awareness different from conscious thought
- associated with right cerebral hemisphere activity
- incorporating subliminal perceptions
- subject to individual interpretations (affected by temperament and experience)
- a source of material for scientific investigation
- feeling-perception ('felt sense') recognised in applied psychology as 'gut feeling, to be noticed and critically questioned.

REFERENCE SECTION

USEFUL ADDRESSES

The following are addresses you can refer to, should you wish to find a qualified person to consult, whether for counselling, personal growth or psychotherapy. They may be able to recommend someone living near to you, or not too far away. Personal development courses, run by some of them, may appeal to you. There may also be local sources of recommendation available, and it is wise to ask about the kind of training undertaken by the person you consult, and to explore at your first interview whether what is offered feels right for you.

The United Kingdom Council for Psychotherapy (UKCP)
Regent's College
Inner Circle
Regent's Park
London NW1 4NS

Telephone: 0171 487 7554

The British Association for Counselling
1 Regent Place
Rugby CV21 2PJ

Write enclosing an A5 stamped, self-addressed envelope to request local lists of counsellors or to enquire about training opportunities in counselling. Prompt replies given.

The Tavistock Institute of Human Relations
120 Bellsize Lane
London NW3 5BA

Telephone: 0171 435 7111 (including family problems)

The National Autistic Society
276 Willesden Lane
London NW2 5RB (Autism and Asperger syndrome)

The Centre for Transpersonal Psychology
7 Pembroke Place
London W2 4XB

Associated with:

The Transpersonal Psychology Study Centre
Bridge House
Culmstock
Cullompton
Devon EX15 3JJ

Both centres provide individual and workshop therapy.

The National Council of Psychotherapists
24 Rickmondsworth Road
Watford WD1 7HT

This organization also lists hypnotherapists. Specify which kind of recommendation you are interested in and check training experience, if in doubt.

NCH Action for Children
85 Highbury Park
London EC2A 3AR

The Children's Society
Edward Rudolf House
Margery Street
London WC1X OJL

RELATE
Herbert Gray College
Little Church Street
Rugby
Warwickshire CV21 3AP (Marriage, partnership and family relations)

Cruse
Cruse House
126 Sheen Road
Richmond
Surrey TW9 1UR (Bereavement)

Your local Citizen's Advice Bureau and central and some local libraries keep updated lists of national and local organizations, nearest branch telephone numbers and other information which may be useful to you.

RECOMMENDED READING AND *TEXTS FOR FURTHER STUDY

ARGYLE, M. *The Psychology of Interpersonal Behaviour*, 4th ed., Penguin, 1983

*ATKINSON, R. C., ATKINSON, R. L., SMITH, E. & BEM, D. *Introduction to Psychology*, 11th ed., Harcourt Brace, Jovanovich, 1993 (comprehensive TEXT)

*CRAIN, W. C. *Theories of Development*, 2nd ed., Prentice-Hall, 1985

ERIKSON, E. *Life Cycle Completed*, Norton, 1985

GIBRAN, K. *The Prophet* (1926), Pan, 1991

GRAHAM, H. *The Human Face of Psychology*, Open University Press, 1986

*GROSS, R. *Psychology: the Science of Mind and Behaviour*, 2nd ed., Hodder & Stoughton, 1992 (comprehensive A-level text)

JUNG, C. G. *Man and His Symbols* (1961), Aldus, 1964

*NORTHEDGE, A. *The Good Study Guide*, Open University Press, 1990

*PENNINGTON, D. C. *Essential Social Psychology*, Arnold, 1986

*REBER, A. S. *Dictionary of Psychology*, Penguin, 1985

ROWAN, J. *The Transpersonal: Psychotherapy and Counselling*, Routledge, 1993

ROWAN, J., DRYDEN, W. (eds.), *Innovative Therapy in Britain*, Open University Press, 1988

RUTTER, M. *Maternal Deprivation Reassessed*, 2nd ed., Penguin, 1981

SCHAFFER, H. R. *Mothering*, Fontana, 1977

STEVENS, R. *Erik Erikson*, Open Uinversity Press, 1983

*TORTORA, G. J., GRABOWSKI, S. R. *Principles of Anatomy and Physiology*, 7th ed., HarperCollins, 1993 (comprehensive biology TEXT)

See also selections from BIBLIOGRAPHY.

BIBLIOGRAPHY

ASSAGIOLI, R. *Psychosynthesis*, Turnstone, 1975

ASSAGIOLI, R. *Transpersonal Development: Dimension Beyond Psychosynthesis*, (Coll. papers, posthum., 1988) Aquarian, HarperCollins, 1993

BANNISTER, D., FRANSELLA, F. *Inquiring Man*, 3rd ed., Croom Helm, 1986

BERNE, E. *Transactional Analysis in Psychotherapy*, Souvenir Press, 1961

BERNE, E. *Games People Play* (1964), Penguin, 1968

BETTELHEIM, B. A. *Good Enough Parent*, Thames & Hudson, 1987

BOWLBY, J. *Child Care and the Growth of Love*, 2nd ed., Penguin, 1965

BROWN, H. *People, Groups and Society*, Open University, 1985

BRUNER, J., SYLVA, K. (eds.), *Play*, Penguin, 1986

BRUNER, J. *Actual Minds, Possible Worlds*, Harvard, 1986

DAWKINS, R. *The Blind Watchmaker* (1986), Penguin, 1988

DOUGLAS, T. *Groupwork Practice*, Tavistock, 1976
EGAN, G. *The Skilled Helper*, 4th ed., Brooks/Cole, 1990
ERIKSON, E. *Childhood and Society* (1950, 1963), Triad/Paladin, 1977
ERIKSON, E. *Young Man Luther*, Faber, 1959
FORDHAM, F. *An Introduction to Jung's Psychology*, Penguin, 1966
FRIJDA, N. *The Emotions*, Cambridge University Press, 1986
GREGORY, R. L. (ed.) *The Oxford Companion to the Mind*, Oxford
    University Press, 1987
HARDY, J. A. *Psychology with a Soul*, Arkana, 1967
HARRIS, T. A. *I'm OK, You're OK*, Pan, 1967
HARRIS, T. A., HARRIS, A. *Staying OK*, Pan, 1986
HEARNSHAW, L. S. *The Shaping of Modern Psychology*, RKP, 1987
JAMES, W. What is an emotion? In *Mind*, 9, 188–205
JAMES, W. *The Principles of Psychology*, Holt, Rinehart & Winston, 1890
JUNG, C. G. *Memories, Dreams, Reflections* (1961), Fontana, 1967
KÜBLER-ROSS, E. *On Death and Dying* (1969), Tavistock, 1970
LAMB, M. E. *The Role of the Father in Child Development*, John Wiley,
    1976
LORENZ, K. *On Aggression* (1963), Methuen, 1967
MASLOW, A. *Motivation and Personality*, 2nd ed., Harper & Row, NY,
    1970
MASLOW, A. *Towards a Psychology of Being*, 2nd ed., Van Nostrand
    Reinhold, 1986
MEDCOF, J., ROTH, J. *Approaches to Psychology*, Open University Press
MURRAY PARKES, C. *See* PARKES
ORNSTEIN. R. *The Psychology of Consciousness*, 3rd ed., Penguin, 1986
PARKES, C. MURRAY *Bereavement*, 2nd ed., Penguin, 1986
PELIKAN, J. *World Treasury of Modern Religious Thought*, Little, Brown
    & Co., 1990
PERLES, F., HEFFERLINE, R., GOODMAN, P. *Gestalt Therapy*, Pelican,
    1973
PIAGET, J. *The Child's Conception of the World* (1929), Paladin, 1973
ROGERS, C. *Client-centred Therapy*, Constable, 1961
ROGERS, C. *On Becoming a Person* (1961), Constable, 1976
ROGERS, C. *A Way of Being*, Houghton Miflin, 1980
ROWAN, J. *The Transpersonal: Psychotherapy and Counselling*,
    Routledge, 1993
RUTTER, M., MADGE, N. *Cycles of Disadvantage*, Heinemann, 1986
SINGER, J. L., POPE, K. S. *The Power of the Human Imagination*, Plenum
    Press, 1978
STORR, A. *The Integrity of Personality* (1960), Penguin, 1963
STORR, A. *Human Aggression*, Penguin, 1968
STORR, A. *Jung: Selected Writings,* Fontana, 1983
STORR, A. *Solitude*, Haning/Collins, 1989
VAN DER POST, L. *Jung and the Story of Our Time*, Penguin, 1978
WINNICOTT, D. W. *The Child, the Family and the Outside World*,
    Penguin, 1964

REFERENCES

AINSWORTH, M. D. *Infancy in Uganda: Infant Care and the Growth of Attachment*, John Hopkins Press, 1967

ARGYLE, M. *The Psychology of Interpersonal Behaviour*, 4th ed., Penguin, 1983

ASSAGIOLI, R. *Psychosynthesis*, Turnstone, 1975

AXLINE, V. *Dibs: in Search of Self*, Penguin, 1971

BANDURA, A. *Principles of Behaviour Modification*, Holt, Rinehart, Wilson, 1969

BANDURA, A. *Social Learning Theory*, Prentice-Hall, 1977

BANDURA, A. *Social Foundations of Thought and Action: A Social Cognitive Theory*, Prentice-Hall, 1985

BANNISTER, D., FRANSELLA, F. *Inquiring Man*, 3rd ed., Croom Helm, 1986

BERNE, E. *Transactional Analysis in Psychotherapy*, Souvenir Press, 1961

BERNE, E. *Games People Play* (1964), Penguin, 1968

BETTELHEIM, B. *A Good Enough Parent*, Thames & Hudson, 1987

BOWLBY, J. *Child Care and the Growth of Love*, Penguin, 1953

BOWLBY, J. *Forty-four Juvenile Thieves: Their Characters and Home Life*, Balliere, Tindall & Cox, 1946

BRUNER, J., SYLVA, K. (eds.) *Play*, Penguin, 1986

BRUNER, J. *Actual Minds, Possible Worlds*, Harvard, 1986

BUSS, A. H., PLOMIN, R. *Temperament Theory of Personality Development*, Wiley, 1975

CANNON, W. B. The James-Lange theory of emotions: a critical examination and an alternative theory (1927), In *American Journal of Psychology*, 39, 106–24

COOK. M. *Perceiving Others: the Psychology of Interpersonal Perception*, Methuen, 1979

CUMMING, E., HENRY, W. E. *Growing Old*, Basic Books, 1961

DAWKINS, R. *The Blind Watchmaker* (1986), Penguin, 1988

DEVORE, I. (ed.), *Primate Behaviour*, Holt, Rinehart & Winston, 1965

ERIKSON, E. *Childhood and Society* (1950, 1963), Triad/Paladin, 1977

ERIKSON, E. *Insight and Responsibility* (1952), Norton, 1964

ERIKSON, E. *Young Man Luther* (1958), Faber, 1959

ERIKSON, E. *Life Cycle Completed* (1982), Norton, 1985

FESTINGER, L., PEPITONE, A., NEWCOMB, T. A. Some consequences of deindividuation in a group (1952). In *Journal of Abnormal and Social Psychology*, 47, 383–89.

FLAVELL, J. H. *Cognitive Development*, Prentice-Hall, 1977

FORDHAM, F. *An Introduction to Jung's Psychology*, 3rd ed., Penguin, 1966

FREUD, S. *Interpretation of Dreams* (1900), trans. J. Strachey, Basic Books, 1965

FREUD, S. *Three essays on the theory of sexuality* (1905). In *Complete Psychological Works of Sigmund Freud*, Vol. 7, Chatto & Windus, 1962

FREUD, S. *Beyond the Pleasure Principle* (1920). In *Standard Edition*, Vol. 18, Hogarth Press, 1955

FREUD, S. *The Ego and the Id* (1923), trans. J. Rivière, W. W. Norton & Co., 1960

FREUD, S. *Civilization and its Discontents* (1930). *Standard Edition,* 21, 59–145, Hogarth Press, 1961

FRIJDA, N. H. *The Emotions,* Cambridge University Press, 1986

FRITH, U. (ed.), *Autism and Asperger Syndrome,* Cambridge University Press, 1991

GOLDSMITH, H. H., GOTTESMAN, I. I. Origins of variation in behavioral style: A longitudinal study of temperament in young twins (1981) In *Child Development,* 52, 91–103

GRAHAM, H. *The Human Face of Psychology,* Open University Press, 1986

GRAHAM, J. A., ARGYLE, M., FURNHAM, A. The goals and goal structures of social situations. In *European Journal of Social Psychology,* Vol. 10, 345–66

HARDY, J. *A Psychology with a Soul,* RKP, 1987, Arkana, 1989

HARRIS, T. A. *I'm OK, You're OK* (1967), Pan, 1973

HARRIS, T. A., HARRIS, A. *Staying OK* (1985), Pan, 1986

HAVIGHURST, R. J. Personality and patterns of ageing. In S. M. Chown (ed.), *Human Ageing,* Penguin, 1968

HAYES, N. *A First Course in Psychology,* 2nd ed., Nelson, 1984

HEARNSHAW, L. S. *The Shaping of Modern Psychology,* RKP, 1987

HOLMES, T. H., RAHE, R. H. The social redjustment rating scale. In *Journal of Psychosomatic Research,* 11, 213–18

JUNG, C. G. On the psychology of the Unconscious (1917, 1926, 1943). In *Two Essays on Analytical Psychology (1953), Complete Works,* Vol. 7, RKP 1969

JUNG, C. G. *Memories, Dreams, Reflections* (1961), Fontana, 1967

JUNG, C. G. *Man and his Symbols,* Aldus, 1964

KAGAN, J., ROSMAN, B. L., DAY, D., ALBERT, J., PHILLIPS, W. Information processing in the child: significance of analytic and reflective attitudes (1964). In *Psychological Monographs* 78, (Whole no. 578)

KOHLBERG, L. *Essays on Moral Development* (1955), Vol. 1, Harper & Row, 1981

KÜBLER-ROSS, E. *On Death and Dying* (1969), Tavistock, 1970

LAZAR, I., DARLINGTON, R. Lasting effects of early education: A report for the Consortium of Longitudinal Studies (1982). In *Monograph for the Society for Research in Child Development,* 47, 2–3

LAZARUS, R. S. *Psychological Stress and the Coping Process,* McGraw Hill, 1966

LAZARUS, R. S., FOLKMAN, S. *Stress, Appraisal, Coping,* Springer, 1984

LORENZ, K. *On Aggression* (1963), Methuen, 1967

MARCIA, J. *Identity in adolescence.* In J. Adelson (ed.), *Handbook of adolescent psychology,* Wiley, 1980

MASLOW, A. *Motivation and Personality* (1954), 2nd ed., Harper & Row, 1970

MASLOW, A. *Towards a Psychology of Being* (1968), 2nd ed., Van Nostrand Reinhold, 1986

MEAD, M. *Male and Female* (1949), Victor Gollancz Ltd., 1950

MILGRAM, S. *Obedience to Authority* (1963, 1974), Harper & Row, 1974

MURRAY PARKES, C. *See under* Parkes, C. M.

NEIMARK, E. P. Longitudinal development of formal operations thought (1975). In *Genetic Psychology Monographs*, 91, 171–225

PARKES, C. M. *Bereavement*, 2nd ed., Penguin, 1986

PAVLOV. I. P. *Conditioned Reflexes*, Oxford University Press, 1927

PERLES, F., HEFFERLINE, R., GOODMAN, P. *Gestalt Therapy*, Pelican, 1973

PIAGET, J. *The Child's Conception of the World* (1929), Paladin, 1973

REICHARD, S., LIVSON, F., PETERSEN, P. *Ageing and Personality*, Wiley, 1962

ROBERTSON, J., BOWLBY, J. Responses of young children to separation from their mother. In *Courr. Cent. Int. Enf.*, Vol. 2, 131–42 (Tavistock)

ROGERS, C. The use of electrically recorded interviews in improving psychotherapeutic techniques (1942). In *American Journal of Orthopsychiatry*, 12, 429–34

ROGERS, C. Some observations on the organization of personality (1947). In *American Psychologist*, 21, 358–368

ROGERS, C. *Client-centred Therapy*, Constable, 1951

ROGERS, C. *On Becoming a Person* (1961), Constable, 1976

ROGERS, C. *Becoming Partners: Marriage and its Alternatives,* Delacorte, 1972

ROGERS, C. *A Way of Being*, Houghton Miflin, 1980

ROWAN, J. *The Transpersonal: Psychotherapy and Counselling*, Routledge 1993

RUTTER, M. *Maternal Deprivation Reassessed* (1972), Penguin, 1981

RUTTER, M., MADGE, N. *Cycles of Disadvantage*, Heinemann, 1976

RUTTER, M., QUINTON, D. Long-term follow-up of women institutionalized in childhood: Factors promoting good functioning in adult life (1984). In *British Journal of Developmental Psychology*, Vol. 2, 191–204

SAMUELS, A., SHORTER, B., PLAUT, F. *Critical Dictionary of Jungian Analysis*, RKP, 1986

SCHACHTER, S., SINGER, J. Cognitive, social and physiological determinants of emotional state (1962). In *Psychological Review*, 63: 379–99

SCHAFFER, H. R. *Mothering*, Fontana, 1977

SCHAFFER, H. R., EMERSON, P. E. The development of social attachments in infancy, *Monog. Soc. Res. Child Devel*, Vol 29, 94

SELIGMAN, M. *Helplessness*, Freeman, 1975

SELYE, H. *The Stress of Life*, McGraw-Hill, 1956, *also* revised edition, Van Nostrand Reinhold, 1979

SKINNER, B. F. *The Behaviour of Organisms*, Appleton-Century-Crofts, 1938

SPERRY, R. W. Lateral specialization in the surgically separated hemispheres. In SCHMITT, F. O., WORDEN, G. (eds.), *The Neurosciences Third Study Program*, pp. 5–19, MIT Press, Massachusetts, 1974

STERN, D. *The First Relationship: Infant and Mother,* Harvard University Press, 1977

STORR, A. *Human Aggression*, Penguin, 1968

THOMAS, A., CHESS, S. *Temperament and Development*, Brunner/Mazel, 1977

THORNDIKE, E. L. Animal Intelligence: and experimental study of associative learning in animals (1898) In *Psychological Review Monograph Supplement 2*, No. 8.

WATSON, J. B. *Behavior: An introducion to comparative psychology* (1914). Revised and incorporated in WATSON, J. B. *Behaviorism*, Norton, 1970

WATSON, J. B. *Behaviourism*, Lippincott, 1924

WEIKART, D. P. *Relationship of Curriculum Teaching and Learning in Pre-School Education*, John Hopkins University Press, 1972

WEINER, B. *Achievement Motivation and Attribution Theory*, General Learning Press, 1974

WING, L. Asperger Syndrome: a clinical account. In *Journal of Psychological Medicine*, No.11, pp. 115–129, 1981

WINNICOTT, D. W. *The Child, the Family and the Outside World*, Penguin 1964

ZIGLER, E. F., BERMAN, W. Discerning the future of early childhood intervention (1983). In *American Psychologist*, 38, 894–906

ZIMBARDO, P. G. Pathology of imprisonment. In *Society*, April 1972

INDEX

PICTURE CREDITS

The author and publisher would like to thank the following copyright holders for photographic material used in this book:

Figure 1.1 (p. 9) © **Collections/Anthea Sieveking**; Figure 2.1 (p. 20) © **Collections/Anthea Sieveking**; Figure 3.1 (p. 24) © **Collections/Sandra Lousada**; Figure 4.1 (p. 35) © **Collections/Anthea Sieveking**; Figure 4.2 (p. 38) © **Collections/Anthea Sieveking**; Figure 5.1 (p. 46) © **Collections/ Anthea Sieveking**; Figure 5.2 (p. 51) © **Collections/Anthea Sieveking**; Figure 6.1 (p. 67) © **Collections/Anthea Sieveking**; Figure 7.1 (p. 73) © **Sally & Richard Greenhill**; Figure 8.1 (p. 88) © **Sally Greenhill, Sally & Richard Greenhill**; Figure 9.1 (p. 94) © **Mary Evans Picture Library**; Figure 10.1 (p. 108) © **Collections/Anthea Sieveking**; Figure 11.1 (p. 121) © **Sally & Richard Greenhill**; Figure 12.1 (p. 131) © **Collections/Anthea Sieveking**; Figure 13.1 (p. 145) © **Mallet's Northern Antiquities (Mary Evans Picture Library)**